Artificial Intelligence and Safety

In a world where machines learn, evolve, and sometimes outthink us, *Artificial Intelligence and Safety* offers a rare, integrated lens into both the power and peril of intelligent systems. Drawing on the authors' unique blend of programming mastery and enterprise risk leadership, this guide is your compass in the age of intelligent machines.

This book goes beyond traditional risk management frameworks by integrating the latest advancements in artificial intelligence (AI) and generative AI. Combining real-world case studies, Socratic questioning, and the wisdom of AI governance pioneers, it journeys through the evolution of AI, the rise of deep learning, and the practical implications of large language models (LLMs) and retrieval-augmented generation (RAG). The authors translate complex technical knowledge into actionable insights and teach how to use Python not just for prediction, but for protection—turning code into a risk management ally. Readers will understand how to embed ethics by design, assess emerging risks, and confidently apply AI governance frameworks.

This guide demystifies AI for everyone—from software architects to policymakers and risk managers. Whether you're crafting LLMs or setting enterprise policy, this book empowers you to not only ask the right questions but build the right systems, because the future of AI isn't just about building intelligence, it's about building it responsibly.

Charu Khanna is director of risk management at a global financial institution. She has extensive experience in risk management, data and operational risk, and analytics.

Sahil Khanna is a senior data scientist and AI governance specialist with extensive experience in designing and deploying machine learning and LLM solutions across healthcare, retail, and technology sectors.

Artificial Intelligence and Safety

A Practical Guide for Programmers and Decision Makers

Charu Khanna and Sahil Khanna

CRC Press
Taylor & Francis Group
Boca Raton London New York

CRC Press is an imprint of the
Taylor & Francis Group, an **informa** business
A CHAPMAN & HALL BOOK

Designed cover image: Web Large Image (Public)

First edition published 2026
by CRC Press
2385 NW Executive Center Drive, Suite 320, Boca Raton FL 33431

and by CRC Press
4 Park Square, Milton Park, Abingdon, Oxon, OX14 4RN

CRC Press is an imprint of Taylor & Francis Group, LLC

ISBN: 978-1-003-86339-7 (hbk)
ISBN: 978-1-003-86338-0 (pbk)
ISBN: 978-1-003-60729-8 (ebk)

DOI: 10.1201/9781003607298

Typeset in Minion
by KnowledgeWorks Global Ltd.

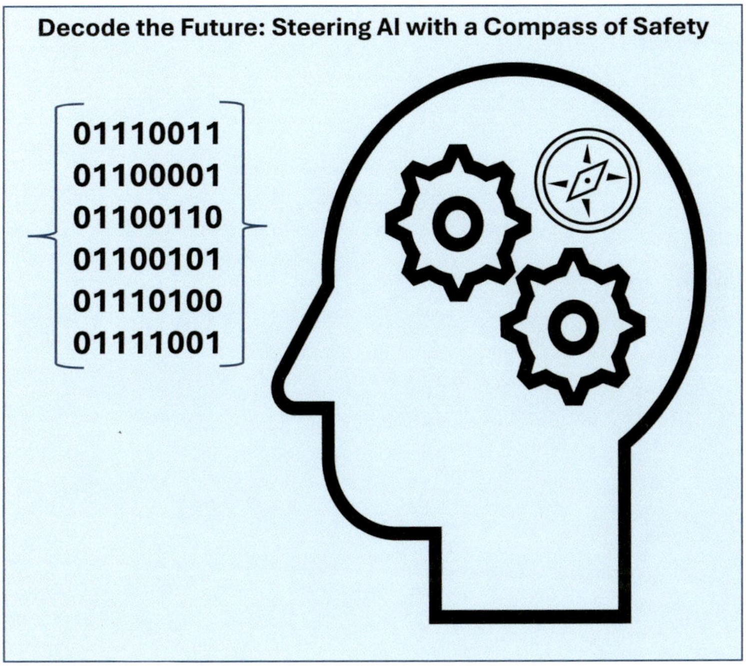

FIGURE 0.1 Decode the future: Steering AI with a compass of safety with a human-brain silhouette and a compass icon guiding binary code—visually capturing navigating code to consciousness, a key concept introduced by authors to enable the dialogue on Artificial Intelligence and Safety

Contents

Preface, ix

Acknowledgments, xiii

Prelude, xv

Why Should You Read This Book?, xvii

Disclaimer, xxxi

Chapter 1 ▪ Mastering Uncertainty: The Strategic Role of Risk Management 1

Chapter 2 ▪ Decoding Intelligence: Your Step-by-Step Guide on Artificial Intelligence 20

Chapter 3 ▪ Machine Learning Foundations: From Theory to Your First Model 43

Chapter 4 ▪ The Rise of Deep Learning 51

Chapter 5 ▪ From Generative AI to Context-Aware Intelligence 100

Chapter 6 ▪ Role of Artificial Intelligence in Risk Management and Vice Versa 138

Chapter 7 ▪ Managing Emerging Risks Using Python: Your Detailed Guide on How to Enable Ethical AI for Better Data Risk Governance 164

CHAPTER 8 ▪ Asking the Right Question: Bridge the Gap Between Risk and Artificial Intelligence 174

CHAPTER 9 ▪ Case Study: Your Practical and Stepwise Guide to Build a RAG-Powered AI Assistant 183

Afterword: The Future of Risk Management in the Era of Artificial Intelligence 188

INDEX, 193

Preface

Risk management has always been a discipline grounded in the known, using patterns, probabilities, and established frameworks to predict and mitigate potential threats. But the **landscape has shifted dramatically with the advent of artificial intelligence (AI) and generative AI (Gen AI).** No longer is risk confined to human oversight; it now includes machines that can learn, evolve, and sometimes out-think us.

> This book, *Artificial Intelligence and Safety* takes readers through the core transformation process. **Digits, Direction, and Daring Ideas—Your Journey to Trustworthy AI Starts Here**

This book combines the perspectives of a programmer, **who once saw the world through lines of code, and a modern risk management leader[1] grappling with the ethical, legal, and technical challenges posed by AI.**

By combining their perspectives, we see not only the risks but also the potential to reshape protection methods while empowering innovation within the intelligent system-driven world.

The book draws inspiration from personal learnings, research, and experiences of the authors and the leading publications in the field of risk management and AI, aiming to become a seminal resource for professionals and students alike.

This book consolidates the critical concepts and practices into a cohesive and comprehensive guide, **addressing both foundational principles and cutting-edge applications.**

The book goes beyond traditional risk management frameworks by integrating the latest advancements in AI and Gen AI.

This book covers a wide range of topics, from understanding and implementing risk management and data privacy risk strategies to applying

AI/Gen AI tools for risk identification and management. **Practical case studies and real-world applications** are emphasized, providing readers with scientifically sound solutions to contemporary challenges.

Professionals will find this book both theoretically grounded and tremendously practical because it delivers actionable insights to solve real-world problems.

Alongside foundational topics such as risk governance and controls, the **book explores the significant impact of AI in transforming risk management practices.**

The book emphasizes the need to **balance innovative approaches and risk management through AI governance principles and ethical AI use** alongside specific risk management tools and techniques (illustrated in Figure 0.2) for data-driven environments. This book establishes itself as a vital reference for senior executives and risk managers along with data privacy officers, AI specialists and compliance professionals.

Whether you are a programmer writing code or a leader making strategic decisions, understanding AI and risk management are the critical steps in navigating the complexities of our modern world.

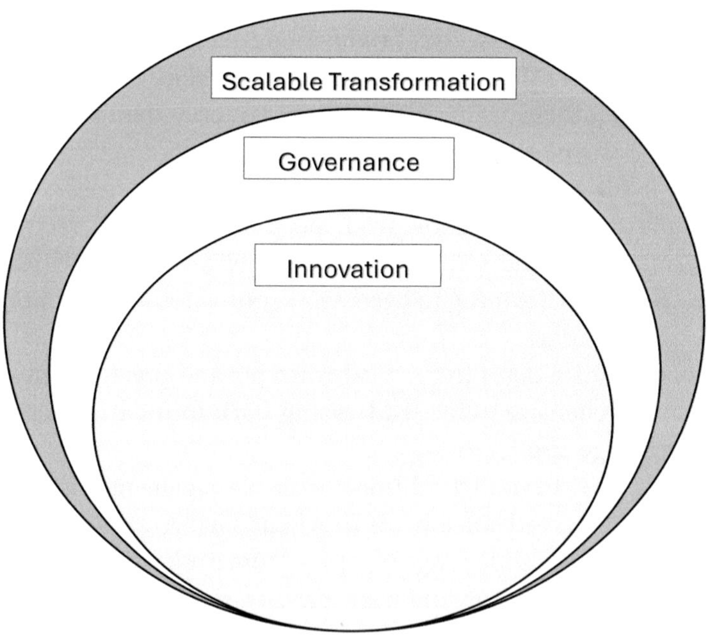

FIGURE 0.2 Balancing innovation and risk.

The comprehensive analysis reveals that about 3.85 million professionals and students around the world work in AI or data privacy risk management or participate in both fields.

The calculated figure includes essential sectors like financial services together with healthcare and technology as well as corporate and academic institutions. The financial services industry which covers banks, insurance companies, hedge funds, investment firms and fintech companies contains about 500,000 institutions worldwide.

Each of these institutions typically employs an average of five relevant professionals, leading to a total of 2.5 million potential in this sector (source: World Bank: Global Financial Development Database; Statista: Number of banks worldwide).

In the healthcare sector, with approximately 100,000 large institutions globally and an average of three relevant professionals each, we estimate about 300,000 professionals (World Health Organization (WHO): Global Health Observatory data; Statista: Number of hospitals worldwide). The technology sector, comprising around 50,000 large IT and cybersecurity firms globally, with an average of five relevant professionals each, adds another 250,000 potential readers (Gartner: IT Industry Statistics; International Data Corporation (IDC): Worldwide IT Industry).

Corporate entities, including approximately 200,000 large multinational corporations globally, with an average of three relevant professionals each, contribute an additional 600,000 professionals to the audience (United Nations Conference on Trade and Development (UNCTAD): World Investment Report; Statista: Number of multinational companies worldwide).

In academia, with roughly 10,000 universities and research institutions globally, and an average of 20 relevant students and academics each, we estimate about 200,000 potential readers (UNESCO: Global Education Monitoring Report; Times Higher Education: World University Rankings).

Acknowledgments

Some books are written in silence. This one was written in echoes—of mentors' questions, late-night algorithm debates, and quiet encouragement from those who saw in me what I had not yet dared to see in myself.

To my husband—your quiet genius, tireless support, and relentless pursuit of excellence have shaped the architecture of this work. You not only challenged my thinking but illuminated new paths when I stood at conceptual dead ends. You saw the book in me long before I did, and your belief became my scaffolding.

To my mother-in-law—thank you for your enduring strength, your faith in my voice, and your whispered reminders to be bold, not just brilliant. You showed me that being "enough" isn't about capacity, but about courage.

To my parents—every page is layered with the values you wove into my childhood: discipline, inquiry, and the freedom to ask "why." You invested your lives into our minds, and I carry that legacy forward with reverence.

To my co-author, Sahil—your mathematical genius and analytical precision enriched the soul of this book. Your ability to translate abstract theory into technical clarity elevated every chapter, and I'm grateful for your partnership in this intellectual journey.

To my mentors—thank you for seeing beyond potential and guiding me with wisdom, tough questions, and patient correction. Your belief in rigorous thinking and ethical practice continues to shape my path. You taught me not only how to build systems, but how to question them. Your insights, feedback, and brainstorming sessions have been invaluable. You helped me not just interpret risk, but embody resilience.

To the thinkers who came before—Richard Feynman, Fei-Fei Li, Stuart Russell, Timnit Gebru—your words resonate in these chapters, reminding us that ethics must scale with intelligence, and that risk is not a constraint, but a compass.

To the invisible frameworks—the recursive loops, stochastic gradients, and bias-variance tradeoffs—thank you for being my metaphors as much as my models. You taught me that systems, like people, must be trained not just on data, but on values.

To the regulators, researchers, and policy architects—especially those shaping the EU AI Act, NIST AI RMF, and California's pioneering legislation—your work formed the backbone of Chapter 4. You proved that governance can be a design principle, not just an afterthought.

To the sacred process itself—those solitary mornings parsing through fairness metrics, those evenings revising case studies for clarity and context—thank you for demanding precision without ever letting go of wonder.

And to the late Toni Morrison—your words, *"If there's a book that you want to read, but it hasn't been written yet, then you must write it,"* became both a mirror and a mandate. Your life story and this quote reminded me that unmet needs are not voids, but invitations—to rise, to write, to contribute.

This book is my offering. To those who protect the boundaries of innovation with ethics, and who see in the structure of code the soul of conscience—*may it serve as both a mirror and a map.*

—Charu Khanna
New York, June 2025

Prelude

Growing up as an introvert child of middle class & working parents, who dedicated their life (and almost all their savings) in bringing the right balance of theoretic knowledge and learning through experience in their 2 impressionable children, which probably began my journey (or what I like to call my love story) with **balancing risk & innovation**.

My journey of developing a deeper understanding of "Risk" started with Socratic questioning in hyper-loop of **"What?" and "Why!"**

A series of "what" and "why" questions is often referred to as an "inquiry" or "inquiry-based learning." In educational contexts, it may also be called "**Socratic questioning**"[2] when it involves a systematic and disciplined questioning process to stimulate critical thinking and draw out ideas and underlying presuppositions. An example of how Socratic "what/why" dialogue unfolds in a real AI ethics review scenario is presented in Table 0.1.

Another term that might be used, particularly in problem-solving and investigative contexts, is "**root cause analysis**," which involves asking successive "why" questions to uncover the fundamental cause of a problem. This method (visually represented in Figure 0.3) encouraged me in continuous questioning and dialogue to explore complex concepts and uncover underlying assumptions.

In the realm of science, the **physicist Richard Feynman** is renowned for his emphasis on curiosity and questioning. Feynman encouraged people to always ask "why" and not accept things at face value, promoting a deep and inquisitive approach to understanding the world.

Now, let's begin our journey together and ask our first of many questions—"**How do I master the uncertainty**"

TABLE 0.1 Below is an example scenario-based demonstration of Socratic "what/why" dialog. Represented as a mini-script in which a facilitator (F) leads a group (G) or individual (I) through successive questions, gradually surfacing deeper assumptions, evidence gaps, and alternative viewpoints

Scenario: AI-Ethics Review: Predictive Policing Algorithm (*Setting—A city ethics board evaluating a vendor's crime-risk model)*

Step	Socratic Prompt (Facilitator)	Typical Response (Group or Individual)	Underlying Insight Surfaced
1	What outcome does the algorithm claim to predict?	Burglary "risk scores" by neighborhood block.	Clarifies target variable.
2	Why might that prediction matter to citizens?	Helps allocate patrols and reduce crime rates.	Surfaces assumed benefit.
3	What data feed the model?	Police incident logs, census demographics.	Identifies Inputs
4	Why were those particular data chosen over, say, 911 calls or insurance claims?	readily available and historically consistent.	Reveals a convenience bias
5	What biases might be baked into historic arrest data?	Over-policing of certain minority neighborhoods	Acknowledges potential skew.
6	Why should that bias worry us if the goal is crime reduction?	Risk of reinforcing unfair patrol patterns, eroding trust.	Links bias to social impact
7	What safeguards could mitigate the bias?	Re-weight data, incorporate independent victim reports, add fairness constraints.	Generates solution space
8	Why would those safeguards be credible to the public?	Provide audit logs, publish fairness metrics.	Establishes accountability lens.
	Result: The board postpones deployment, requesting bias-mitigation experiments and public transparency measures before approving the tool.		

FIGURE 0.3 Illustration to visually capture Socratic "what/why" dialogue style:

- Two silhouettes face each other, symbolizing mentor and learner.
- Speech bubbles show a question mark and a branching tree, hinting at the iterative inquiry that digs deeper.
- A central "question-tree" icon joins the figures, reinforcing the idea of branching reasoning paths.

Why Should You Read This Book?

AI AND RISKS IN THE MODERN WORLD

AI has transformed industries, promising unprecedented efficiency and innovation.

AI-powered diagnostic tools in healthcare have surpassed traditional detection methods by providing more accurate and faster disease identification which results in enhanced patient outcomes. AI systems within financial sectors now analyze millions of transactions in real time to detect fraudulent activities that would remain undetected otherwise. The retail industry uses artificial intelligence to deliver personalized customer experiences while optimizing supply chains and forecasting consumer behavior patterns.

The latest developments demonstrate how AI can transform operational efficiency and decision-making across multiple fields. The increasing deployment of applications brings about corresponding risks.

This book explores four critical landscapes of the modern world:

1. **The New Risk Landscape**
    - Algorithmic biases
    - Data poisoning and adversarial attacks
    - Privacy risks in AI applications
2. **Regulatory and Legal Risks**
    - Current and emerging AI regulations
    - Implications of legal non-compliance

3. **Ethics and Accountability in AI**
   - Frameworks for ethical AI
   - Balancing innovation with moral responsibility
4. **The Technical Landscape**
   - Machine learning, AI and Generative AI
   - Your practical guide to build you AI models from scratch

AI Risks Conceptual Diagram

The following diagram (Figure 0.4) illustrates the three critical areas of AI risks: algorithmic biases, data poisoning and adversarial attacks, and privacy risks. Each area is interconnected and represents a significant challenge for modern AI applications.

The New Risk Landscape

Algorithmic Biases:

Algorithms are only as impartial as the data that trains them. The level of impartiality in algorithms depends directly on the quality of their training data. AI models will necessarily display the biases contained within their training datasets. A recruitment AI system gained public attention when it repeatedly discriminated against women because the underlying historical hiring data it used for training consisted primarily of male applicants. The problem reaches further than gender bias because racial and socio-economic as well as cultural prejudices have become integrated into AI systems thus reinforcing current societal imbalances.

A major event in 2023 revealed biases in AI systems when a leading healthcare AI favored higher-income patients for resource distribution because its training data contained discriminatory patterns.

A study published in *The Lancet Digital Health*[3] revealed that the system, deployed in several major hospitals, used historical billing data as a proxy for health needs, inadvertently disadvantaged economically vulnerable patients. This event sparked widespread criticism and led to a comprehensive audit of AI tools in healthcare. Similar biases were observed in the education sector, where an AI-based grading system disproportionately downgraded students from lower-income schools during the pandemic. These examples underscore the pressing need for fairness and equity in AI system design. Similarly, in the legal sector, ProPublica's

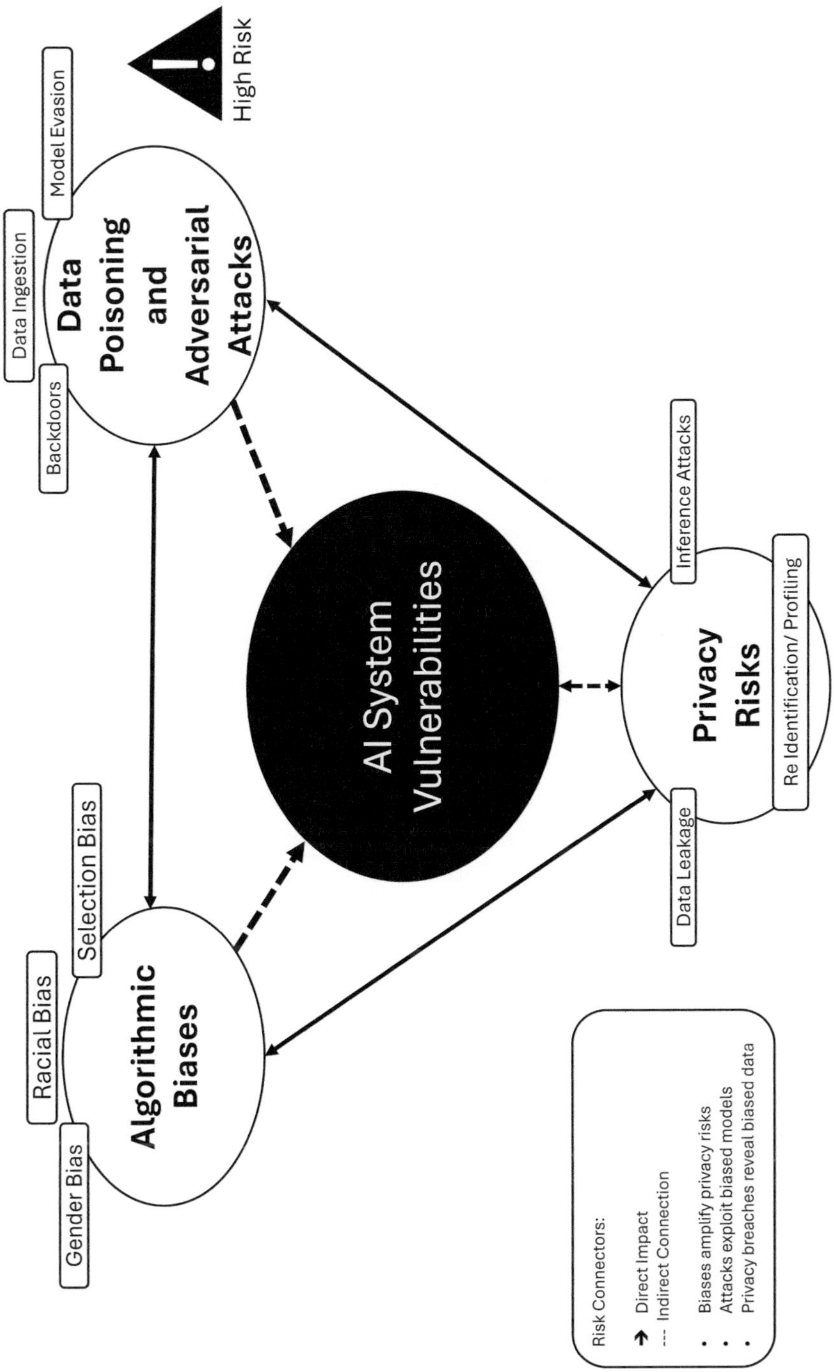

FIGURE 0.4 AI risks conceptual diagram.

ongoing investigation into COMPAS[4], a criminal risk assessment tool, revealed that it unfairly labeled other defendants as high-risk compared to White defendants with similar records.

> Renowned AI researcher Dr. Timnit Gebru[5]emphasizes,
>
> "Bias in AI systems isn't just a technical issue; it's a societal one that reflects the prejudices in our datasets. Addressing it requires systemic change, not just better algorithms."

Data Poisoning and Adversarial Attacks:
Data poisoning[6] and adversarial attacks[7] are emerging threats to AI integrity.

> Data poisoning occurs when malicious actors introduce corrupted data into training datasets, skewing the AI's performance.
>
> For example, a cybersecurity firm discovered that attackers had inserted misleading data into a malware detection system, leading to misclassification of harmful software as benign.

The Tesla autopilot AI underwent scrutiny in 2022 after adversarial attacks led to vehicle misinterpretations of road signs due to minimal alterations like stickers on speed limit signs.

The event showcased extensive weaknesses in autonomous systems because these systems depend mainly on visual data to make decisions. Researchers have shown that small changes to navigation markers can lead drones to deviate significantly from their intended path.

The demonstrated vulnerabilities through these examples show that adversarial inputs pose a widespread threat to autonomous systems which requires strong protective measures like redundant sensor systems and improved adversarial training models for safety and reliability. The deployment of AI in essential applications such as autonomous driving became a safety concern following these findings.

Such incidents underscore the findings of research like "**Adversarial Examples in Machine Learning" by Goodfellow et al.** (***arXiv preprint, 2014***), which first demonstrated the vulnerability of neural networks to adversarial attacks.

Privacy Risks in AI Applications:

Privacy[8] concerns are among the most significant risks in AI adoption. AI systems often require vast amounts of data, including sensitive personal information, to function effectively. Facial recognition systems, for example, have been deployed in public spaces without adequate consent, raising alarms about surveillance and individual freedoms.

In a 2023 investigative report, it was revealed that a major tech company's generative AI model inadvertently exposed sensitive user data during a training session. This incident highlighted the inadequacies of current data governance frameworks. Furthermore, re-identification risks were demonstrated in the "Netflix Prize" controversy, where supposedly anonymized data was cross-referenced with other datasets to identify individual users.

Privacy-preserving techniques such as differential privacy, outlined in the seminal paper "**Learning with Privacy at Scale**" **by Abadi et al.** (*Proceedings on Privacy Enhancing Technologies*, 2016), and federated learning, as discussed in "Communication-Efficient Learning of Deep Networks from Decentralized Data" **by McMahan et al.** (*Proceedings of the AISTATS*, 2017), have gained traction as vital solutions.

For example, Google has implemented federated learning in its Gboard keyboard to enable predictive text and suggestions without transferring user data to central servers. Similarly, Apple employs differential privacy to collect and analyze user data in aggregate for features like emoji suggestions and Safari's tracking prevention. These real-world applications demonstrate how such techniques can enhance functionality while maintaining user privacy, setting a benchmark for privacy-conscious AI development.

Dr. Yoshua Bengio, a Turing Award[9] laureate and one of the pioneers of deep learning, has been at the forefront of advocating for ethical AI development.

> His journey began in 2006 with the breakthrough discovery of deep learning techniques, which revolutionized AI by enabling neural networks to handle vast amounts of data.
>
> By 2018, Bengio began emphasizing the ethical challenges posed by AI, especially after witnessing the societal impacts of biased

algorithms and privacy violations. In that same year, he co-signed the "**Montreal Declaration for Responsible AI,**" a milestone document promoting the ethical use of AI.

In 2020, Bengio publically shared his thoughts during the NeurIPS Conference, calling for greater transparency in AI systems and the integration of fairness metrics into model evaluation. He stated, "Ethical AI demands not just technical safeguards but a culture of respect for privacy. Our innovations must always prioritize human dignity." Beyond academic platforms, Bengio has contributed to global conversations through interviews with major outlets such as *The Guardian* and *MIT Technology Review*, advocating for regulations that ensure AI technologies benefit humanity.

Dr. Bengio's recent research focuses on privacy-preserving methods, including differential privacy and federated learning, to minimize risks associated with data misuse. His leadership in the Responsible AI initiative, launched in 2021, seeks to establish global standards for fairness, accountability, and transparency in AI, offering actionable guidelines to developers and policymakers worldwide.

Regulatory and Legal Risks

As AI systems become increasingly integral to decision-making, governments worldwide are introducing robust regulations to address their associated risks. This section delves into current and emerging AI regulations and examines the profound implications of noncompliance.

Current and Emerging AI Regulations:

AI regulation is a rapidly evolving field. In the European Union, the **General Data Protection Regulation (GDPR),**[10] **implemented in 2018**, set a global benchmark for data privacy.

GDPR mandates organizations to secure user consent, ensure data transparency, and implement robust mechanisms to protect personal data. The regulation has led to fines totaling over $4 billion as of December 2024, highlighting its enforcement rigor.

Building upon GDPR, the EU's proposed **Artificial Intelligence Act** (AI Act)[11] aims to regulate AI technologies based on their risk levels. High-risk applications, such as facial recognition systems and AI in healthcare, are subject to stringent requirements, including mandatory audits, transparency disclosures, and risk mitigation plans. Expected to be fully enforced by 2025, the AI Act is poised to shape AI development and deployment globally.

In the United States, the **National Institute of Standards and Technology (NIST)** released the AI Risk Management Framework (AI RMF) in 2023. This voluntary framework emphasizes transparency, fairness, and accountability, offering a structured approach for organizations to manage AI-related risks.

Additionally, **California's Consumer Privacy Act (CCPA)** and its amendment, the California Privacy Rights Act (CPRA), enforce strict data privacy norms, requiring organizations to disclose data usage and allow users to opt out of data collection.

Implications of Legal Noncompliance:

Noncompliance with AI regulations carries significant repercussions, both financial and reputational.

The largest fine to date, $1.2 billion, was imposed on a global tech company in 2023 for transferring EU citizens' data to non-compliant jurisdictions, violating GDPR.

> Beyond monetary penalties, such breaches erode consumer trust, lead to operational disruptions, and tarnish brand reputation.

Moreover, legal non-compliance often necessitates costly remedial measures. For example, organizations may be required to overhaul their AI systems, conduct extensive audits, and retrain staff to align with regulatory standards. Such measures not only incur direct costs but also delay innovation and market competitiveness.

Recommendations for Compliance:

To thrive in a regulated AI landscape, organizations must prioritize compliance as a strategic imperative.

Key recommendations include:

- Establishing multidisciplinary teams that integrate legal, technical, and ethical expertise.
- Conducting regular audits and impact assessments to identify and mitigate compliance gaps.

- Embedding fairness, accountability, and transparency into AI design and deployment processes.
- Providing comprehensive training programs to ensure all employees understand regulatory requirements.

Ultimately, as explored in this book's theme, **"Code to Consciousness," effective AI governance requires more than adherence to rules— it demands a cultural shift.**

Organizations must view compliance not as a constraint but as an enabler of trust, innovation, and long-term success.

Ethics and Accountability in Artificial Intelligence: A Call to Conscience

AI is no longer an experimental frontier. It is now a fully embedded force in systems that guide financial lending, allocate medical care, filter legal decisions, and even influence hiring or school admissions. As such, **AI has shifted from a technical marvel to a societal actor**—with power and consequence often exceeding human visibility or control.

Yet while AI's reach has grown, so too has its risk—**particularly when it lacks the moral scaffolding of conscious design**.

Unlike traditional code, AI systems learn patterns from data, adapt over time, and act independently of their programmers. These systems are not neutral—they absorb the world's inequalities, biases, and blind spots. If unchecked, they don't just **replicate injustice—they scale it.**

"The question is not whether AI can be good or evil. It's about whether AI can be used by humans for good or evil."

— **Fei-Fei Li**, Stanford University, 2023 World Economic Forum

To design AI without ethical intention is to outsource decision-making to an engine that knows patterns, but not **people**. That is why **conscious coding**—coding with human dignity, fairness, and accountability in mind—must become the **new professional standard**.

"We need to stop assuming that just because something is technical, it is neutral."

— **Timnit Gebru**, Co-founder of DAIR (Distributed AI Research Institute)

The future of AI will not be defined by breakthroughs in compute or scale. It will be defined by whether we build **human-centered** systems that are worthy of trust, safety, and inclusion. And that begins not in boardrooms, but in **the codebase**—line by line.

> "When we fail to question systems, they become enshrined. We must audit not just the code, but the assumptions behind it."—**Joy Buolamwini**, Founder, Algorithmic Justice League

Sidebar: Five Principles of Conscious Coding

1. **Transparency by Design**
   Code must be explainable and auditable by humans at every layer—from data sourcing to model inference.

2. **Bias Anticipation, Not Just Detection**
   Ethical AI development begins with acknowledging that bias is not an exception—it's the baseline. Counter it proactively.

3. **Stakeholder Inclusion**
   Bring affected communities into the development process. Design with—not just for—diverse user populations.

4. **Ethics as Engineering**
   Treat fairness, accountability, and safety as engineering constraints—not post-hoc considerations.

5. **Fail-Safe Architectures**
   Build in override systems, appeal mechanisms, and human-in-the-loop checks for critical AI applications.

REAL LIFE EXAMPLE: COMPAS – WHEN PREDICTIVE POLICING FAILS JUSTICE

COMPAS (Correctional Offender Management Profiling for Alternative Sanctions) was an AI system used by U.S. courts to predict the likelihood of a defendant reoffending. While marketed as objective, an investigation by ProPublica revealed it was **twice as likely to falsely label Black defendants as high-risk compared to white defendants**—based not on behavior, but on patterns embedded in biased historical data.

Source: ProPublica: "Machine Bias" (2016)

This case exemplifies how an opaque algorithm, lacking accountability, can **amplify systemic injustice**—making the case for transparency and conscious coding not optional, but urgent.

CONCLUSION

In an age where code increasingly governs lives, **ethical awareness is the new core competency**. Whether you are a developer, executive, policymaker, or researcher, you hold power—not just to innovate, but to protect. This book invites you to see ethics not as a constraint, but as your greatest contribution to a future shaped by AI.

Because **every line of code is a moral act**—and every system we build is a reflection of what we choose to value. Table 0.2 elegantly summarizes this concept here.

TABLE 0.2 Leadership in AI Risk Management

• **Robust Governance**
• **Ethical AI Design**
• **Transparency and Oversight**
• **Stakeholder Engagement**
• **Risk Assessment**

Key research papers on this topic include:

2018: Luciano Floridi and colleagues, in their landmark research paper, *"AI4People—An Ethical Framework for a Good AI Society" (Floridi et al., 2018),* establish one of the most comprehensive ethical guidelines for the adoption of AI technologies.

Their influential study outlines four key ethical imperatives: **Beneficence**: AI must actively contribute positively to society, going beyond mere harm avoidance to improve human welfare. For technical stakeholders, this translates into the imperative to design algorithms explicitly optimized not only for accuracy or profit but also societal good—such as healthcare diagnostics that maximize patient outcomes rather than cost-effectiveness alone. **Non-maleficence**: AI systems should prioritize avoiding harm. From a policy standpoint, Floridi highlights proactive governance measures like rigorous risk assessments and transparent disclosures of AI limitations, mandating developers to employ robust testing methodologies that identify and mitigate unintended harm before deployment. **Autonomy**: AI must enhance, rather than restrict, human autonomy. Floridi emphasizes designing AI systems with transparent human oversight—particularly crucial in automated financial decision-making, healthcare consent, and employment screening.

Technical experts must integrate explainable AI techniques to maintain human control and informed consent. **Justice**: AI must uphold fairness, transparency, and inclusivity, systematically identifying and mitigating algorithmic biases that may result from skewed datasets or biased human annotations. Floridi suggests technical stakeholders implement fairness-aware machine learning algorithms (such as bias-detection methods like IBM's AI Fairness 360 or Google's Fairness Indicators toolkit) to objectively quantify, disclose, and rectify discrimination.

Floridi's framework aligns seamlessly with policy instruments like the **European Commission's proposed AI Act (2021)**, emphasizing mandatory compliance with explicit guidelines around transparency, fairness, and risk management. This direct linkage makes Floridi's ethical principles practically actionable, guiding both technical teams and policymakers on concrete governance steps.

The urgency of ethical accountability was vividly emphasized by **Geoffrey Hinton during his influential keynote at the Neural Information Processing Systems (NeurIPS, 2018).**

Hinton argued forcefully that current AI developments outpace existing ethical and regulatory frameworks, stating explicitly, "Our technology is rapidly outgrowing our moral and legislative capacities." He recommended the immediate creation of cross-disciplinary governance structures, involving technical AI experts, ethicists, legal scholars, and risk management professionals, ensuring a holistic approach to AI accountability.

Hinton's call to action has directly influenced contemporary policy discussions, most notably informing the establishment of AI ethics committees within leading technology corporations and national regulatory bodies, thus providing a direct reference point for policymakers seeking proactive AI governance frameworks.

2019: Building further upon this insight, **Russell's seminal research (2019)**, presented in **"Human Compatible: Artificial Intelligence and the Problem of Control,"** articulates the pressing necessity to embed human-aligned values within AI. Russell provides a compelling case for creating AI systems that reflect human ethics to mitigate existential and operational risks—a concept central to our exploration. His assertions align powerfully with the discussions in Chapter 2, which introduced the deep ethical dimensions intrinsic to AI's widespread deployment.

2020:

Coeckelbergh (2020), in his impactful paper "AI Ethics", further accentuates the urgency surrounding transparency in AI systems, identifying the "black box" problem as a significant contemporary risk. Decisions generated by deep learning models often lack explainability, posing severe compliance, legal, and reputational risks for organizations. Addressing these complexities forms a cornerstone of our practical exploration within this chapter.

Kaplan and Haenlein's comprehensive analysis (2020) into strategic AI adoption illustrates empirically how organizations utilizing predictive analytics and intelligent automation significantly mitigate financial, operational, and compliance risks. They reinforce the fundamental premise of this chapter—that AI, if effectively governed and integrated within robust ERM frameworks, serves as a potent instrument for proactive risk mitigation.

2021:

"Fairness and Bias in AI Systems" by Harini Suresh and John Guttag (*Communications of the ACM*) Harini Suresh, a computer scientist at Harvard, and John Guttag, a distinguished professor at MIT, collaborated on this paper to address systemic biases in AI systems. Their work provides a comprehensive framework for identifying biases across various stages of the AI pipeline, including data collection, model design, and deployment. By emphasizing strategies like fairness-aware learning algorithms and the use of diverse datasets, the paper has set new benchmarks for ethical AI practices. As of December 2024, this influential research has been cited over 2,300 times, demonstrating its relevance and applicability in academia and industry alike.

Nobel laureate Daniel Kahneman's recent influential book, *"Noise: A Flaw in Human Judgment"* (2021), presents profound insights into how AI can dramatically reduce cognitive biases inherent in human decision-making. However, Kahneman explicitly cautions against the opacity of algorithmic decisions, highlighting the consequential risk of "black box" AI systems. He emphasizes explainability as the critical accountability measure, stressing the necessity for transparent audit trails and detailed disclosure of algorithmic decision processes to regulators, users, and affected stakeholders. For technical audiences, this necessitates rigorous adoption of interpretability methodologies such as Shapley Additive Explanations (SHAP) or Local Interpretable Model-agnostic Explanations (LIME), providing clear visualizations of model decision pathways. Policymakers thus can mandate compliance requirements around interpretability and accountability audits—aligning with Kahneman's recommendations.

Coeckelbergh (2020), in his pivotal paper *"AI Ethics,"* highlights the "black box problem," expanding Kahneman's concerns into a detailed critique of AI's interpretability challenge.

He underscores the technical imperative to adopt "explainable AI" (XAI) as an ethical baseline. Coeckelbergh details how technical teams must integrate transparency by design, utilizing architectures like decision trees, hybrid rule-based models, and attention-based neural networks that inherently support interpretability. For policymakers, Coeckelbergh's emphasis underscores the need to set regulatory standards explicitly mandating AI explainability in high-risk applications—such as healthcare, finance, criminal justice, and recruitment.

Kaplan and Haenlein (2020), through their extensive empirical study on strategic AI adoption, offer conclusive evidence that organizations effectively embedding ethical accountability frameworks within their enterprise risk management (ERM) systems significantly reduce operational, legal, and reputational risks.

Their research identifies clear technical best practices, including continuous model validation, dynamic fairness assessments, and rigorous data governance controls that policy teams can translate directly into enforceable regulatory standards. Their work explicitly quantifies the organizational benefit of integrating ethical accountability into risk management, providing policymakers concrete justification for stricter compliance and governance standards.

Taken collectively, these foundational works—Floridi's ethical principles, Russell's human-value alignment, Hinton's governance urgency, Kahneman's emphasis on transparency, Coeckelbergh's detailed advocacy for explainability, and Kaplan and Haenlein's empirical validations—illustrate how embedding ethics and accountability into AI is not merely desirable but technically achievable and legally imperative.

This nuanced understanding equips technical experts to implement ethically responsible AI design proactively, empowers policymakers with actionable regulatory frameworks, and ultimately ensures AI's profound transformative power remains aligned with enduring human values. In doing so, organizations not only mitigate risks but unlock AI's fullest potential—ethical, accountable, and sustainable innovation that benefits humanity collectively.

Disclaimer

This book is a synthesis of publicly available information, including news articles, academic journals, industry reports, regulatory publications, real-world incidents, and the authors' own professional research and experience. We have also used AI tools, for example ChatGPT, Claude, GrokAI, etc. to generate select visual content and images to help elaborate key topics and improve reader understanding. While every effort has been made to ensure the accuracy, relevance, and integrity of the content, the authors do not claim ownership or responsibility for the accuracy or views expressed in external sources. The content presented herein is intended solely for informational purposes—to serve as a practical guide for scientists, policymakers, risk managers, and AI practitioners. It does not constitute legal, technical, or financial advice. The authors have exercised due diligence in evaluating and referencing source materials but do not accept liability for any direct or indirect consequences arising from the interpretation or application of this content. The aim is to empower readers with critical thinking around the responsible and ethical development of AI technologies. Any mention of specific tools, organizations, or events is illustrative and not intended as endorsement or critique. The views expressed in this book are solely those of the authors and do not reflect the views, strategies, or positions of their current, former, or future employers. Readers are encouraged to consult original sources and seek professional advice where appropriate.

NOTES

1. Authors are industry experts in the technical and risk domains. However, this book is based on their own research - perceived and experienced - during their personal experiments. *Content of the book and related, does not reflect the viewpoint of their past, current and future employers.* As such authors encourage and advise their readers to do self-research before

applying any concept from this book, and consider the content of this book and related, as only for general information in a way to help in elevating and encouraging them to gain knowledge on risk and emerging technology.

2. Excerpts from Wikipedia: Socrates (c. 470 – 399 BC) was a Greek philosopher from Athens who is credited as the founder of Western philosophy and considered as among the first moral philosophers of the ethical tradition of thought. Socrates did not document his teachings. All that is known about him comes from the accounts of others and at times from each reader's interpretation. As such, this reference of "Socratic questioning" in this book should be perceived as the authors' opinion and one of many methods to encourage holistic and deeper thinking. **Socratic questioning** is authors' preferred and time-tested technique for having meaningful discussions that get to the heart of what people truly believe and why by engaging in mindful questioning (and answering) without accusations or debating. Ask clarifying questions, respectfully challenge assumptions, seek evidence/reasons, consider alternative perspectives, explore impacts, question the question itself, etc could be few ways one can arrive at deeper understanding. There are limitations to this technique.
3. The Lancet Digital Health is an open-access, peer-reviewed monthly journal dedicated to the rapidly evolving field of digital health. The journal addresses the intersection of technology and health, focusing on how digital tools can inform and improve clinical practices and outcomes worldwide.
4. Correctional Offender Management Profiling for Alternative Sanctions (COMPAS) is a case management and decision support software developed and owned by Northpointe (now Equivant), used by U.S. courts to assess the likelihood of a defendant becoming a recidivist.
5. Dr. Timnit Gebru is a prominent AI researcher known for her work on ethical AI, algorithmic bias, and the social implications of AI. She's a co-founder of Black in AI, a non-profit organization aimed at increasing the presence and visibility of Black individuals in the field of AI. Gebru is also the founder and executive director of the Distributed AI Research Institute (DAIR), an organization dedicated to ethical AI research. Her work has been recognized with various accolades, including being named one of Nature's Ten people who shaped science.
6. Data poisoning involves intentionally corrupting the training data used to build AI/ML models. Attackers inject malicious or misleading data into the training dataset, influencing the model's learning process. This can lead to inaccurate predictions, biased outcomes, and security vulnerabilities.
7. Adversarial Attacks exploit vulnerabilities in AI systems by crafting malicious inputs (adversarial examples) that deceive the model into making incorrect decisions. Attackers subtly modify input data in a way that is imperceptible to humans but significantly impacts the AI model's output. This can compromise security, privacy, and safety, especially in critical applications like autonomous vehicles or medical diagnosis systems.

8. Privacy risks refer to the potential harm individuals or organizations face due to the improper handling of their personal data. These risks can range from data breaches and unauthorized access to data misuse, identity theft, and reputational damage. It's important to understand and mitigate these risks to protect individuals' privacy and ensure compliance with relevant regulations. Mitigating Privacy Risks techniques can include implementing strong security measures, cybersecurity training, conduct privacy risk assessments, monitor and respond to breaches, staying informed about regulations, or, exploring and implementing technologies that can help protect privacy, such as encryption, anonymization, and differential privacy.
9. The Turing Award, often called the "Nobel Prize of Computing," is the highest honor in computer science. It's an annual award given by the Association for Computing Machinery (ACM) to recognize individuals who have made major, lasting contributions to the field. The award is named after the British mathematician and computer scientist Alan Turing, whose work laid the foundation for modern computer science.
10. https://gdpr-info.eu/ Here you can find the official PDF of the Regulation (EU) 2016/679 (General Data Protection Regulation) in the current version of the OJ L 119, 04.05.2016; cor. OJ L 127, 23.5.2018 as a neatly arranged website. All Articles of the GDPR are linked with suitable recitals in this link. The European Data Protection Regulation is applicable as of May 25th, 2018 in all member states to harmonize data privacy laws across Europe. If you find the page useful, feel free to support us by sharing the project.
11. https://ai-act-law.eu/?utm_source=gdpr-info.eu: Here you will find the PDF of Artificial Intelligence Act (AI Act) neatly arranged. The final text of the AI Act is available both in English and German. The Regulation (EU) 2024/1689 of the European Parliament and of the Council of 13 June 2024 laying down harmonised rules on Artificial Intelligence will apply from 2 August 2026 with some exceptions (cf. Art. 113 AI Act).

CHAPTER 1

Mastering Uncertainty

The Strategic Role of Risk Management

> "The only true wisdom is in acknowledging and understanding that you essentially know nothing"

This profound statement was made by Socrates, the classical Greek philosopher, who, through his philosophical journey, emphasized the importance of questioning everything and continuously seeking knowledge.

INTRODUCTION

This inaugural chapter of this book is designed to do far more than just welcome you to a familiar discipline. It is an invitation to reimagine risk management as the connective tissue that binds ingenuity to resilience in an age defined by volatility.

Today, quantum-speed technological[1] shifts, fractal geopolitical realignments, and cascading environmental disruptions collide to form what complexity scientists call a "*risk spiral*": a feedback loop in which seemingly isolated hazards amplify one another and propagate across global systems.

Against this backdrop, the **practice of managing risk** is no longer a defensive ledger of losses to avoid; **it is the primary language through which leaders articulate strategy, allocate scarce resources, and spark responsible innovation.**

DOI: 10.1201/9781003607298-1

This chapter therefore opens with a provocation: ***What if uncertainty were not a threat to be feared, but raw material to be sculpted into opportunity?***

From this question, we embark on a narrative that merges centuries-old actuarial wisdom with the bleeding-edge insights of artificial intelligence (AI) and safety, revealing risk management as both an intellectual framework and a lived philosophy.

Whether you are a graduate student decoding your first Monte Carlo simulation[2] or a board-room veteran overseeing multibillion-dollar capital allocation, the pages ahead challenge you to *adopt risk thinking as a daily habit*—much like reading financial statements or practicing situational awareness on a factory floor.

To ground this habit, we weave *three* distinct threads:

First, we trace the historical arc of risk—from the Phoenicians' earliest maritime insurance contracts to the probabilistic revolution ignited by Pascal and Fermat, through the 20th-century synthesis of modern portfolio theory, and finally into today's AI-augmented predictive analytics. This lineage underscores a vital truth: *while tools evolve, the human imperative to make sense of uncertainty remains constant.*

Second, we present contemporary case studies drawn from cybersecurity, supply chain resilience, public health preparedness, and climate finance stress testing. Each story demonstrates how forward-leaning organizations transformed looming perils into competitive advantage—sometimes by spotting weak signals before rivals, other times by engineering organizational cultures that reward transparent communication of "bad news."

Third, we project forward, sketching the contours of emerging risk domains such as synthetic media misinformation, quantum decryption threats, and algorithmic liability regimes. Readers come away with a panoramic vision: *yesterday's lessons, today's imperatives, and tomorrow's frontiers form a seamless continuum* that any risk-literate professional must traverse.

Yet narrative alone is insufficient. Throughout this book we embed actionable frameworks that translate philosophy into practice.

You will encounter the taxonomy that distinguishes *inherent* risk[3] from *residual*[4] risk, the bow-tie diagram[5] that visualizes causal pathways, and maturity models that benchmark organizational capabilities across governance, data, and culture.

We examine the expanding role of digital twins and scenario generators that now allow executives to "time travel" across thousands of plausible futures before committing a single dollar of capital. At every step, we pair conceptual depth with practical heuristics—rules of thumb that seasoned practitioners rely on when data are incomplete and the clock is ticking.

Importantly, we reject the notion that risk management is the solitary province of auditors or compliance officers. Rather, **it is a multidisciplinary craft that thrives at the confluence of data science, behavioral psychology, ethics, and systems engineering.**

To illustrate, consider the cross-functional "**fusion cells**" adopted by leading aerospace firms: cybersecurity analysts, AI ethicists, and supply chain economists gather in the same war-room to map how a malicious software update might not only ground aircraft but also trigger insurance claims, reputational damage, and regulatory scrutiny. Such holistic foresight demands a workforce fluent in risk vocabulary—precisely the literacy this chapter aims to cultivate.

By the chapter's midpoint, you will recognize that effective risk management hinges as much on *mindset* as on *method.*

We **explore cognitive biases—from normalcy bias to the illusion of control**—that silently erode judgment, and we introduce antidotes such as pre-mortems, red-team exercises, and devil's advocate roles.

These tools democratize vigilance, empowering every employee—factory technician, machine learning engineer, or regional sales director—to become an early warning sensor. When amplified by transparent governance structures and psychologically safe cultures, their collective intelligence elevates the entire enterprise's ability to absorb shock and rebound stronger.

No introductory chapter would be complete without charting the professional pathways available to aspiring programmers and risk leaders.

We therefore curated a living compendium of certifications[6] and learning journeys: ISO 31000, Project Management Institute-Risk Management Program (PMI-RMP,) Certified Information Privacy Professional (CIPP), National Institute of Standards and Technology (NIST) *Artificial Intelligence Risk Management Framework (AI RMF 1.0)*

NIST AI RMF Practitioner, Certified Third-Party Risk Professional (CTPRP), and more. Each credential is mapped to a capability domain—quantitative analytics, regulatory mastery, cyber-resilience, ethical AI—offering readers a self-directed syllabus tailored to their career aspirations. In an era where credentials multiply as quickly as hazards, our guidance helps you invest your time and tuition strategically, selecting those programs that deliver both intellectual rigor and market credibility.

The chapter culminates with a forward-looking manifesto. *We argue that the organizations which will flourish in the coming decade are those that position risk officers not as corporate alarm bells but as innovation catalysts.*

When **risk appetite**[7] is articulated clearly and monitored continuously, engineers gain the confidence to experiment, strategists gain the clarity to seize fleeting market windows, and stakeholders gain the assurance that progress will not come at the expense of safety or trust.

In this sense, risk management becomes the "**trust infrastructure**" of the digital economy—an invisible yet indispensable foundation upon which bold ideas are built.

By the final paragraph, you will have journeyed well beyond definitions. You will have seen risk management reframed as a strategic dialogue between uncertainty and ambition, and as a muscle that grows stronger with every scenario tested and every lesson learned. You will understand why enterprises that embedded risk culture prior to the COVID-19 pandemic pivoted faster, protected revenue, and even expanded market share, while laggards struggled to interpret weak signals amidst the noise. And you will appreciate that the most sophisticated AI model is only as trustworthy as the risk governance that shepherds its lifecycle—from dataset curation to post-deployment monitoring.

> **Mastering Uncertainty** thus sets the intellectual tone for the entire book.
>
> It equips you with a mental compass oriented toward possibility, a toolkit of methodologies to navigate complexity, and a community of practice built on shared language and ethical conviction.

Our aspiration is that when you finish this book, you are not merely informed but transformed—eager to implement its insights in your next project, to explore the deeper technical vistas of subsequent chapters, and to recommend this volume to peers and protégés alike. In accepting this invitation, you become part of a global movement: professionals and scholars who refuse to be passive recipients of disruption, choosing instead to shape a future where uncertainty is not the enemy of progress but its most potent ally.

This chapter is divided into four carefully curated sections:

Section A: Introduction to Risk Management & Framework

Section B: Why managing Risk is Non-negotiable in Today's Era

Section C: Applications in Real World & How *You* can Master These

Section D: Chapter Summary

SECTION A: INTRODUCTION TO RISK MANAGEMENT & FRAMEWORK

In today's interconnected and rapidly evolving world, organizations and individuals alike are faced with uncertainties that are as unpredictable as they are impactful.

According to a 2023 report by the U.S. Government Accountability Office (GAO), the federal government incurred estimated annual financial losses due to fraud ranging from $233 billion to $521 billion between fiscal years 2018 and 2022. This staggering figure underscores the critical importance of robust risk management frameworks in mitigating financial and operational risks across sectors. Whether it's a global pandemic halting supply chains, a cybersecurity breach exposing sensitive data, or an economic downturn shaking financial markets, risks are ever-present and increasingly multifaceted.

Risk management, therefore, emerges as a vital practice—an art and science of foreseeing, evaluating, and addressing these uncertainties to safeguard objectives and create opportunities.

The **origins of risk management** trace back to ancient times when early societies devised strategies to navigate uncertainty.

> From Babylonian merchants insuring their goods against loss to the first financial risk models during the Renaissance, humanity has always sought to anticipate and mitigate risk. These traditional approaches laid the groundwork for the modern discipline of risk management, which evolved to encompass structured methodologies for addressing financial, operational, and strategic threats. While traditional risk management focused heavily

on measurable and predictable risks, today's approach must also account for emerging risks—those that arise from rapid technological advancements, geopolitical shifts, and environmental changes.

For example, the global financial crisis of 2008 highlighted the importance of comprehensive risk frameworks in understanding interconnected risks. Similarly, the rapid adoption of AI has brought new challenges, such as algorithmic bias and data misuse, emphasizing the need for modern, adaptive risk strategies. Some big tech companies have implemented AI risk frameworks to assess ethical implications, while some banks are leveraging machine learning to predict credit defaults. In recent times, we have noticed how organizations are pivoting toward risk management practices that are both agile and technologically driven.

Modern risk management extends beyond threat mitigation to include the strategic use of risks for organizational growth and innovation.

The fundamental purpose of risk management involves **a structured approach to discover events that can either obstruct or unexpectedly advance organizational goals followed by analyzing the chance and consequences of these events and developing strategies to safeguard value and seize opportunities.**

The history of risk management begins with 17th-century maritime insurance records and extends through 20th-century financial probability models to present-day AI predictive analytics. Yet the essence remains unchanged: ***Risk management represents humanity's united effort to create stability amidst market fluctuations.***

For programmers, this could mean writing secure, robust code that mitigates the risk of breaches, while for seasoned executives, it's about embedding risk principles into decision-making to navigate market volatility.

Why Begin Our Book Here?

This is because every subsequent chapter—whether exploring machine learning triage systems or ethics frameworks for generative AI—relies on the vocabulary and thought patterns forged in this discipline.

We start by unpacking the standard risk lexicon: inherent risk versus residual risk, threat versus vulnerability, and impact versus likelihood. By grounding readers in these fundamental distinctions, we build fluency that will make later discussions about *algorithmic bias scores or Monte Carlo simulations* instantly intelligible.

Moreover, this introductory chapter highlights the human dimension of risk. Behind every heat map and dashboard lies judgment: the collective intuition, experience, and ethics of professionals who must decide whether to accept, mitigate, transfer, or exploit uncertainty.

You will encounter vignettes of risk managers who successfully detected early warning signs—think of the epidemiologists who modeled pandemic spillovers years before COVID-19—as well as cautionary tales where risks were ignored, leading to catastrophic losses. These narratives remind us that risk management is as much an art of perception as **it is a science of measurement.**

Key Components of Risk Management Framework

A well-designed risk management framework provides a structured approach to identify, assess, mitigate, and monitor risks. These components not only build organizational resilience but also ensure strategic alignment.

Let's dive into each key component with detailed methodologies and real-world applications.

These interdependent components of a modern risk management framework are illustrated using a wheel-and-spoke model in Figure 1.1.

Table 1.1 operationalizes this framework by mapping each risk management domain to its core tasks and enabling mechanisms.

A consolidated taxonomy of these core risk concepts, along with definitions and practical examples, is provided in Table 1.2. This taxonomy serves as a reference point throughout the book.

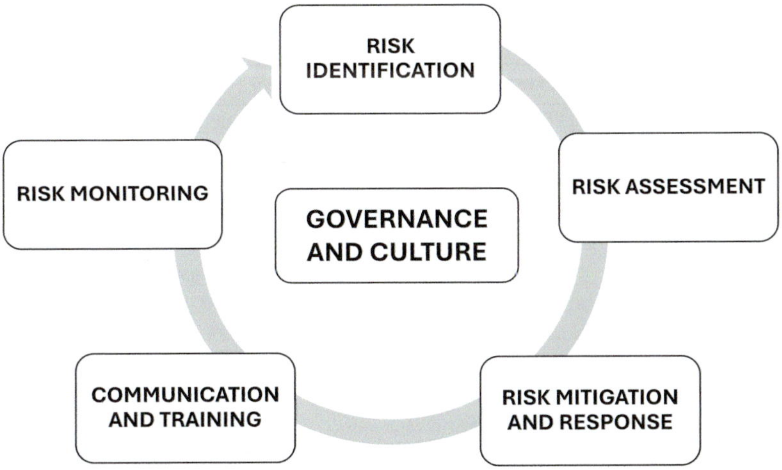

FIGURE 1.1 This wheel-and-spoke layout underscores that effective governance drives—and is reinforced by—every other domain.

TABLE 1.1 The Wheel-and-Spoke Layout. This Holistic Table Underscores that Effective Governance Drives—and Is Reinforced by—Every Domain

Domain	Tasks	Enablers
Governance and culture	Define risk vision and policy, roles and risk appetite	Tone at-the-top, ISO 31000/ COSO ERM
Risk identification	Scan internal/external context, surface threats and vulnerabilities, and maintain risk register	Workshops, SWOT/PEST, scenario planning, data mining and AI anomaly detection
Risk assessment	Qualitative scoring, quantitative models (VaR, Monte Carlo), prioritize via heat map	Taxonomy, scales, statistical tools, FAIR, simulation software
Risk response/ mitigation	Choose strategy (Avoid, Reduce, Transfer, Accept, Exploit), design and implement controls, create action plans and budgets	Policies, control libraries, cyber-insurance, automation, IAM, SDLC gates
Monitoring and reporting	Track KRIs and residual risk, dashboard and board reporting, independent assurance/audit	GRC platforms, BI dashboards, internal audit, continuous controls monitoring
Communication and training	Enterprise-wide awareness, targeted skill programs, stakeholder engagement	LMS and micro-learning, playbooks, crisis-comms plans
Continuous improvement	Post-incident reviews, benchmarking and maturity assessments, updating framework and controls	Lessons-learned databases, capability models, external standards refresh

TABLE 1.2 Key Risk Taxonomy. This Holistic Table Equips Practitioners and Learners with a One-Stop Reference for the Core Vocabulary, Measurement Methods, and Governance Concepts That Anchor Modern Risk Management Practice

Term	Simple Definition	Example
Risk	The effect of uncertainty on objectives (positive or negative)	A sudden spike in raw material prices threatens profit margins
Inherent risk	The level of risk in a process *before* any controls are applied	A payment system exposed directly to the internet that faces high cyber-attack risk
Residual risk	The remaining risk *after* controls and mitigations are in place	After installing a web-application firewall, the same system still carries moderate cyber risk
Threat	An external actor or force that can exploit a weakness	Phishing campaign, hurricane
Vulnerability	An internal flaw or gap that a threat can exploit	Unpatched software, single-person approval for payments

(*Continued*)

TABLE 1.2 (*Continued*) Key Risk Taxonomy. This Holistic Table Equips Practitioners and Learners with a One-Stop Reference for the Core Vocabulary, Measurement Methods, and Governance Concepts That Anchor Modern Risk Management Practice

Term	Simple Definition	Example
Impact	The magnitude of loss or gain if a risk event occurs	$10 million in lost revenue from one week of downtime
Likelihood/ probability	The chance that a risk event will occur within a time frame	5% annual probability of a Category-4 storm hitting the data center
Risk heat map	A two-dimensional grid (impact × likelihood) used to visualize and rank risks	Red cells flag high-impact/ high-probability events for executive attention
Risk appetite	The amount of risk an organization is willing to pursue or retain to meet its goals	Board approves up to 2% of annual revenue at risk in R&D bets
Risk tolerance	Acceptable variation around objectives within the risk appetite	IT outage tolerance <4 hours; anything longer triggers incident escalation
Risk threshold	A specific cut-off point that, once exceeded, requires action	If residual cyber risk score exceeds 70/100, mandatory remediation is launched
Risk capacity	The maximum level of risk an organization can absorb without jeopardizing viability	A bank's capital adequacy rules limit credit-loss capacity to 12% of equity
Risk profile	The overall composition and relative weighting of an entity's risks	40% market, 30% operational, 20% credit, 10% strategic
Risk register	A living log of identified risks, assessments, and responses	Spreadsheet or GRC tool listing each risk, owner, KRI, treatment plan
Risk management plan	Document that outlines processes for identification, analysis, response, monitoring, and governance	Project charter includes a section detailing how risks will be logged and escalated
Risk identification techniques	Structured approaches to surface risks	**Brainstorming workshops, SWOT/PEST analyses, Delphi surveys**, checklists, AI anomaly detection
Risk measurement and assessment techniques	Methods for quantifying or qualifying risk levels	Qualitative 3×3 matrix; quantitative **Monte Carlo simulation**; value-at-risk; fault-tree analysis

(*Continued*)

TABLE 1.2 (*Continued*) Key Risk Taxonomy. This Holistic Table Equips Practitioners and Learners with a One-Stop Reference for the Core Vocabulary, Measurement Methods, and Governance Concepts That Anchor Modern Risk Management Practice

Term	Simple Definition	Example
Monte Carlo simulation	Monte Carlo simulation is a type of computational algorithm that uses repeated random sampling to obtain the likelihood of a range of results of occurring	How to create a Monte Carlo simulation: • Choose a formula. The first step in creating a Monte Carlo simulation is to choose a formula to represent a predictive model. • Define inputs. The inputs of your formula are the variables you identify for your specific purpose. • Start the simulation. • Analyze the results.
Risk response/ mitigation strategies	Actions to address risk: Avoid, Reduce, Transfer, Accept, Exploit	Transfer: buy cyber-insurance; Reduce: patch servers; Accept: low-impact supplier delay
Controls	Policies, procedures, or technical safeguards that reduce risk likelihood or impact	Multi-factor authentication, segregation of duties, encryption at rest
Control effectiveness	Degree to which a control achieves its intended risk-reduction objective	Pen-test shows MFA blocks 99% of credential-stuffing attacks—highly effective
Key risk indicator (KRI)	A metric that provides early signal of increasing risk exposure	Percentage of critical servers not patched within 30 days
Risk frameworks and standards	Structured guidance for enterprise risk programs	**ISO 31000**,[a] **COSO ERM**, **NIST AI RMF**, **Basel III/IV**, **FAIR** for cyber value-at-risk
Risk governance	Roles, responsibilities, and oversight structures that steer risk activities	Board Risk Committee, three-lines-of-defense model
Algorithmic bias score	Metric that quantifies disparity in an AI model's outcomes across demographic groups—treated as residual model risk	Model shows 1.8× higher denial rate for applicants from ZIP codes with minority populations

(*Continued*)

TABLE 1.2 (*Continued*) Key Risk Taxonomy. This Holistic Table Equips Practitioners and Learners with a One-Stop Reference for the Core Vocabulary, Measurement Methods, and Governance Concepts That Anchor Modern Risk Management Practice

Term	Simple Definition	Example
ISO (International Organization for Standardization)	ISO brings global experts together to agree on the best way of doing things—for anything from making a product to managing a process. As one of the oldest non-governmental international organizations, ISO has enabled trade and cooperation between people and companies all over the world since 1946	Approximately 25,795 International Standards and other deliverables covering almost all aspects of technology, management and manufacturing
NIST AI RMF	NIST is the National Measurement Institute (NMI) for the United States. Also sometimes called National Metrology Institute, NMI is a unique organization authorized by a country's government to: • Maintain the country's primary measurement standards • Provide traceability for all national measurement needs • Represent the country in the international system of units for trade and science • Advance measurement science to support the country's economic competitiveness • Use measurement expertise to support the development of technically sound documentary standards	One of NIST's best-known documentary standards is the NIST Cybersecurity Framework. For additional details and standards, refer to https://www.nist.gov/

[a] ISO 31000 is an international standard that provides principles and guidelines for risk management, applicable to any organization, regardless of size or sector. It focuses on helping organizations integrate risk management into their business processes and activities. The standard covers principles, a framework, and a process for identifying, analyzing, evaluating, and treating risks. Standard is reviewed every five years. Read the last published (ISO 31000:2018) guideline on https://www.iso.org/standard/65694.html.

Now that we have covered what risk management is, let us dive in where this is most critical and how you can master this skill.

SECTION B: WHY MANAGING RISK IS NON-NEGOTIABLE IN TODAY'S ERA

Risk management functions as an essential requirement for all organizations and individuals today.

Today's organizational landscape demands risk management as a fundamental requirement rather than an optional or desirable function. Risk management has become an essential element that shapes strategic decisions and operational resilience for both organizations and individuals in our complex modern world.

Businesses today function within settings that feature swift tech progress, expanded network connections, and massive data distribution. Risks in modern settings stem not only from traditional areas such as market volatility and operational failures but also from advanced digital threats including cybersecurity breaches and data privacy violations along with biases and errors in AI.

The failure of organizations to actively manage these risks results in financial losses along with the potential for devastating reputation harm and regulatory fines.

The National Institute of Standards and Technology (NIST) demonstrates that traditional software risks get heightened by the unique complications presented by AI systems. AI systems require data that frequently becomes obsolete or fails to match real-world scenarios which produces unforeseen outcomes including biased decisions and erroneous conclusions. AI-related risks present distinct challenges because their effects develop through intricate socio-technical system interactions which influence diverse stakeholder groups beyond direct users.

Risk management remains essential today because it plays a crucial role in building stakeholder trust.

The NIST AI Risk Management Framework (AI RMF) explains how effective risk management practices build system trustworthiness through accountability and transparency while maintaining ethical standards in technology deployments. Trust remains essential to secure user acceptance and meet regulatory requirements which directly impacts an organization's ability to sustain operations over time while maintaining competitive market status.

- Organizations must now focus on risk prioritization and proper management because their resources are limited.
- Organizations need to differentiate between critical and minor risks because not all risks merit equal attention and misallocation of resources arises from treating them the same.
- Organizations need to establish strategic prioritization frameworks which focus on the identification and resolution of top-priority risks that have the potential to cause significant damage.
- Strategic prioritization helps maintain organizational resources while enhancing the protection of essential business operations and vital infrastructure.

Examine how insufficient risk management practices affect essential sectors such as healthcare and finance. The mishandling of risks in critical industries results in significant ramifications that extend from personal life effects to disruptions within societal structures. Improper patient data management combined with inaccurate AI financial risk evaluations can result in serious privacy breaches and major financial disturbances.

Today's risk management approaches stress the importance of constant adaptation and learning processes. Organizations must build adaptable systems which enable them to detect new risks and adjust to them quickly.

Modern organizations must develop agile responses and sturdy risk cultures because threats continue to evolve technologically and sociopolitically along with regulatory changes.

Organizations need adaptability to transition from reactive to proactive approaches in risk mitigation.

A strong risk management system remains fundamental for both organizational success and the welfare of society within our fast-paced and interconnected world today.

Organizations that actively adopt advanced risk management models, like the NIST AI RMF, prepare themselves for successful complex navigation while building stakeholder confidence and securing sustainable growth over time.

Risk management has become so crucial that it now stands as a key strategic imperative beyond its previous role as an operational support function.

In summary, here's why:

1. **Protecting assets and reputation**: Unmanaged risks can lead to financial losses, legal liabilities, and reputational damage—often with lasting consequences. For example, the U.S. GAO reported that financial losses due to fraud across federal programs ranged from $233 billion to $521 billion annually between 2018 and 2022 (GAO Report : https://www.gao.gov/). Effective risk management safeguards resources and mitigates reputational harm.
2. **Ensuring business continuity**: Natural disasters, cyber-attacks, or supply chain disruptions can bring operations to a halt. A 2022 report by FEMA highlighted that 40% of businesses do not reopen after a disaster, emphasizing the importance of proactive risk management (https://www.fema.gov/). Robust strategies ensure resilience and operational continuity in the face of such crises.
3. **Driving decision-making**: Risk management provides leaders with actionable insights to make informed decisions. Organizations like IBM leverage AI-powered risk tools to identify vulnerabilities in supply chains and optimize responses, demonstrating how modern risk management enhances decision-making (https://www.ibm.com/us-en).
4. **Enhancing stakeholder confidence**: Employees, customers, investors, and regulators are more confident in organizations that proactively manage risks. The NIST published guidelines in 2022 emphasizing the role of transparent risk frameworks in building trust, particularly in AI and cybersecurity domains (https://www.nist.gov/).
5. **Compliance and regulatory obligations**: In an era of stringent regulations, risk management helps organizations meet compliance requirements and avoid penalties. For instance, the California Consumer Privacy Act (CCPA) and the European Union's General Data Protection Regulation (GDPR) mandate strict data privacy measures, underscoring the need for strong compliance frameworks (CCPA, https://gdpr-info.eu/).

6. **Empowering individuals**: Risk management extends beyond organizations. On a personal level, understanding risk can help individuals manage their finances, health, and career decisions more effectively. The Consumer Financial Protection Bureau (CFPB) offers tools to help individuals assess and mitigate personal financial risks (https://www.consumerfinance.gov/).

7. **Managing AI-driven risks**: With the rise of AI, unique risks like algorithmic bias, data misuse, and ethical challenges have emerged. The National Artificial Intelligence Initiative Act of 2020 aims to address these issues by promoting transparency, accountability, and ethical AI development. Understanding these risks and mitigating them is critical to ensuring that AI serves society responsibly.

SECTION C: APPLICATIONS IN REAL WORLD AND HOW *YOU* CAN MASTER THESE

Risk management is not confined to a single domain. Its principles apply across industries and functions, reflecting its universal relevance. The following sections outline key domains, relevant laws, and government policies, providing both historical and current context:

- **Financial risk management**: This domain focuses on managing credit, market, liquidity, and operational risks. In the United States, the Dodd-Frank Wall Street Reform and Consumer Protection Act of 2010 was introduced to prevent financial crises by increasing transparency and oversight in the financial sector. The act is enforced by the Securities and Exchange Commission (SEC) and the Commodity Futures Trading Commission (CFTC). Financial institutions today leverage AI models for credit scoring and fraud detection, balancing innovation with compliance.

- **Cybersecurity and data privacy**: As data breaches and ransomware attacks grow, laws like the CCPA (effective 2020) and the Cybersecurity Information Sharing Act (CISA, 2015) are critical. The Federal Trade Commission (FTC) and the Cybersecurity and Infrastructure Security Agency (CISA) oversee implementation. These regulations require organizations to adopt robust data protection measures and transparency in handling consumer data. Emerging AI technologies also face scrutiny under these laws for algorithmic bias and privacy violations.

- **Operational risk management**: Operational risks arise from internal failures, process inefficiencies, or external events. **The Sarbanes-Oxley Act (SOX, 2002)** mandates internal controls and risk assessments for public companies, monitored by the Public Company Accounting Oversight Board (PCAOB). Organizations are also adopting AI-driven tools for real-time monitoring of operational risks.
- **Enterprise risk management (ERM)**: ERM aligns risk management with strategic objectives, considering the full spectrum of risks. COSO's ERM Framework (updated 2017) provides a globally recognized standard, emphasizing governance, strategy, and performance integration.
- **Supply chain risk management**: The COVID-19 pandemic highlighted vulnerabilities in supply chains, leading to government initiatives like the Executive Order on America's Supply Chains (2021). Agencies such as the Department of Commerce and the Department of Defense oversee supply chain resilience programs.
- **Health and safety risk management**: Industries like manufacturing and healthcare prioritize employee and customer safety. The Occupational Safety and Health Administration (OSHA) enforces the Occupational Safety and Health Act (1970), ensuring workplace safety standards are upheld.
- **Reputation risk management**: Reputation risks stem from public perception, product recalls, or ethical missteps. The FTC enforces truth-in-advertising laws to protect consumers and brands from reputational harm due to false claims or unethical practices.
- **Environmental and climate risk management**: The Environmental Protection Agency (EPA) enforces the Clean Air Act (1970) and the Clean Water Act (1972) to address environmental risks. The 2021 Infrastructure Investment and Jobs Act includes climate resilience funding, reflecting increased government focus on sustainability.
- **AI and technology risk management**: This domain examines challenges like algorithmic bias, data security, and ethical AI use. The National Artificial Intelligence Initiative Act (2020) promotes ethical AI development, overseen by the National AI Initiative

Office. The NIST AI RMF (2023) provides guidelines for mitigating AI risks.

- **Personal risk management**: On an individual level, risk management helps with financial planning and health decisions. The CFPB offers tools to manage personal financial risks. Policies like the Affordable Care Act (ACA, 2010) reduce health-related financial risks for individuals.

These domains demonstrate how risk management, supported by robust laws and policies, is integral to addressing the challenges of a rapidly changing world. Understanding the regulatory landscape empowers organizations and individuals to adopt proactive and compliant risk strategies.

We will delve deeper into the realms of risk management and AI in following chapters.

Here are few certifications that establish mastery in these areas:

Financial Risk Manager (FRM), issued by the Global Association of Risk Professionals (GARP), is a globally recognized qualification for mastering financial risk management domain.

Certified Information Systems Security Professional (CISSP), governed by (ISC), is essential for professionals in cybersecurity domain.

Certified in Risk and Information Systems Control (CRI/SC), offered by ISACA, is tailored for operational risk professionals.

Risk Management Professional certification, offered by Project Management Institute PMI.org, is tailored for project risk management expertise.

Enterprise Risk Management Professional Certification (ERMCP) by the ERM Academy is ideal for gaining expertise in ERM area.

Certified Supply Chain Professional (CSCP), issued by APICS, validates expertise in SCM domain.

Certified Safety Professional (CSP), administered by the Board of Certified Safety Professionals (BCSP), is widely recognized.

Public Relations Society of America Accreditation (APR) can be useful for mastering reputation risk management domain.

Certified Environmental Risk Assessor (CERA) is a valuable credential for professionals in environmental and climate risk management domain.

Certified Artificial Intelligence Practitioner (CAIP) from CertNexus is ideal for professionals focused on AI-related risks.

Certified Financial Planner (CFP) is highly regarded for personal financial risk management expertise.

NOTES

1. Quantum-based communications reproduce a naturally occurring phenomenon in which light particles (photons) can be linked or "entangled" such that any change in one of the photons is instantaneously mirrored by its "twin" even when they are separated by great distances. As per the World Economic Forum article on emerging technologies, published on July 3, 2024, **quantum technology** is based on the principles of quantum mechanics. These are the laws of physics that apply to sub-atomic particles, going back to the work of physicists including Niels Bohr, Werner Heisenberg, and Erwin Schrödinger in the 1920s. Quantum technology is not new. It first came into play with the development of nuclear power, and it is fundamental to the semiconductors you find in your phone and many other devices. Read the full article on https://www.weforum.org/stories/2024/07/explainer-what-is-quantum-technology/.
2. Monte Carlo simulation is a way to answer, "What might happen?" by playing out thousands (or millions) of random but realistic scenarios and seeing how often each outcome shows up. In simple words, Monte Carlo simulation is like running lots of "what-if" experiments with digital dice so you can see the full range of possible futures instead of betting on a single guess.
3. In business terms, inherent risk is the level of threat a process, project, or system naturally carries if you do nothing special to control or mitigate it.
4. Residual risk is the danger that remains after you've put your safety measures in place. In business, residual risk is the level of threat that lingers once policies, controls, or safeguards have been applied. It reminds you that no system is ever 100% risk-free—there's always some uncertainty you must accept, monitor, or insure against.
5. Bow-tie diagram shows what happens after the critical event and where you can place barriers. It shows how something bad could happen, what could trigger it, and what damage it might cause. Not to be confused with a **fishbone/Ishikawa** concept which analyzes root causes that lead to a particular effect.

6. Readers are expected to consider this list as general reference. We urge readers to perform their own research and analysis before signing up for any course or certification. Authors by no means are endorsing any listed certifications or courses.
7. **Risk appetite** is the amount of danger—or uncertainty—you're *comfortable* taking on to reach your goals. For example, a company might say, "We're willing to invest in new tech projects that could lose up to $2 million, but not more." That dollar limit is its risk appetite.

CHAPTER 2

Decoding Intelligence

Your Step-by-Step Guide on Artificial Intelligence

This chapter is divided into four sections:

Section A: Introduction to Artificial Intelligence

Section B: Evolution of Intelligence in Modern Science

Section C: New 'Core' of Innovation: How AI is Helping Humanity and Business

Section D: Ethical Consideration in Developing and using AI

But let us first understand what artificial intelligence (AI) versus generative AI is – may be like a 5-year-old! (see Figure 2.1)

FIGURE 2.1 Robot learning through human interactions and data.

DOI: 10.1201/9781003607298-2

Imagine you have a **robot friend**.

This robot can't think like a human by itself, but you teach it some **rules** and give it **lots of examples**—like showing it a ball and saying "this is a ball," a cat and saying, "this is a cat." After seeing enough examples, the robot starts to **notice patterns**. It can now **guess**:

> If it sees a ball, it says "ball!"
> If it sees a cat, it says "cat!"

Artificial intelligence is just **machines learning to think a little bit like humans** – by copying, guessing, and using patterns we teach them (see Figure 2.2).

AI learns from examples and gets better at guessing things.

FIGURE 2.2 Robot which is creative in learning new things.

Now imagine your robot friend becomes very **creative**.

Instead of just recognizing things (like "this is a ball"), it can now **create something new** by itself!

For example:

> It writes a story about a cat who flies to the moon.
> It draws a picture of a rainbow unicorn.
> It makes up a new song you've never heard before.

This is **generative AI** – **AI that doesn't just understand** things, but can **make brand-new things**: stories, pictures, music, videos, even conversations!

GenAI is creative. It uses what it learned to **create new things**.

Now, let us understand the concepts via a more formal definition.

SECTION A: INTRODUCTION TO ARTIFICIAL INTELLIGENCE

Artificial intelligence (AI) stands as the key technological force of the 21st century because it has transformed entire industry and reshaped economies while creating significant effects on our daily lives that were previously unimaginable.

The AI has developed from being a theoretical idea to become an actual driving force behind innovations seen in self-driving cars and smart assistants as well as areas such as predictive analytics and healthcare breakthroughs.

What does AI represent and what mechanisms enable its functionality?

The essential purpose of AI involves machines replicating human intellectual capabilities.

A variety of technologies and methodologies give machines the ability to learn data patterns and solve problems while making autonomous decisions.

It is believed that researchers introduced the term "artificial intelligence" at the Dartmouth Conference in 1956 when they predicted machines would one day replicate human cognitive functions. Thanks to improvements in computing power and data availability alongside algorithm development, AI has transformed into a sophisticated field with practical applications in multiple industries.

The development of AI started during the mid-20th century with **symbolic reasoning and rule-based systems.**

Early systems, such as ELIZA (a natural language processing program developed in 1966), demonstrated the potential of AI to simulate human-like interactions. However, limited computing power and a lack of large datasets hindered progress.

The turn of the 21st century marked a new era for AI, driven by **three** key factors (shown in Figure 2.3):

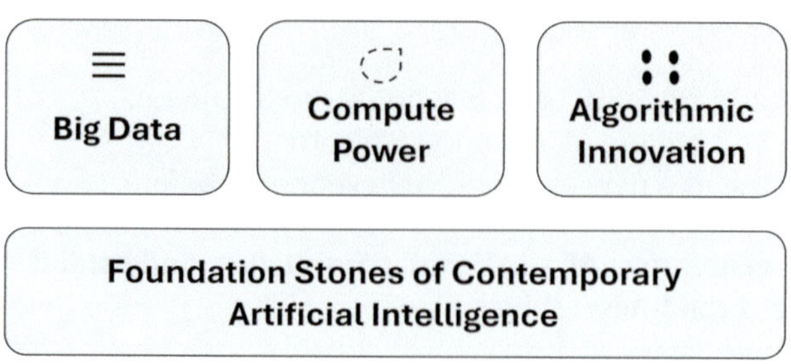

FIGURE 2.3 Synergy that powers today's AI landscape: data × compute × algorithms.

Before we dive deeper in ethical AI considerations, it is important to understand the difference between algorithms, machine learning, AI, and generative AI (summarized in Figure 2.4).

- **Algorithms**: These are the step-by-step instructions or rules to solve a problem. Algorithms are the building blocks of AI and machine learning.
- **Machine learning (ML)**: A subset of AI focused on algorithms that allow systems to learn from data and improve without explicit programming.
- **AI**: A broader field that encompasses ML, deep learning, and other techniques aimed at simulating human intelligence.
- **Generative AI**: A specialized subset of AI that uses models like generative adversarial networks (GANs) and transformers to generate new content such as text, images, or videos.

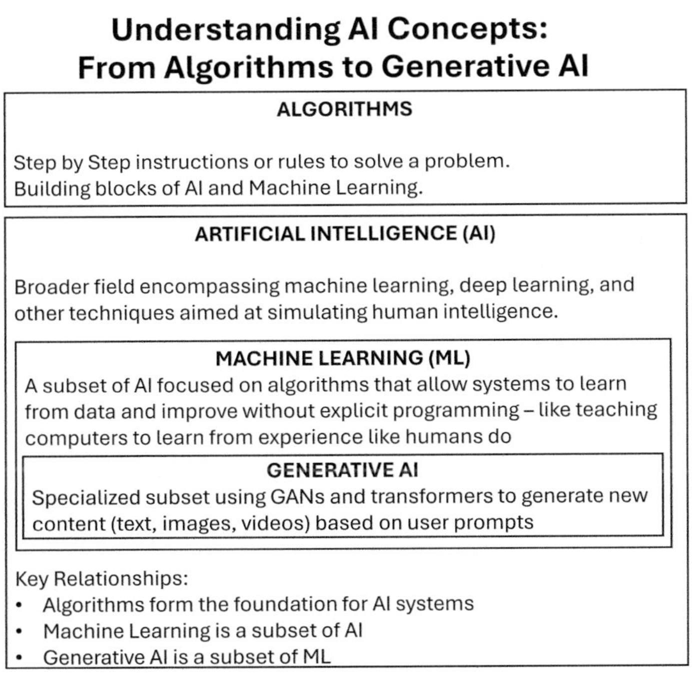

FIGURE 2.4 Understanding machine learning, AI, and gen AI.

AI rests on three mutually reinforcing pillars—**big data, computational power, and algorithmic innovation**—each with its own technical heartbeat.

1. **Big data:** As described in a Harvard Online blog,[1] one hundred years ago, only a few data points on a person were collected over the span of their lifetime: when they were born, if they got married, and when they died. These details, brief enough to fit on a headstone, give us little insight into what daily life was like for the population in a time before advanced technology and computer development. Imagine the work of researchers and social scientists of the time; they developed and conducted formal studies that took weeks, months, or even years to complete to gain more detailed insight on the daily habits and needs of people and communities.

   Today, data of every kind is readily available. The large amount of data collected and accessed every second across the globe is often referred to as "**big data**" and is used by every kind of industry and organization to shape businesses, cultures, and communities.

   Big data is characterized by its volume, velocity, variety, veracity, and value. It involves the analysis of large, complex datasets that traditional data processing systems cannot efficiently handle. The major categories of machine learning that operate on such large-scale data are illustrated in Figure 2.5.

   The technologies used to manage, store and analyze it, such as Hadoop, Spark and cloud computing.

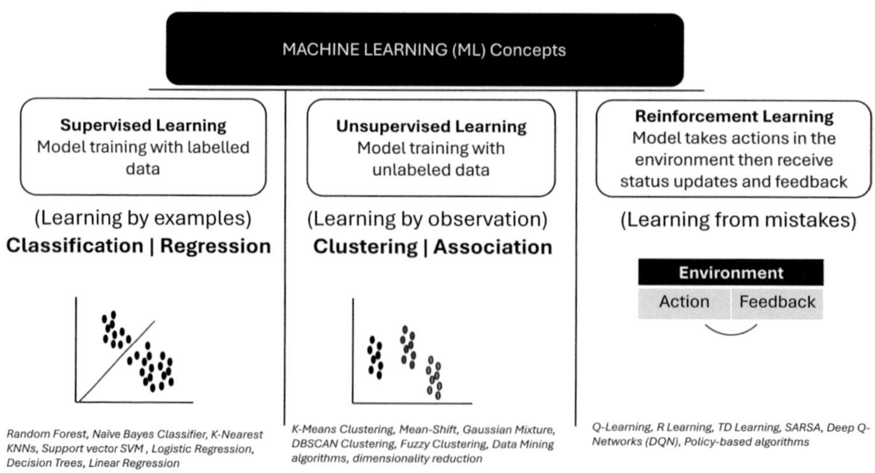

FIGURE 2.5 Types of machine learning.

Modern models drink from oceans of text, images, sensor feeds, and clickstreams, shrinking statistical noise through sheer volume. By the law of large numbers, a sample mean x converges to the true mean μ as

$$Pr(|\underline{x} - \mu| < \varepsilon) \geq 1 - \delta \ when \ n > \frac{1}{2\varepsilon^2} ln \frac{2}{\delta},$$

showing how a ten-fold increase in observations n cuts error almost by a third. Big-data pipelines therefore focus less on "perfect" curation and more on scalable ingestion, feature versioning, and privacy-preserving sampling (e.g., differential privacy).

We have illustrated the "big data" concepts in greater detail in following chapters.

2. **Computational advancements:** A significant enabler of AI's recent explosive growth has been advances in computational hardware and architectures. **Graphics processing units (GPUs)**, originally designed to render high-quality video game graphics, have proven remarkably effective for parallelized computations required in ML.

   GPUs leverage thousands of cores to handle multiple calculations simultaneously, drastically reducing training times for complex neural networks. For instance, NVIDIA's CUDA[2] platform facilitates parallel computing, making GPUs accessible to researchers and developers for AI applications.

   More specialized hardware, such as **tensor processing units** (TPUs),[3] has further accelerated ML tasks. Introduced by Google, TPUs are application-specific integrated circuits optimized explicitly for tensor calculations common in neural network training. Google's TPUs can deliver significantly faster training and inference times compared to traditional GPUs and CPUs, enabling rapid iteration and deployment of ML models.

   In addition, cloud computing has dramatically altered the computational landscape by offering scalable resources on demand. Elastic cloud clusters provided by platforms like Amazon Web Services, Google Cloud, and Microsoft Azure allow organizations to adjust computational resources dynamically based on their requirements, ensuring efficiency and cost-effectiveness. This elasticity enables both small startups and large enterprises to access powerful computational resources without substantial upfront investments, democratizing access to AI technologies.

GPUs, TPUs, and elastic cloud clusters translate data hunger into tractable training times. The practical speed-up is captured by:

$$T_{GPU} \approx \frac{T_{CPU}}{k\eta},$$

where k is the number of parallel cores and $\eta \leq 1$ the utilization efficiency. Mixed-precision arithmetic, model sharding, and on-device inference further bend the cost–performance curve, making billion-parameter networks feasible for startups as well as hyperscalers.

3. **Algorithmic breakthroughs:** At the heart of modern AI lie significant algorithmic advancements that transform vast datasets and computational power into actionable insights. **Deep neural networks (DNNs)**, inspired by human neural architecture, have proven exceptionally adept at identifying patterns and making predictions from both structured and unstructured data. Innovations in DNN architectures, such as **convolutional neural networks (CNNs)** for image processing and **recurrent neural networks (RNNs)** for sequence data, have vastly improved model performance across various domains.

   A particularly transformative development has been the introduction of transformer architectures,[4] exemplified by **models like BERT and generative pre-trained transformer (GPT)**. Transformers leverage attention mechanisms, allowing models to weigh the importance of different data segments contextually. This capability has revolutionized **natural language processing (NLP)**, enabling models to generate highly coherent and contextually relevant text.

   Reinforcement learning (RL), another pivotal algorithmic innovation, empowers AI systems to learn optimal actions through trial-and-error interactions with their environments.

   Notable successes like DeepMind's AlphaGo,[5] which mastered the complex game of Go by playing against itself, highlight the potential of RL to solve intricate, real-world problems through iterative optimization techniques. DNNs, transformers, and RL policies form the cognitive layer that turns data × compute into insight. At their core lies iterative optimization such as gradient descent:

$$\theta_{t+1} = \theta_t - \alpha \nabla_\theta L(\theta_t),$$

where θ are learnable weights, L a loss function, and α the learning rate. Architectural leaps—attention mechanisms, residual connections, diffusion processes—have slashed sample complexity and enabled models to generalize from language to protein folding.

Together, these three foundation stones create a virtuous cycle:

1. Richer data improve models,
2. Better hardware trains them faster, and
3. Smarter algorithms squeeze more value from every byte and flop, propelling AI from laboratory curiosity to enterprise mainstay.

AI has evolved significantly from traditional data science—which focuses primarily on extracting insights from structured data—to ML, which empowers systems to learn from both structured and unstructured data, and finally to **generative AI**, a *transformative* technology capable of creating entirely new content like text, images, and music. Table 2.1 maps major AI components to their underlying techniques, applications, and real-world examples.

TABLE 2.1 AI Technologies and Components

AI Component	What Is It?	Techniques/ Technologies	Applications	Examples
Machine learning (ML)	A subset of AI that focuses on creating algorithms capable of learning and improving from data	Supervised learning, unsupervised learning, reinforcement learning	Fraud detection, personalized recommendations, predictive maintenance	Predicting customer churn, spam email detection
Deep learning	A subset of ML that uses artificial neural networks modeled after the human brain	Neural networks	Image recognition, speech synthesis, and autonomous vehicles	Self-driving cars, image classification in healthcare
Natural language processing (NLP)	The ability of machines to understand, interpret, and generate human language	Sentiment analysis, machine translation, chatbots	Virtual assistants like Siri and Alexa, automated customer support	ChatGPT, Google Translate

(*Continued*)

TABLE 2.1 (*Continued*) AI Technologies and Components

AI Component	What Is It?	Techniques/ Technologies	Applications	Examples
Computer vision	Enabling machines to interpret and process visual information from the world	Image segmentation, object detection, facial recognition	Medical imaging, autonomous drones, security systems	X-ray analysis, autonomous drone navigation
Generative AI	AI systems capable of generating new content, such as text, images, and music	Transformer models like generative pre-trained transformers (GPT)	Content creation, code generation, design prototyping	DALL-E for images, GPT-4 for text generation

For introductory purposes, it is vital for readers to understand these concepts and terminologies thoroughly. Figure 2.6 provides a consolidated view of the key components and subfields that together constitute modern artificial intelligence.

Today, AI encompasses subfields such as:

- **ML**: The practice of training algorithms to learn from data. Officially defined as the *science of training algorithms* to perform tasks by learning from data. ML involves processes such as data collection, feature extraction, model training, and validation.

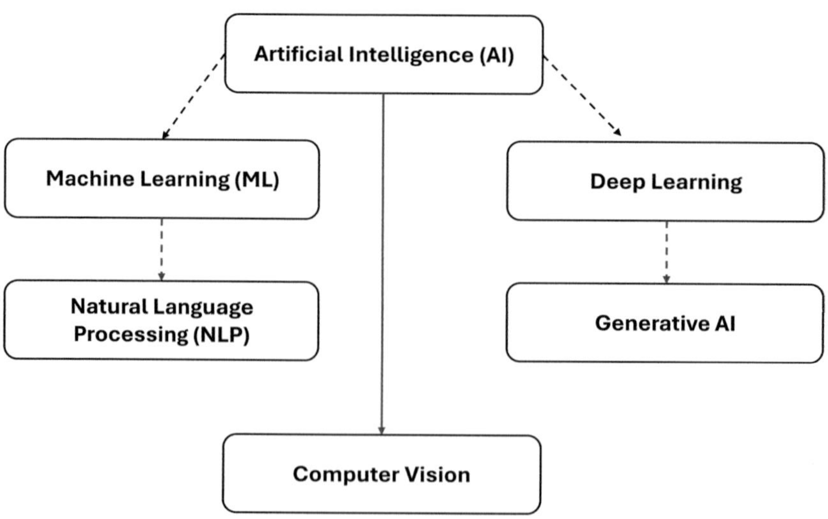

FIGURE 2.6 Key components of artificial intelligence.

- **NLP**: Enabling machines to understand and generate human language. A subfield dedicated to enabling machines to understand, interpret, and generate human language. NLP employs linguistic algorithms, statistical methods, and neural network architectures like transformers to *parse language and respond contextually.*
- **Computer vision**: Teaching machines to interpret and process visual information. This field involves enabling machines to *interpret visual data*. Techniques such as CNNs are used to recognize patterns in images and videos, facilitating applications like facial recognition, autonomous vehicles, and medical imaging diagnostics.
- **Robotics**: Combining AI with physical systems to perform tasks autonomously. It combines AI algorithms with physical robotic systems, enabling autonomous task execution. Robotics integrates sensor data, control systems, and ML algorithms to *perform complex physical tasks without human intervention.*
- **Generative AI**: Creating new and unique content with advanced neural networks like GPT models. Focused on creating novel content using advanced neural networks. Models like GPT *generate human-like text, images, or even music*, opening new frontiers in creative industries and content automation.

Categories of AI

AI can be broadly classified into *three* categories:

1. **Narrow AI (weak AI):** These systems are designed to perform a specific task, such as facial recognition or language translation. They are limited in scope and cannot perform tasks outside their designated function.
2. **General AI (strong AI):** This is a theoretical concept of AI that possesses the ability to understand, learn, and apply knowledge across a wide range of tasks, similar to human intelligence. General AI does not yet exist in the public domain per say; *well, not until this book was being drafted!*
3. **Superintelligent AI:** This refers to AI that surpasses human intelligence across all domains. It is currently a speculative concept and a subject of significant debate and ethical consideration.

SECTION B: EVOLUTION OF INTELLIGENCE IN MODERN SCIENCE

The Shifting Lens: From Natural to Artificial Intelligence

The concept of intelligence began as a characteristic of human thought before extending into areas of biological research and psychological studies. The Dartmouth Conference of 1956 introduced the term "artificial intelligence" which reshaped scientific perspectives by defining intelligence as a replicable function in machines beyond its biological roots.

In modern science, **the evolution of intelligence** has unfolded through the convergence of several fields. Three scientific disciplines work together to advance intelligence research where neuroscience studies the nature of cognition while computer science creates machine-based replications and statistics develops models to handle uncertainty.

> Recent advances in machine learning and deep neural networks enable machines to simulate processes of human perception and rational thought processes.
>
> Just as fire, once a discovery of nature, was first harnessed by humans and later delivered to homes through electric stoves—intelligence has now made a similar journey. From being an exclusive trait of living beings, it has evolved into a utility—'**Intelligence-as-a-Service**'—available on-demand, delivered by machines.

Timeline of AI Evolution and Major Scientific Phases

The evolution of AI can be traced through several key scientific and technological phases (visualized in Figure 2.7), marked by significant breakthroughs and research paradigms.

1. **Early foundation and theoretical work (before 1950s):**

   - **Ancient philosophers**: Philosophers like Aristotle explored formalized reasoning, providing a foundation for symbolic manipulation later used in AI.

   - **Calculating machines**: Throughout history, mathematicians and inventors such as Gottfried Leibniz and Charles Babbage developed mechanical calculating machines, paving the way for digital computers.

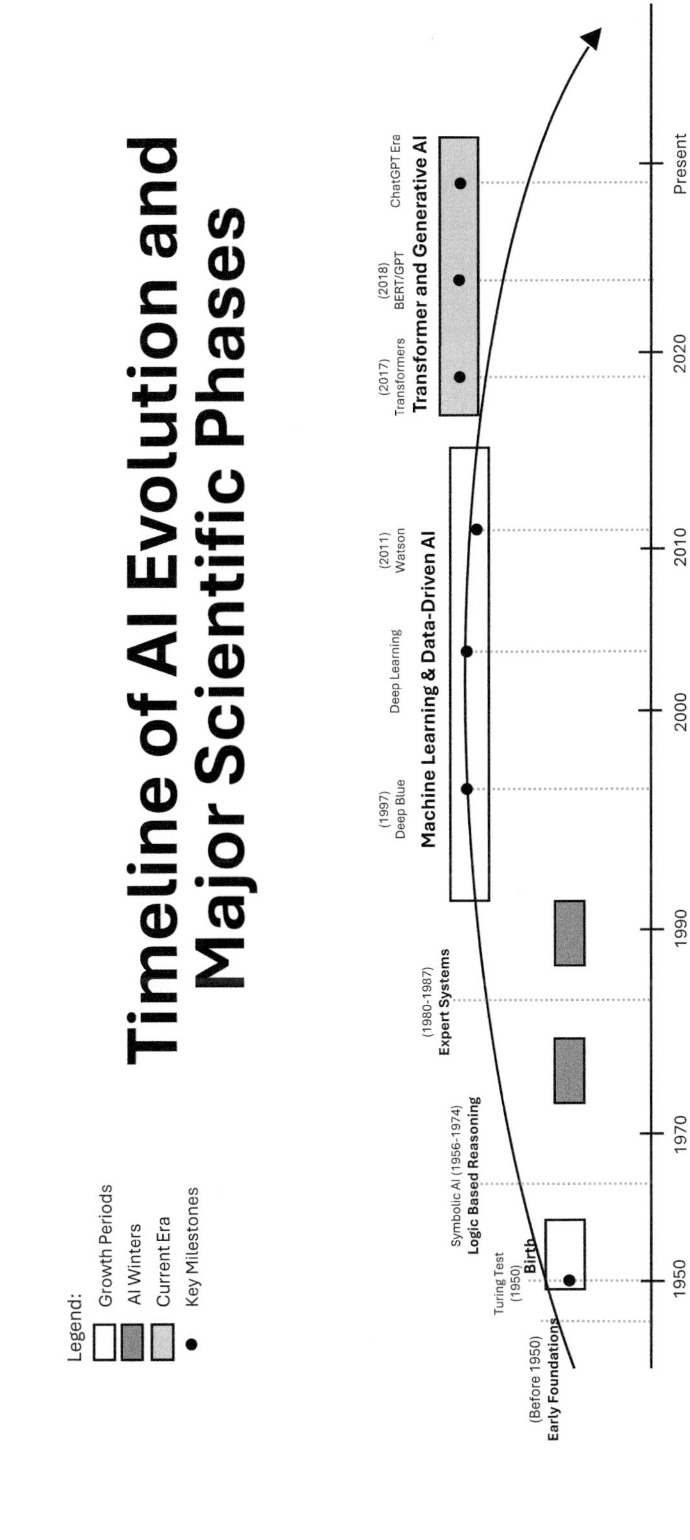

FIGURE 2.7 AI evolution timeline.

- **Theory of computation**: Alan Turing's work on computable numbers and the Turing machine laid the theoretical basis for a mechanical device simulating any form of mathematical deduction.
- **First artificial neural network model:** Warren McCulloch and Walter Pitts introduced their model of artificial neurons in 1943, which was considered an early form of AI even before the term was coined.

2. **The birth of AI (1950s):**

- **Turing test (1950):** Alan Turing proposed the Turing test to assess a machine's ability to exhibit intelligent behavior indistinguishable from a human.
- **Dartmouth workshop (1956):** Widely considered the birthplace of AI as an academic discipline, the term "artificial intelligence" was coined by John McCarthy at this conference.
- **Logic Theorist (1956):** Developed by Newell and Simon, this program proved mathematical theorems, demonstrating the power of symbolic AI.
- **Perceptron (1957):** Frank Rosenblatt introduced this single-layer neural network model capable of recognizing patterns, sparking interest in connectionist approaches.

3. **Early successes and symbolic AI (1956–1974):**

- **Optimism and funding:** Significant progress was made in AI research, leading to substantial funding from government agencies like DARPA.
- **General Problem Solver (GPS):** Newell and Simon developed this program aiming for a general algorithm for problem-solving using search and heuristics.
- **ELIZA (1966):** Joseph Weizenbaum developed this **early chatbot** that simulated conversations using NLP.
- **Shakey the Robot (1966):** Shakey was the first mobile robot capable of autonomous navigation and decision-making, showcasing integration of perception, planning, and execution.

4. **The first AI winter (1974–1980):**
   - **Critiques and funding cuts**: Overly ambitious claims and limitations of symbolic AI led to reduced funding and public skepticism, marking the first "AI winter".
5. **AI boom and expert systems (1980–1987):**
   - **Revival through expert systems**: AI experienced a resurgence with the development and commercialization of expert systems like XCON, capable of emulating human expertise.
   - **Japanese fifth-generation computer project (1982):** This initiative aimed to create computers with advanced AI capabilities, further boosting AI research.
6. **The second AI winter (1987–1994):**
   - **Market collapse and funding decline**: The collapse of the market for specialized AI hardware and continued challenges in achieving general intelligence led to a decline in funding and interest, creating another AI winter.
7. **Machine learning and data-driven AI (1990s–2010s):**
   - **Emergence of ML**: The 1990s saw a renewed focus on ML algorithms like support vector machines and neural networks, which offered new approaches to AI.
   - **Deep Blue vs. Kasparov (1997):** IBM's Deep Blue defeated the world chess champion, showcasing AI's capability in complex problem-solving.
   - **Rise of deep learning**: Advancements in computing power and data availability led to breakthroughs in deep learning, enabling significant progress in areas like image and speech recognition.
   - **IBM Watson wins jeopardy! (2011):** Watson demonstrated advancements in NLP and question answering capabilities.
   - **Birth of AI assistants (2010s):** Apple released Siri, marking the advent of widely popular AI assistants.

8. **The transformer era and generative AI (2017–present):**
    - **Transformer architecture (2017):** The "**Attention Is All You Need" paper** introduced the transformer model, revolutionizing NLP.
    - **BERT and GPT (2018):** Google's BERT and OpenAI's GPT models advanced language understanding and generation, leading to new NLP applications.
    - **Generative AI boom**: Models like DALL-E, MidJourney, and ChatGPT emerged, showcasing AI's ability to generate text, images, and other content, captivating a wider audience.
    - **Accelerated investment**: Venture capital funding for AI companies, particularly in generative AI, saw explosive growth.
9. **Future of AI:**
    - **Multimodal AI**: The next wave of innovation focuses on AI systems capable of processing and integrating information across various modalities like text, images, and audio.
    - **Artificial general intelligence (AGI):** The pursuit of AGI—AI that can match or surpass human-level cognition across all domains—remains a sought-after goal.
    - **AI ethics and regulation**: As AI becomes more integrated into society, concerns about bias, misinformation, and ethical implications necessitate addressing potential risks and developing responsible AI development.

Empirical scaling laws demonstrate that model performance increases predictably with compute, data, and model size. This observation has fueled the development of general-purpose AI models using compute-intensive training regimes.

Both the US Executive Order and EU AI Act now use training compute thresholds as early indicators of potential societal risk.

This timeline highlights the significant progress AI has made from theoretical concepts to practical applications, demonstrating its potential to transform various industries and aspects of human life.

SECTION C: NEW 'CORE' OF INNOVATION: HOW AI IS HELPING HUMANITY AND BUSINESSES

This section focuses on two most important domains where AI has been particularly transformative.

1. **Humanity**:
   - AI-powered diagnostics in healthcare are detecting diseases earlier, saving lives.
   - Climate modeling powered by AI helps predict and mitigate environmental disasters.
   - Education is becoming more accessible with AI-driven platforms providing personalized learning experiences.
2. **Businesses**:
   - AI optimizes operations, reduces costs, and improves decision-making.
   - Predictive analytics enable better inventory management and demand forecasting.
   - Customer service is enhanced with AI chatbots providing 24/7 assistance.

Amplifying Human Potential

AI is no longer a niche capability; it is a horizontal enabler across sectors as illustrated in Figure 2.8. In healthcare, AI-driven diagnostic tools like AlphaFold and radiology AIs enhance precision and reduce diagnosis time. In finance, fraud detection models and algorithmic trading systems revolutionize risk analysis and capital allocation. AI empowers **digital public infrastructure (DPI)** by improving access, efficiency, and equity in government services.

Strategic Edge for Enterprises

AI confers a **strategic edge** through automation, prediction, and personalization. Recommendation engines (e.g., Netflix, Amazon), chatbots (e.g., customer service), and generative AI tools (e.g., design assistants) increase productivity and customer satisfaction.

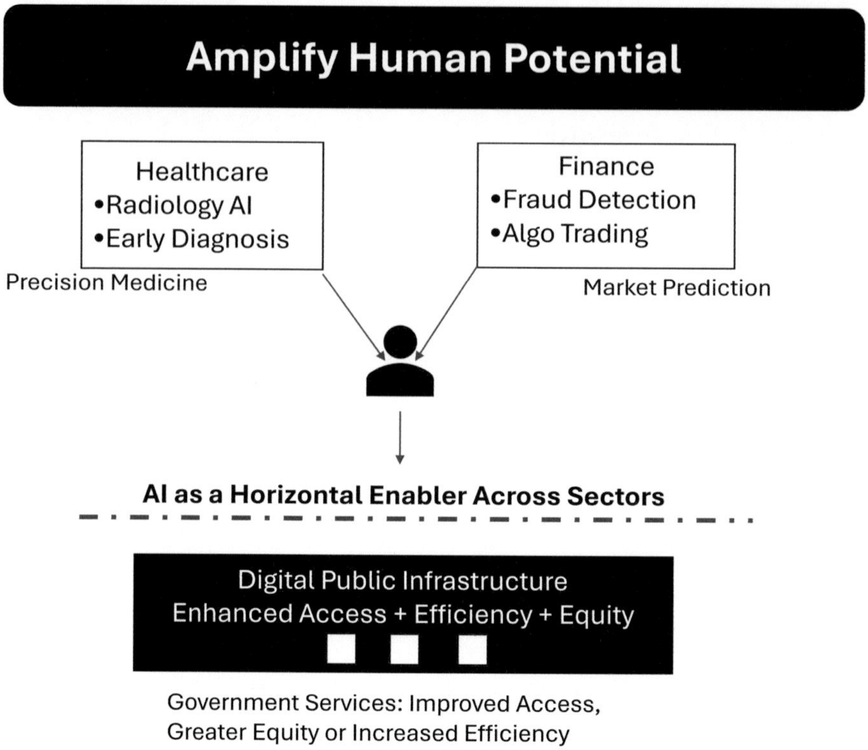

FIGURE 2.8 Human potential with AI.

For business leaders, integrating AI with **Enterprise Risk Management (ERM)** leads to proactive decision-making, anomaly detection, and predictive modeling. The strategic enterprise benefits enabled by AI integration are depicted in Figure 2.9. MIT's AI risk taxonomy outlines how organizations are using AI for safe deployment while addressing domain-specific risks like misinformation, data breaches, and system failure.

Socioeconomic Impacts

While AI democratizes access to services, it also introduces power asymmetries. Large-scale adoption may lead to **employment polarization**, surveillance, and centralized control. Figure 2.10 highlights the balance between AI-driven benefits and emerging societal challenges such as employment polarization and privacy risks. Responsible innovation requires balancing growth with sustainability and equitable access.

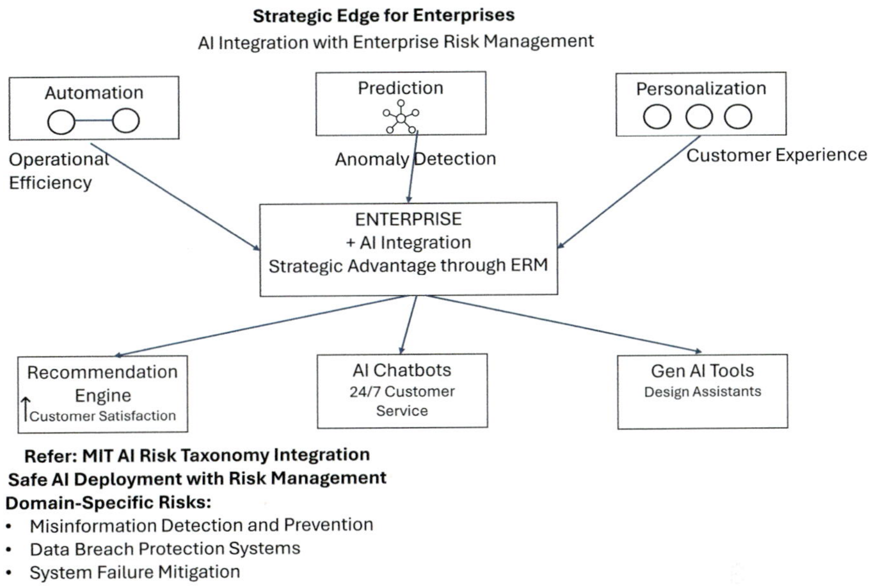

FIGURE 2.9 Benefit for the enterprises.

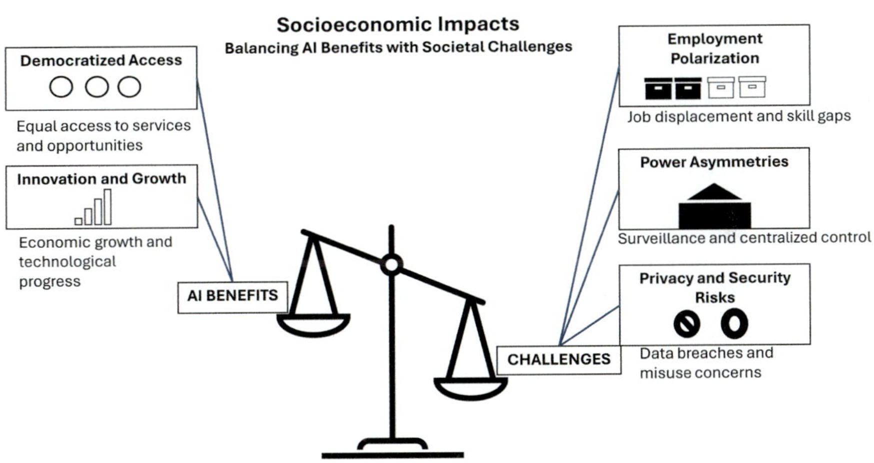

FIGURE 2.10 Balancing AI with social challenges.

SECTION D: ETHICAL CONSIDERATIONS IN DEVELOPING AND USING AI

As AI becomes integral to modern society, significant ethical considerations emerge, impacting individuals, communities, and global systems.

Thus, in our opinion, ethical coding must be more than reactive compliance; **it should form the core ethos guiding every AI practitioner's daily work, ensuring thoughtful, responsible, and human-centric technology development.**

Regulatory frameworks such as the **EU AI Act**, **OECD Principles**, and the **AI Bill of Rights (U.S.)** call for embedding ethics from design to deployment. Techniques include:

- Bias mitigation during data collection and model training
- Model interpretability (e.g., LIME, SHAP)
- Algorithmic impact assessments and stakeholder engagement
- NIST AI_RMF_Playbook

As AI becomes more integrated into society, it raises critical ethical questions and challenges. These are discussed as follows:

1. **Bias and fairness**:
    - AI systems can inherit biases from their training data, leading to unfair or discriminatory outcomes.
    - Example: Facial recognition systems misidentifying individuals based on race or gender.
2. **Transparency and accountability**:
    - The "black box" nature of AI models makes it difficult to understand how decisions are made.
    - Organizations must prioritize explainability and ensure accountability for AI-driven outcomes.
3. **Privacy and security**:
    - AI systems often require access to sensitive personal data, raising concerns about data misuse and breaches.
    - Regulations like GDPR and the California Consumer Privacy Act (CCPA) aim to address these concerns.

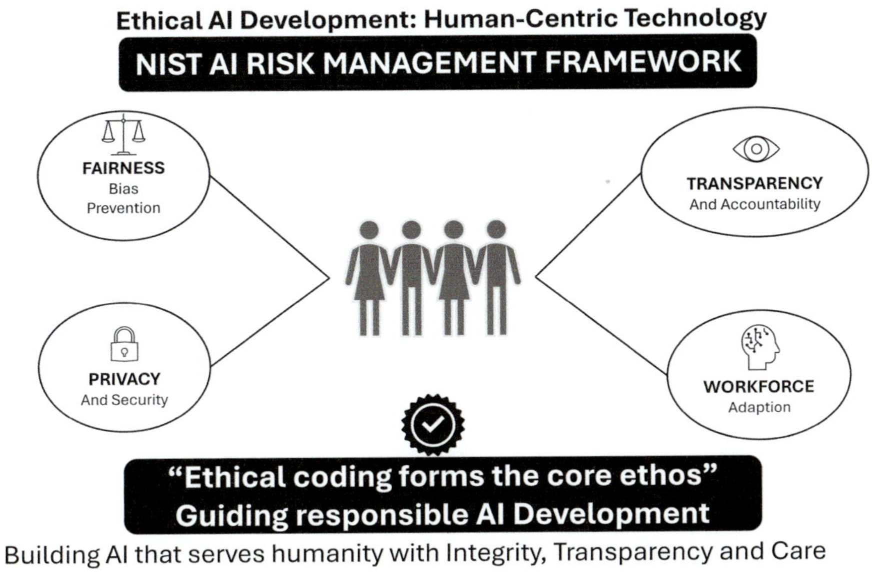

FIGURE 2.11 Building AI that serves humanity with integrity, transparency, and care.

4. **Job displacement**:
    - Automation driven by AI could disrupt labor markets, necessitating workforce reskilling and adaptation.
5. **Ethics by design:**
    - Initiatives like the NIST[6] AI Risk Management Framework emphasize ethical design and deployment of AI systems.

Figure 2.11 reinforces the importance of building AI systems grounded in integrity, transparency, and human-centric design. We have delved deeper into the ethical design concept in the following chapters.

CONCLUSION I: BECOMING PROFICIENT IN AI

To develop expertise in AI, consider the following steps:

1. **Learn the fundamentals**:
    - Start with programming languages like Python and libraries such as TensorFlow and PyTorch.

- Build a strong foundation in mathematics, particularly linear algebra and statistics.

2. **Understand AI frameworks and tools**:
   - Familiarize yourself with ML frameworks and cloud-based AI tools like Google Cloud AI and AWS SageMaker.
3. **Work on real-world projects**:
   - Apply your knowledge to solve practical problems, such as building a recommendation system or developing a chatbot.
4. **Stay updated on trends and regulations**:
   - Follow industry publications and guidelines, including ethical AI frameworks and data privacy laws.
5. **Pursue certifications**:
   - Consider certifications like Google's Professional Machine Learning Engineer or Microsoft Certified: Azure AI Engineer Associate.

CONCLUSION II: CHAPTER SUMMARY

AI is not just a technological breakthrough; it is a paradigm shift that is redefining how we live, work, and solve problems. This chapter has dived deep into the concepts, technologies, and ethical considerations surrounding AI. The future of AI and generative AI holds immense potential and promise. As these technologies continue to advance, they will likely become increasingly integrated into everyday life, driving innovation across industries and transforming how we interact with the digital world. However, it is crucial to navigate the ethical and societal implications thoughtfully to ensure the responsible and beneficial development of AI.

As you move forward, the next chapters will build on this foundation, exploring the integration of AI with risk management and other domains.

Whether you are a programmer writing code or a leader making strategic decisions, understanding AI is a critical step in navigating the complexities of our modern world.

In the next chapters, you will delve deeper into some of the topics covered in this chapter. This will empower you with much-needed knowledge and understanding of this emerging technology and how to balance innovation with consciousness.

NOTES

1. Published in 2024, Pros and Cons of Big Data: https://www.harvardonline.harvard.edu/blog/pros-cons-big-data Harvard Online describes **big data** as a transformative force reshaping how organizations derive value, make decisions, and drive innovation. More than just volume, big data encompasses the **velocity**, **variety**, and **veracity** of data generated across digital interactions, IoT devices, social platforms, and enterprise systems. Harvard emphasizes the strategic importance of data literacy, analytical thinking, and ethical data governance as foundational skills in the age of AI. As industries increasingly depend on data-driven insights, understanding big data is no longer optional—it's essential for leadership, competitiveness, and responsible innovation.
2. NVIDIA's CUDA (Compute Unified Device Architecture) technology transformed the landscape of high-performance computing by enabling general-purpose parallel processing on GPUs. Introduced in 2006, CUDA allows developers to harness the massive parallelism of NVIDIA GPUs using familiar programming languages like C, C++, and Python. This innovation unlocked dramatic speedups for complex computational tasks—from scientific simulations to deep learning—fueling breakthroughs across AI, data science, and graphics-intensive industries. As the backbone for many modern AI frameworks, CUDA remains a cornerstone in accelerating ML, computer vision, and generative AI at scale.
3. Google's TPUs are custom-built application-specific integrated circuits (ASICs) designed to accelerate ML workloads, especially those using TensorFlow. Purposefully engineered for high-throughput matrix operations at scale, TPUs dramatically speed up the training and inference of deep neural networks while optimizing power and cost efficiency. Since their debut in 2016, TPUs have powered some of Google's most advanced AI systems—from Google Translate to large-scale language models—enabling cutting-edge performance for both research and production AI. Their integration into Google Cloud makes enterprise-grade AI acceleration accessible across industries.
4. Breakthrough research paper "Attention Is All You Need" by Vaswani et al., 2017: https://arxiv.org/abs/1706.03762 introduced the transformer architecture, revolutionizing the field of natural language processing by eliminating the need for recurrence or convolution in sequence modeling. Vaswani et al. proposed a novel self-attention mechanism that enables models to weigh the relevance of all words in a sequence simultaneously, allowing for unparalleled scalability, speed, and contextual understanding. This breakthrough laid the foundation for modern large language models like BERT and GPT, making it one of the most influential papers in AI. The simplicity and power of the transformer have redefined how machines learn language—and, by extension, how they understand the world.

5. The DeepMind AlphaGo project marked a historic milestone in AI by becoming the first computer program to defeat a world champion at the ancient and complex game of Go. Combining deep neural networks with reinforcement learning, AlphaGo showcased the power of self-play and strategic foresight, pushing the boundaries of AI's cognitive capabilities. Its success stunned the AI and gaming communities alike, not only for its raw strength but also for its creativity and adaptability—challenging centuries of human expertise. AlphaGo's development underscored the transformative potential of AI in solving problems that were once thought to be uniquely human. Read more on https://deepmind.com/research/case-studies/alphago-the-story-so-far
6. The National Institute of Standards and Technology (NIST) develops measurements, technology, tools, and standards to advance reliable, safe, transparent, explainable, privacy-enhanced, and fair AI so that its full commercial and societal benefits can be realized without harm to people or the planet. NIST, which has conducted both fundamental and applied work on AI for more than a decade, is also helping to fulfill the 2023 Executive Order on Safe, Secure, and Trustworthy AI. NIST established the U.S. AI Safety Institute and the companion AI Safety Institute Consortium to continue the efforts set in motion by the E.O. to build the science necessary for safe, secure, and trustworthy development and use of AI.

CHAPTER 3

Machine Learning Foundations

From Theory to Your First Model

Machine learning (ML) sits at the heart of today's artificial intelligence (AI) revolution. Yet newcomers often encounter two barriers:

1. **Conceptual fog**: disparate terminology (features vs. embeddings, bias vs. inductive bias) that makes the landscape feel fragmented.
2. **Mathematical intimidation**: equations emerge abruptly, leaving many readers disengaged.

In this chapter, we will formally (and mathematically) define supervised, unsupervised, and reinforcement learning problems and situate generative AI and foundation models within the broader ML taxonomy. This chapter is divided into the following four sections:

Section A: What Does it Really Mean to "Learn"?

Section B: Big Data: From Ledger Lines to Zettabytes

Section C: What Exactly Is Machine Learning?

Section D: Machine Learning and AI Governance—Coding Responsibly

DOI: 10.1201/9781003607298-3

SECTION A: WHAT DOES IT REALLY MEAN TO LEARN?

Imagine a barista (let us call her 'Rebecca') is learning to perfect latte art. Each morning, Rebecca observes the swirl patterns left by steamed milk (input), receives instant feedback from customers (label: *beautiful* or *needs improvement*), and tweaks her pouring angle.

Over weeks, she internalizes a mapping from milk viscosity, cup tilt, and pour velocity to the final aesthetic score. **This mapping is a hypothesis.**

Learning, at its core, is the process by which a system—biological or artificial—improves its ability to achieve a goal through experience.

- **Every-day intuition:** A child wobbling on a bicycle eventually rides smoothly because repeated interaction with pedals, balance, and feedback reshapes muscle memory.
- **Human ↔ Machine parallel:** Both humans and machines (i) receive streams of data, (ii) build internal representations, and (iii) adjust decision rules to minimize future error. The difference is substrate: neurons versus silicon.

In psychology this is framed as stimulus-response adaptation; in computer science we formalize it as updating parameters inside an algorithm.

In other words, *experience supplies evidence, and the system reshapes itself to reduce future error.*

Humans achieve this through electrochemical signals that reinforce or dampen synaptic pathways. Machines accomplish the same goal via numerical optimization—iteratively nudging parameters to minimize a loss function. Both processes create an **internal model of the world** capable of forecasting outcomes before they happen: the barista can *imagine* tomorrow's pour, and a spam filter can *anticipate* tomorrow's phishing email.

A practical definition, in our opinion, that can be useful throughout this chapter is Tom Mitchell's LEP triad: *A computer program is said to learn from* ***Experience*** *E with respect to some class of* ***Tasks*** *T and performance measure* ***P*** *if its performance at tasks in T, as measured by P, improves with experience E.* We will revisit each boldface term—experience as data, task as hypothesis space, performance as loss—grounding them first in intuition and later in mathematics.

Our formal machinery—loss functions, hypothesis spaces, VC-dimension—merely codifies this intuitive simulator so that it can run on silicon at planetary scale.

SECTION B: BIG DATA: FROM LEDGER LINES TO ZETTABYTES

Before we delve deeper into ML, AI, and gen AI, it is important to understand what feeds these advanced technologies—data (or in today's terms "big data").

The Traditional View: "Large" but Containable

Before the 21st century, "big" data usually meant structured, relational records whose volume strained a single server but still lived inside an enterprise data warehouse. Banks archived millions of daily transactions; telecom operators stored call detail records (CDRs); retailers logged point-of-sale receipts.

An Oracle or Teradata cluster, batch-loaded overnight and queried with SQL, was state-of-the-art. Velocity was measured in hours, and schemas were meticulously designed upfront to guarantee referential integrity.

The Modern Reality: Volume, Velocity, Variety, and Veracity

Today's definition is governed by the famous "4 Vs" as shown in Table 3.1 (some add Value and Variability).

Evolution examples:

- **Weather prediction**: from hourly surface readings to petabyte-scale satellite imagery and Doppler radar cubes.

TABLE 3.1 Benchmarks and Examples of 4 Vs of Big Data

V	1990s Benchmark	2020s Benchmark	Example
Volume	GB > TB	PB > EB > ZB	Facebook ingests approximately 4 PB of new data per day (images, video, logs)
Velocity	Batch nightly	Millisecond streams	NYSE tick feeds product approximately 1TB/sec across equities
Variety	Rows and columns	Text, voice, images, sensor time-series, graph edges	Autonomous vehicles generate LiDAR point clouds + camera frames + CAN-bus logs
Veracity	Curated, mostly correct	Noisy, redundant, biased	Social media sentiment requires natural language processing (NLP_ cleaning, bot filtering, and language detection

- **Genomics**: the first human genome (2003) took 13 years and $3 billion; now one Illumina NovaSeq run outputs >6 TB of raw reads in <24 hours.
- **E-commerce**: clickstream trails, A/B test logs, product images, and customer chats create **multimodal** datasets that cannot fit traditional ER models.

Big Data as a Pillar of Modern (Generative) AI

Large-scale AI models—from **BERT** (3.3 B words) to **GPT-4o** and image-diffusion generators—are **data-hungry**. Without terabytes of curated text, code, audio, or video, even the most sophisticated architecture would **overfit** or hallucinate.

Big data also fuels:

- **Retrieval-augmented generation (RAG)**: vector-search over billions of embeddings to ground responses in fresh documents.
- **Self-supervised vision:** contrastive learning on unlabeled image crops; ImageNet-21K (≈14 M images) is now dwarfed by LAION-5B.
- **Synthetic data engines**: using generative models to augment minority classes or simulate rare edge-cases for autonomous-driving safety tests.

Looking Ahead

Edge sensors, 6G networks, and federated-learning hubs will push global data volume toward **yottabyte** scales. Post-quantum cryptography and privacy-enhancing tech (homomorphic encryption, secure enclaves) will make "big" not just *large* but *secure.*

Yet the core principle endures **data × compute × algorithms**. Each advance in storage efficiency, data-governance policy, or scalable visualization widens the runway for the next leap in AI. Mastery of big-data engineering is therefore no longer an IT specialization—it is a strategic imperative for any organization that seeks to build, deploy, or even *trust* modern AI and generative-AI solutions.

To know more on Big Data and related technologies, we recommend reading an open access survey article published by Abdalla, H.B. "A Brief Survey on Big Data: Technologies, Terminologies and

Data-Intensive Applications". *J Big Data* **9**, 107 (2022). Read more on this article at: https://journalofbigdata.springeropen.com/articles/10.1186/s40537-022-00659-3

SECTION C: WHAT EXACTLY IS MACHINE LEARNING?

ML is a sub-field of AI in which *algorithms improve with experience.*

> Think of ML as a clever robot-chef that keeps tasting its own soup and adjusting the recipe till it gets a thumbs-up from the diners.
>
> Formally, an ML system takes data (the ingredients), chooses a model (a recipe written in Maths), and tweaks that model so the loss (the "yuck-factor" when the taste is wrong) is as small as possible.

We recommend reading the innovative article from School of Computer Science, Carnegie Mellon University, "The Discipline of Machine Learning" by Tom M. Mitchell (July 2006 CMU-ML-06-108).

Mitchell surveys ML's aims, successes, and futures—e.g., never-ending learners and self-supervised curricula—while explicitly discussing privacy trade-offs versus societal benefit and urging open, informed debate on responsible application.

Mitchell's LEP Triad (Task–Performance–Experience)

Definition (Mitchell, 2006)

A machine "learns" when, for a particular **Task** T, its **Performance** P improves with **Experience** E as illustrated in Figure 3.1. In other words, improvement on P at T follows from exposure to E.

Task (T): *What capability?*

Specify the input–output mapping or control objective: classification (spam vs. harm), regression (forecast demand), generation (draft a summary), or control (navigate a robot). A precise task description fixes the hypothesis space and data interfaces.

Performance (P): *According to which yardstick?*

Choose measurable criteria aligned to the task: accuracy/F1, calibration error, regret/reward, latency/cost—often multi-objective (e.g., accuracy **and** fairness or privacy). P becomes the operational "north star" for training and evaluation.

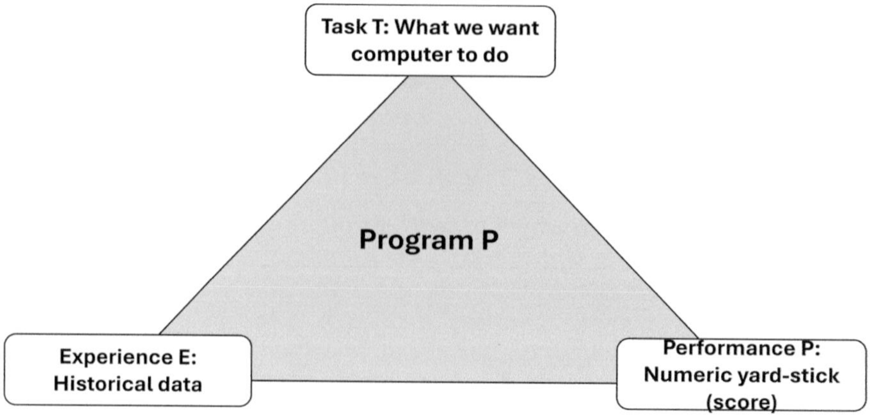

FIGURE 3.1 Three pillars of a program.

Experience (E): *What evidence fuels improvement?*
Curated signals the system learns from. For example, labeled datasets, interaction logs, demonstrations, simulated rollouts, or self-supervised masks. E must be representative and governed (lineage, consent, quality) to avoid biased or brittle learning.

How the pieces fit?

- **E shapes T:** The richness and coverage of experience constrain which tasks are realistically learnable.
- **P shapes learning:** Your metric induces the loss/optimization target—optimize the wrong P, learn the wrong behavior.
- **E ↔ P coupling:** Feedback design (labels, rewards, critiques) is the *mechanism* by which E drives improvements in P.

Quick project template
"We aim to improve **P** (e.g., factuality @ Top-k) on **T** (policy Q&A) using **E** (audited policy docs + retrieval traces), verified on a held-out evaluation suite."

This compact framing keeps teams aligned—from data collection to model training and governance checkpoints—while staying faithful to Mitchell's original definition.

SECTION D: MACHINE LEARNING AND AI GOVERNANCE—CODING RESPONSIBLY

Why Governance Matters?

As models shift from academic curiosities to mission-critical infrastructure, issues of bias, robustness, privacy and accountability dominate board-room agendas (Figure 3.2). Regulation such as the **EU AI Act 2024** and the **NIST AI-RMF** impose life-cycle-wide risk management obligations.

1. **Data governance:** Differential privacy, lineage tracking, opt-out compliance (e.g., copyright filtering).
2. **Model development:** Parameter-Efficient Fine-Tuning (LoRA, IA^3) keeps audit trails; DPO aligns human preferences without RL instability.
3. **Evaluation:** Red-teaming, domain-shift stress-tests, and systemic-risk thresholds (compute $>10^{25}$ FLOPs triggers EU obligations).
4. **Monitoring:** Telemetry for hallucination rate, toxicity spikes; automated rollback and model-editing patches.

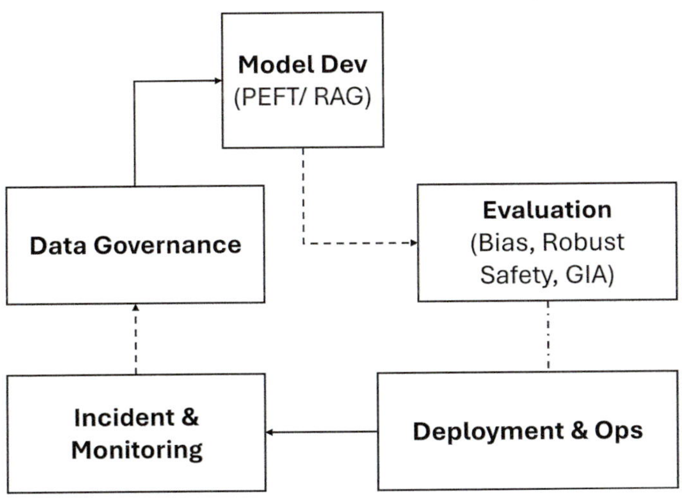

FIGURE 3.2 Governance structure.

CONCLUDING THOUGHTS

ML's journey from linear regression to self-refining agentic systems illustrates a recurring theme: ***scale amplifies capability*, but also risk**.

Understanding the theoretical bedrock (statistics, optimization, information theory) empowers practitioners to innovate responsibly, while governance frameworks anchor those innovations to societal values.

The remainder of this book will build upon these principles, diving deeper into algorithms, risk management playbooks, and hands-on coding laboratories that position you—whether student, engineer, or researcher—at the forefront of the AI renaissance.

CHAPTER 4

The Rise of Deep Learning

INTRODUCTION

From Linear Functions to Deep Intent: The Evolution of Machine Learning

When people hear the term "machine learning," they often imagine something futuristic—a system that understands language, diagnoses disease, or detects fraud with uncanny precision. But machine learning, at its heart, is an old idea:

If data contains patterns, then machines should be able to learn those patterns and make decisions accordingly.

At its core, **machine learning** is the practice of learning a function from examples. More formally, given input data x and desired outputs y, we want to find a function $f(x)$ that approximates the relationship between them. This chapter explores how that idea evolved into the modern machine learning systems that now power much of today's risk management, decision intelligence, and artificial intelligence (AI)-enabled services.

The field is typically broken into three paradigms (summarized in Figure 4.1):

1. **Supervised learning**: Given labeled data (x_i, y_i), the model learns to predict y for new x. Common tasks include classification (e.g., fraud detection) and regression (e.g., credit risk scoring).

DOI: 10.1201/9781003607298-4

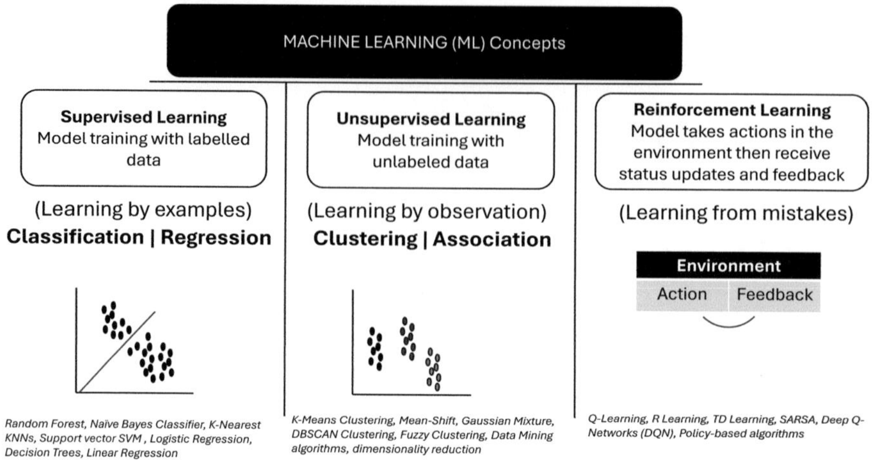

FIGURE 4.1 Types of machine learning.

2. **Unsupervised learning**: The model identifies patterns in data without labels. For example, grouping similar customers or reducing dimensionality for visualization.
3. **Reinforcement learning**: An agent learns by trial and error, maximizing rewards over time (used in robotics or decision-making).

Supervised Learning

Now we will begin our journey with the foundational paradigm which is supervised learning. A consolidated overview of essential generative AI terminology used throughout this chapter is provided in Figure 4.2.

SUPERVISED LEARNING: THE FOUNDATIONAL PARADIGM

Imagine you are teaching a child to distinguish apples from oranges by showing them many examples of each fruit, labeled clearly.

In the world of AI, **supervised learning** works the same way: we train a model on a dataset of **features** (input data) paired with known **labels** (desired outputs), so that it can infer a general rule—called the **model**—to classify or predict unseen data.

In this approach, a model is trained on a dataset containing labeled examples. If we want a machine to classify emails as spam or not, we provide thousands of emails tagged accordingly. The model learns a mapping between inputs (email contents) and outputs (labels). Once trained, this mapping can be generalized to new, unseen examples.

LLM Large Language Model Advanced AI system trained on massive text corpora to understand and generate human- like language	Synthetic Data Augmentation Model-generated samples used to expand, balance, or anonymize real datasets	Prompt Engineering AI Instruction Design Crafting prompts that steer a model toward accurate, context-aware outputs	Fine-tuning Model Specialization Adapting a foundation model to a narrow task by training on smaller domain data	Guardrails Moderation Filters Safety layers that block unsafe, biased, or non-compliant outputs before release
Transformers Neural Architecture Self-attention networks that process sequences in parallel, powering today's state-of-the-art NLP	Tokens Text units Smallest chunks (sub-words or characters) that model reads, determine context length	Zero-shot Generalization Performing unseen tasks using broad knowledge without explicit task training	RLHF Human-Aligned Training Reinforcement learning that tunes model behavior using human preference feedback	Perplexity Quality Metric Lower perplexity indicates better predictive performance on next-token tasks
Neural Network AI Foundation Layered nodes that learn patterns from data, mimicking brain-like processing	Context Window Input Capacity Maximum tokens the model can ingest at once, governs long-context handling	Few-Shot/ ICL In-Context Learning Generalizing from just a few examples embedded in the prompt (no weight updates)	Back Propagation Gradient Computation Method Algorithm for training deep neural networks to learn complex patterns and relationships in data	Jailbreaks Constraint Evasion Attacks that trick models into bypassing safety or policy filters
API Integration Interface Standard endpoints that let apps call model functions and embed AI features	Embeddings Vector Representation Dense numeric encoding of text, images or code enabling semantic search and retrieval	Soft Prompts Prompt Tuning Learned virtual tokens that guide the model without changing main weights	Top-K/Top-p/Beam Decoding Strategy Sampling or search methods balancing diversity v/s quality in generation	Temperature Randomness Control Hyper-parameter balancing deterministic v/s creative token sampling
Multimodal Mixed Inputs Models jointly processing text, vision, audio, or other modalities	Embedding Index Vector Store Database (eg FAISS) storing embeddings for fast semantic similarity search	Chain-of-Thought Reasoning Prompt Asking the model to think step-by-step, improving logic and transparency	Generative Adversarial Networks (GANs) Approach including two competing neural networks: a generator that creates new data (e.g., images, text) and a discriminator that tries to distinguish between real and generated data	Hallucination AI Fabrication When a model outputs fluent but factually incorrect information
RAG Retrieval-Augmented Generation Combines external knowledge retrieval with generation to ground answers in fresh facts	Grad Checkpoint Memory Saver Saves RAM by recomputing activations during back-prop, enables training bigger nets	CoT "Vote" Self-consistency Sampling multiple reasoning paths and selecting the majority answer for robustness		Hyperparameter Model training Configuration set before training the model

FIGURE 4.2 Must know: Gen AI terms and definitions.

Supervised learning introduces several critical terms. The inputs are referred to as features and the outputs are labels. The function that maps inputs to outputs is called a model. Learning, in this context, means adjusting the internal parameters of the model to minimize the error between the predicted and true outputs. A loss function, such as mean squared error for regression or cross-entropy for classification, governs this minimization. Supervised learning underpins countless AI applications: email spam filters, medical diagnosis, credit-risk scoring, and more. Its strength lies in its ability to **generalize** from examples, allowing systems to make reliable predictions on new inputs

Core Components

- **Features**: Quantitative representations of inputs (e.g., word frequencies in an email).
- **Labels**: The ground-truth annotations (e.g., "spam" vs. "not spam").
- **Model**: The function $f_\theta(x)$ parameterized by θ, mapping features to labels.
- **Loss function**: A measure of error—like **mean squared error** for regression or **cross-entropy** for classification—that the learning algorithm minimizes by adjusting θ.

Supervised learning remains the bedrock of AI because it leverages human-annotated data to teach machines precise mappings from inputs to outputs. So, it is important to understand this in detail.

Supervised learning is the bedrock paradigm of machine learning in which a model learns to predict outputs (labels) from inputs (features) by example. Given a dataset of input–output pairs (x_i, y_i), the learner seeks a mapping h:X→Y that will generalize to new, unseen x. Unlike unsupervised methods (which find structure without labeled examples) or reinforcement learning (which learns via reward signals in an environment), supervised learning offers direct feedback on exactly "what went wrong" whenever the model's prediction deviates from the true label.

Historical Milestones

- **1950s–1960s**: Early perceptrons (Rosenblatt, 1958) demonstrated that single-layer neural nets could learn simple binary classification tasks.

- **1986**: Rumelhart, Hinton & Williams' backpropagation paper reignited multi-layer neural network research.
- **1995**: Introduction of Support Vector Machines (Cortes & Vapnik), which robustly handle high-dimensional data.
- **2000s**: Kernel methods, ensemble techniques (random forests, boosting), and large-scale convex solvers matured.

Why Supervised Learning Matters Today?

Nearly every high-impact AI application—spam detection, medical diagnosis, credit scoring, image recognition, speech transcription—relies on supervised learning. Its direct mapping from annotated data to predictive behavior remains the most reliable route for building systems whose performance can be measured and controlled.

Core Algorithms

1. Linear regression
   i. Ordinary least squares
   ii. Gradient descent variants
   iii. Regularized regression (Ridge, Lasso)
2. Logistic regression
3. k-Nearest neighbors
4. Decision trees and ensembles
   i. CART
   ii. Random forests
   iii. Gradient-boosted trees
5. Support vector machines
6. Neural networks and deep feedforward models
7. Advanced models: Gaussian processes, Bayesian linear models

But not all learning is supervised.

Unsupervised Learning

In **unsupervised learning**, models work without labeled outputs, instead learning from the inherent structure of the data. **Clustering**, dimensionality reduction, and anomaly detection are common examples.

Unsupervised learning discovers structure in unlabeled data. The "core" algorithms fall into two broad categories—clustering (finding groups of similar points) and dimensionality reduction (finding low-dimensional structure or representations)—plus a few hybrids. Here are the main ones:

1. **k-Means clustering**: Splits data into k groups by assigning each point to the nearest cluster center.
2. **Hierarchical clustering**: Builds a tree of nested clusters by repeatedly merging or splitting groups based on similarity.
3. **DBSCAN**: Finds groups of any shape by linking points that are close together and marking others as noise.
4. **Gaussian mixture models (GMM)**: Represents data as a mix of bell-shaped distributions and clusters points by their likely source distribution.
5. **Principal component analysis (PCA)**: Reduces data dimensions by rotating to new axes that capture the most variance.
6. **Autoencoders**: Neural networks that learn to compress data into a smaller representation, then reconstruct it back.
7. **t-SNE**: Maps high-dimensional data into two or three dimensions so that similar points stay close together.
8. **UMAP**: Projects data into low dimensions by preserving both local and global structure more efficiently than t-SNE.
9. **Latent Dirichlet allocation (LDA)**: Discovers topics in document collections by modeling each document as a mixture of topics.
10. **Nonnegative matrix factorization (NMF)**: Decomposes data into parts-based representations by factoring matrices into nonnegative factors.

These algorithms form the backbone of unsupervised learning. In practice, one often combines them—for instance, reducing dimensionality with

PCA or an autoencoder *before* clustering with k-Means or DBSCAN—to tame high-dimensional data and reveal cleaner structure.

Reinforcement Learning

It is a paradigm in which an "agent" learns to make decisions by interacting with an "environment" and receiving feedback in the form of rewards or penalties. Rather than being told the correct action (as in supervised learning) or simply discovering structure without feedback (as in unsupervised learning), a reinforcement learning (RL) agent must explore and exploit its environment to discover which sequences of actions **maximize its long-term cumulative reward**. For example, consider training a robot to navigate a maze: each time it moves closer to the exit, it receives a small positive reward; and if it bumps into a wall, it receives a penalty. Over many trials the robot learns which turns and paths yield the highest total reward and eventually finds the shortest route.

The core components of any RL system are:

- **Agent**: The learner or decision-maker (e.g., the robot),
- **Environment**: Everything the agent interacts with (e.g., the maze),
- **State**: A representation of the current situation (e.g., robot's location),
- **Action**: Choices the agent can make at each state (e.g., move north, south),
- **Reward**: Scalar feedback signal indicating the desirability of the outcome (e.g., +1 for progress, –1 for collisions).

> Unlike supervised learning—where models learn from labeled examples of "right" answers—or unsupervised learning—where they discover hidden patterns without external feedback—RL's unique strength lies in its ability to **learn optimal behavior through trial and error**, making it indispensable for tasks like game playing (e.g., DeepMind's AlphaGo), robotics, and autonomous control systems.

Features, Representations, and the Limits of Shallow Models

Early machine learning relied heavily on manual feature engineering—the art of transforming raw data into informative inputs for algorithms. A data scientist building a risk detection model might normalize values, extract ratios, or convert categorical fields into one-hot vectors. Once the features were defined, simple models such as logistic regression,[1] decision trees,[2] or support vector machines (SVMs)[3] were used to classify or score new data.

Let's break down the core concepts:

- **Features**: Measurable inputs (e.g., age, income, image pixels).
- **Labels**: Known outcomes used for training (e.g., approved/denied, 0/1).
- **Model**: A function that maps features to labels, denoted as $f_\theta(x)$, where θ represents the model's parameters.
- **Loss function**: Measures the difference between predicted and true labels. For example:
    - **Mean squared error (MSE):**
    The MSE measures the amount of error in statistical models. It assesses the average squared difference between the observed and predicted values. When a model has no error, the MSE equals zero. As model error increases, its value increases.

    $$\mathbf{MSE} = \sum_{i=1}^{n} (y_i - \widehat{y_i})^2$$

    In simple words, MSE is a way for the computer to measure how far off its guesses are. It looks at each mistake (how wrong a prediction is), squares the size of the mistake (to make sure big errors count more), and then takes the average of all those squared mistakes. It is like baking cookies and checking how far off each one is from the perfect size, then averaging those differences to see how well you did overall. The smaller the MSE, the better the computer is doing!

    - **Cross-entropy (for classification):** The cross-entropy measures the difference between the discovered probability distribution of a classification model and the predicted values.

    $$\textbf{Cross-Entropy} = \sum_{i=1}^{n} y_i \, \boldsymbol{log}\left(\widehat{y_i}\right)$$

    In simple words, cross-entropy is how a computer measures how surprised it is by its wrong guesses in a classification task (like picking the right animal in a photo). If it was very confident but totally wrong, it gets a big penalty. If it was unsure but still wrong, the penalty is smaller. It compares what the computer *thought* the answer was with what the *correct* answer is. The goal is to reduce surprise (or confusion) over time—just like how we learn better when we understand why we were wrong. The lower the cross-entropy, the better the model is at classifying things.

These models, sometimes referred to as shallow learners, are interpretable and efficient, and they still have their place in risk-sensitive applications. However, they often struggle with unstructured data—such as text, images, or audio—and can only capture relatively simple relationships unless features are handcrafted with great care.

To move beyond these limitations, machine learning needed models that could learn not only mappings from inputs to outputs, but also the features themselves. This is the promise of deep learning.

Now that we have covered the basics and introduction, let us dive further into "The Rise of Deep Learning".

This chapter is divided into five sections:

Section A: Artificial Neural Networks

Section B: Training Neural Networks

Section C: Convolutional Neural Networks

Section D: Recurrent Neural Networks

Section E: Practical Case Study of NLP using RNN, LSTM, DistilBERT and RoBERTa

SECTION A: ARTIFICIAL NEURAL NETWORKS

The Rise of Deep Learning

For years, most machine learning relied on shallow models like decision trees, SVMs, and logistic regression. These models worked well when engineered features were strong, but they struggled when data complexity grew. The solution came from a resurgence of an older idea: neural networks.

What is an Artificial Neural Network?

Deep learning refers to a class of models known as artificial neural networks[4] (ANNs). ANNs mimic the structure of biological brains (very

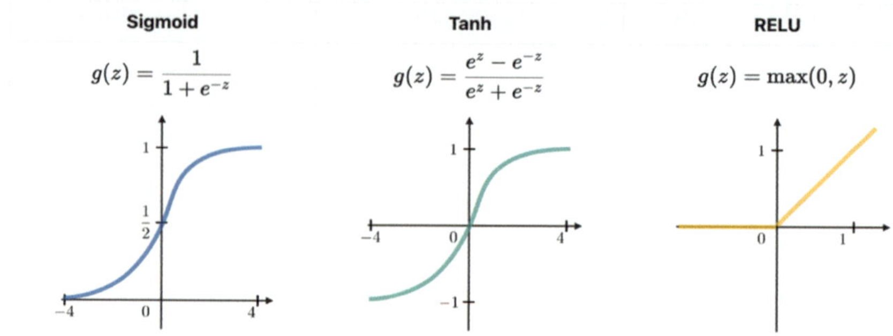

FIGURE 4.3 Common activation functions.

loosely). These models are composed of layers of neurons, where each neuron performs a weighted sum of its inputs.

Each neuron computes:

$$z = w \cdot x + b$$

where x is input vector, w is weight vector, and b is bias.

We pass z through a **nonlinear activation function** $a = \sigma(z)$, common activation functions. The shapes and output ranges of common activation functions are illustrated in Figure 4.3. These functions behave differently during training:

- **ReLU** (rectified linear unit): $\sigma(z) = max(0, z)$
  - Output range: $[0, \infty)$
- **Sigmoid**: $\sigma(z) = \frac{1}{1+ e^{-z}}$
  - Output range: $(0, 1)$
- **Tanh**: $\sigma(z) = tanh(z) = \frac{e^{z} - e^{-z}}{e^{z} + e^{-z}}$
  - Output range: $(-1, 1)$

These nonlinearities allow networks to represent **complex, curved** relationships—unlike a straight line.

The power of a neural network comes from stacking multiple layers—hence the term "deep".

Each layer learns increasingly abstract representations of the input. In a vision task, for instance, the first layer might detect edges, the second corners, the third shapes, and so on until the network can recognize an entire object.

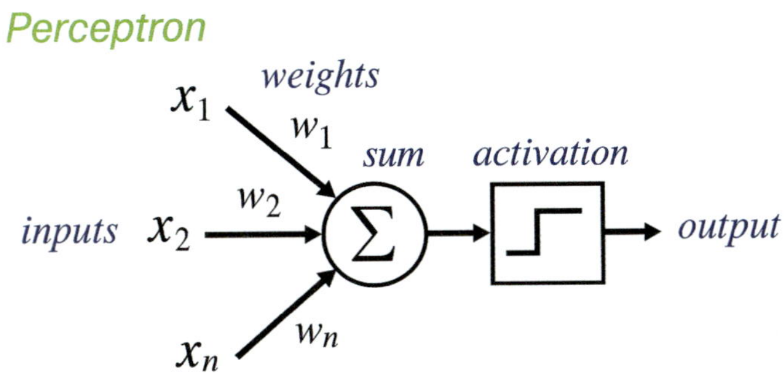

FIGURE 4.4 Single perceptron model.

A neural network with one hidden layer (as shown in Figure 4.4) looks like this:

$$f(x) = W_2 \cdot \sigma(W_1 \cdot x + b_1) + b_2$$

where, W_1, b_1 are weights and biases for the first (hidden) layer and W_2, b_2 are for the output layer.

Each layer adds flexibility. More layers → more abstraction → more expressive power. A multi-layer neural network architecture illustrating this hierarchical abstraction is shown in Figure 4.5.

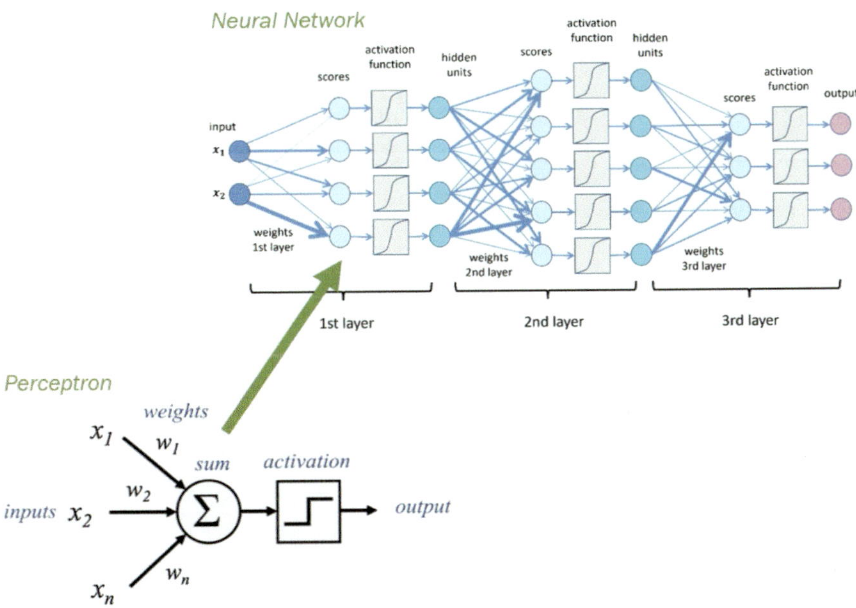

FIGURE 4.5 Neural network architecture.

SECTION B: TRAINING NEURAL NETWORKS

Training a neural network means adjusting all weights[5] in every layer to minimize the loss. This is done using **backpropagation,**[6] which applies the **chain rule** from calculus to compute gradients layer by layer. Here's the intuition:

- **Forward propagation**: where the input flows through the network and generates a prediction.
- **Loss calculation**: a loss function compares the prediction $\hat{y}$ with the true label y.
- **Backpropagation and gradient descent**: where to minimize loss, we update weights using **backpropagation**, which applies the chain rule:

$$\frac{\partial L}{\partial w} = \frac{\partial L}{\partial \hat{y}} \cdot \frac{\partial \hat{y}}{\partial w}$$

  Then update the weights using: $w = w - \eta \cdot \frac{\partial L}{\partial w}$
  where, η is the learning rate.

The optimization is typically done using gradient descent,[7] which nudges each parameter in the direction that reduces error, and often with variants like Adam, which adjust learning rates dynamically to speed convergence.

Installing TensorFlow[8] and Required Packages

Prerequisites:

- Python 3.8+
- pip[1]

Installation (CPU)

```
pip install tensorflow
pip install keras
pip install pandas
pip install numpy
pip install seaborn
pip install matplotlib
```

Check GPU availability

```
import tensorflow as tf
print("Num GPUs Available: ", len(tf.config.list_physical_devices('GPU')))
```

Example: Building an ANN in TensorFlow/Keras using fashion mnist dataset

```
import tensorflow as tf
import pandas as pd
from tensorflow import keras
import numpy as np
import matplotlib.pyplot as plt
import seaborn as sns

%matplotlib inline

fashion_mnist = keras.datasets.fashion_mnist

(X_train, y_train), (X_test, y_test) = fashion_mnist.load_data()

X_train = X_train / 255.0
X_test = X_test / 255.0

from tensorflow.keras.models import Sequential
from tensorflow.keras.layers import Dense, Activation, Flatten

# Simple ANN with one hidden layer

## Feedforward part
model = Sequential()

model.add(Flatten(input_shape=[28,28]))
model.add(Dense(128, activation='relu'))    ## First Dense or Hidden  layer

model.add(Dense(10,  activation='softmax'))  ##  Output  layer  (binary
classification)

## Backpropagation Part
model.compile(loss='sparse_categorical_crossentropy',
        optimizer='adam',
        metrics=['accuracy'])

## Train the model
model.fit(X_train, y_train,
      epochs=10, validation_data=(X_test, y_test))
```

- models.Sequential([…])
    - This creates a simple feedforward ANN (also called a multilayer perceptron [MLP]).
    - Data flows forward through the layers (input → hidden → output).
- model. compile(...) sets up the loss function and optimizer.
- model.fit(...) triggers the **training process**, where TensorFlow uses **backpropagation** to:
    - Compute the gradient of the loss wrt weights
    - Update weights using **Adam optimizer**[9]
    - Minimize the binary_crossentropy loss

```
losses = pd.DataFrame(model.history.history)
losses[['accuracy','val_accuracy']].plot(figsize = (10,5), title="Accuracy vs Val_Acc")
```

Key Observations:

- Accuracy steadily climbs with training, while validation accuracy stabilizes, indicating good model performance, this learning behavior is visualized in Figure 4.6.

```
predictions = np.argmax(model.predict(X_test), axis=-1)
from sklearn.metrics import classification_report, confusion_matrix

print("############### Classification Report ###############\n\n", classification_report(y_test, predictions))
```

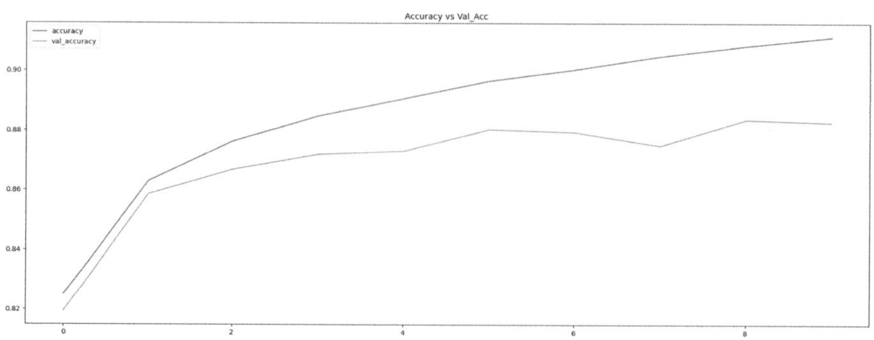

FIGURE 4.6 Training vs. validation accuracy graph.

```
plt.figure(figsize=(15,6))
sns.heatmap(confusion_matrix(y_test, predictions),annot=True,cmap="Bl
ues", fmt='g')
plt.ylabel('True label')
plt.xlabel('Predicted label')
plt.title('Confusion matrix - ANN with one hidden layer')
plt.show()
```

Key Observations:

- Precision, recall, and F1-scores across all classes, showing balanced model performance with strong accuracy overall. The resulting classification metrics and confusion matrix are reported in Figure 4.7 and Figure 4.8, respectively.

Deep networks allow for impressive flexibility, but they introduce new challenges. One major issue is overfitting—a model that learns the training data too well, including its noise. To counter this, regularization techniques like dropout (randomly disabling neurons during training), early stopping, and L2 regularization are used.

```
# ANN structure with Dropout layer, EarlyStopping

import numpy as np
import pandas as pd
import tensorflow as tf
from tensorflow import keras
from tensorflow.keras import layers, models, Sequential
```

############### Classification Report ###############

	precision	recall	f1-score	support
0	0.86	0.83	0.84	1000
1	0.98	0.98	0.98	1000
2	0.80	0.77	0.79	1000
3	0.89	0.91	0.90	1000
4	0.78	0.81	0.80	1000
5	0.99	0.93	0.96	1000
6	0.70	0.70	0.70	1000
7	0.93	0.94	0.94	1000
8	0.97	0.97	0.97	1000
9	0.92	0.97	0.95	1000
accuracy			0.88	10000
macro avg	0.88	0.88	0.88	10000
weighted avg	0.88	0.88	0.88	10000

FIGURE 4.7 Classification report.

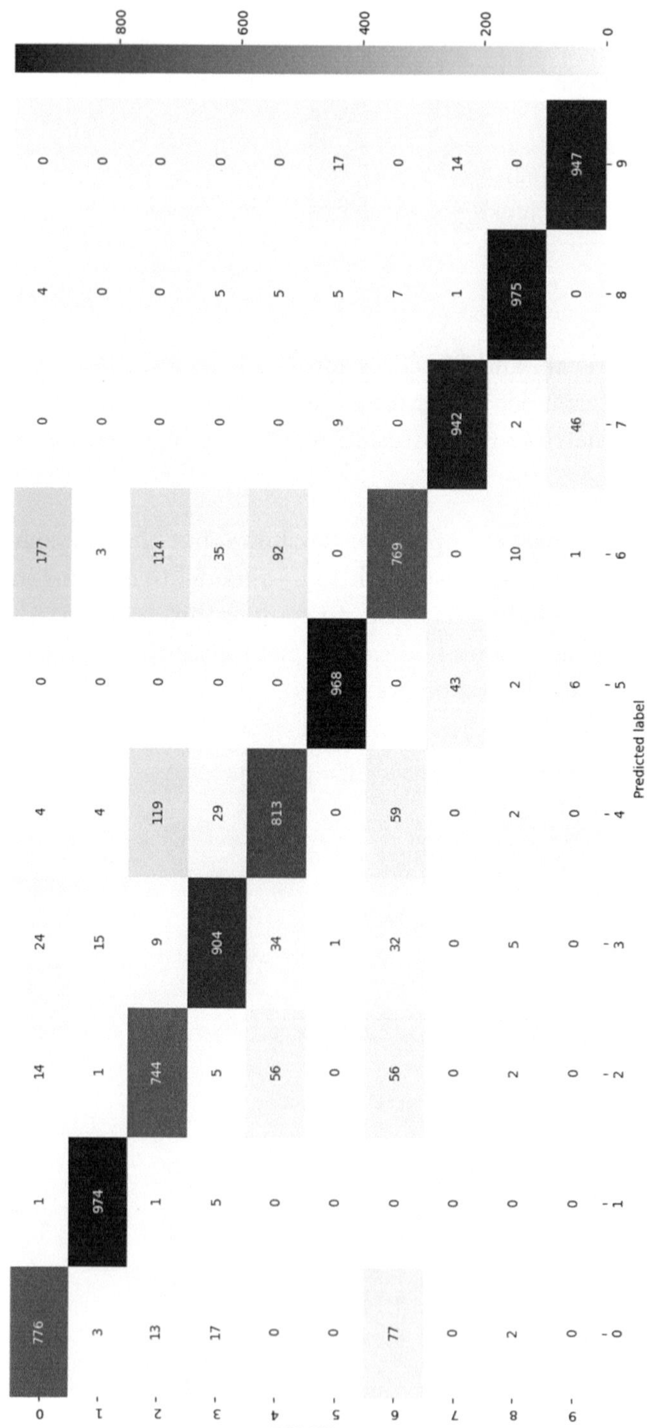

FIGURE 4.8 Confusion matrix: ANN with one hidden layer.

```
from tensorflow.keras.layers import Dense, Activation, Flatten, Dropout,
BatchNormalization
from tensorflow.keras.callbacks import EarlyStopping

## Set up early stopping
early_stop = EarlyStopping(monitor='val_loss',mode = "min", patience=3,
verbose=1)

model = Sequential()
model.add(Flatten(input_shape=[28, 28]))
model.add(Dense(128, activation='relu'))          ## Hidden Layer 1
model.add(Dropout(0.3))                           ## Dropout layer

model.add(Dense(128, activation='relu'))          ## Hidden Layer 1
model.add(Dropout(0.3))

model.add(Dense(128, activation='relu'))          ## Hidden Layer 1
model.add(Dropout(0.3))

model.add(Dense(10, activation='softmax'))        ## Output layer

model.compile(loss='sparse_categorical_crossentropy',
          optimizer='adam',
          metrics=['accuracy'])

model.fit(X_train, y_train,
       epochs=10, batch_size = 32,
       validation_data=(X_test, y_test), callbacks=[early_stop])

losses = pd.DataFrame(model.history.history)
losses[['accuracy','val_accuracy']].plot(figsize = (10,5), title="Accuracy vs
Val_Acc")
```

Key Observations:

- Compared to the previous training vs. validation accuracy plot, this one shows (see Figure 4.9) slightly lower initial accuracy but steadier validation performance, suggesting improved generalization as training progresses.

```
predictions = np.argmax(model.predict(X_test), axis=-1)

print("############### Classification Report ###############\n\n",
classification_report(y_test, predictions))
```

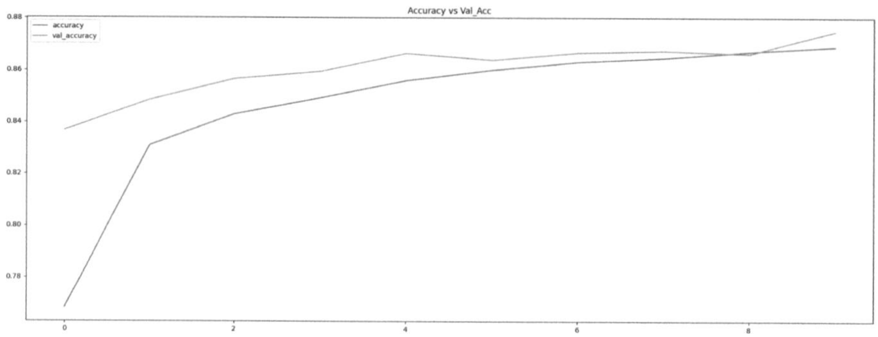

FIGURE 4.9 Training vs. validation accuracy graph.

```
plt.figure(figsize=(15,6))
sns.heatmap(confusion_matrix(y_test, predictions),annot=True,cmap="Bl
ues", fmt='g')
plt.ylabel('True label')
plt.xlabel('Predicted label')
plt.title('Confusion matrix - ANN with three hidden layer')
plt.show()
```

Key Observations:

- Metrics remain consistent with overall accuracy at 87%, suggesting stable performance. The corresponding classification report and confusion matrix are presented in Figures 4.10 and 4.11, respectively.

```
############### Classification Report ###############

              precision    recall  f1-score   support

           0       0.81      0.85      0.83      1000
           1       0.99      0.96      0.98      1000
           2       0.78      0.81      0.79      1000
           3       0.86      0.89      0.88      1000
           4       0.79      0.79      0.79      1000
           5       0.97      0.95      0.96      1000
           6       0.71      0.63      0.67      1000
           7       0.91      0.97      0.94      1000
           8       0.95      0.97      0.96      1000
           9       0.97      0.93      0.95      1000

    accuracy                           0.87     10000
   macro avg       0.87      0.87      0.87     10000
weighted avg       0.87      0.87      0.87     10000
```

FIGURE 4.10 Classification report.

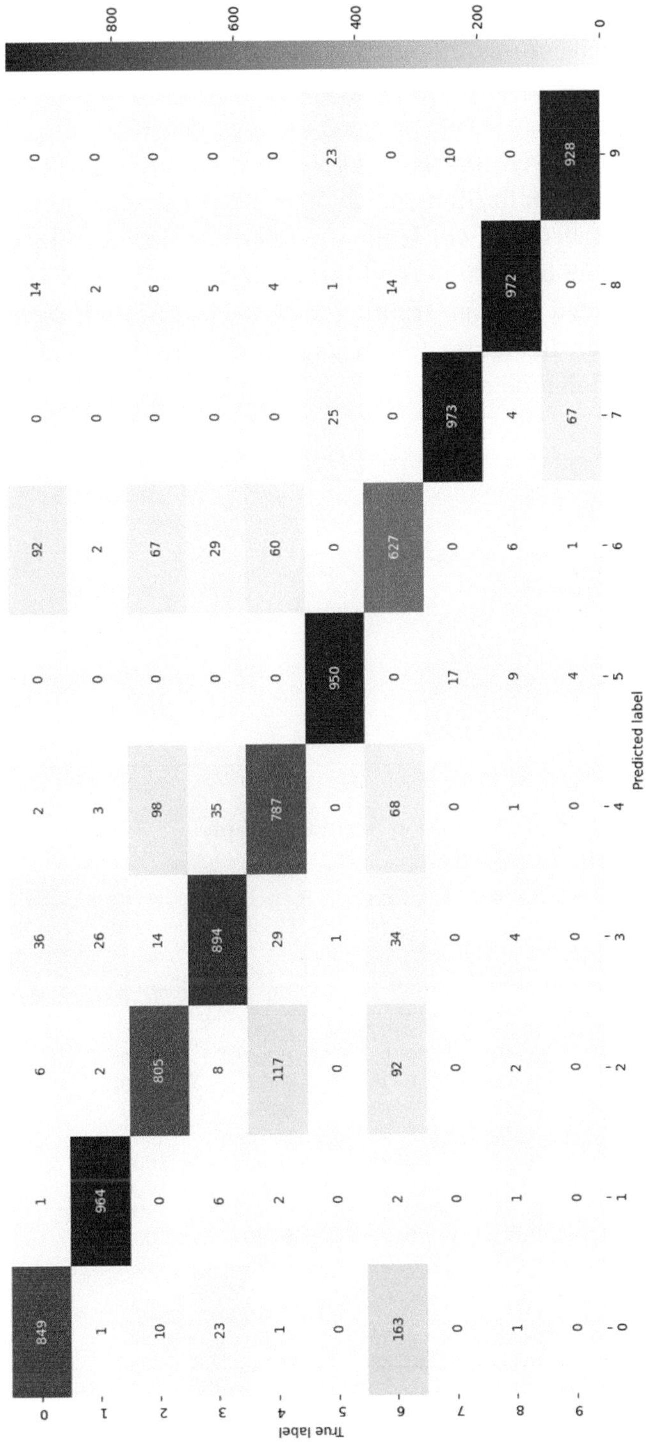

FIGURE 4.11 Confusion matrix: ANN with three hidden layers.

Another challenge, particularly in earlier architectures, was the vanishing gradient problem—as the number of layers increased, the gradients became too small to effectively update the early layers. This made training deep models difficult.

These problems were partially solved through architectural innovations like batch normalization (which normalizes the input to each layer) and residual connections (which allow gradients to flow directly to earlier layers). The impact of batch normalization on model stability and performance is illustrated through training curves, classification metrics, and confusion matrices in Figures 4.12 through 4.14. With these tools, the deep learning revolution took off.

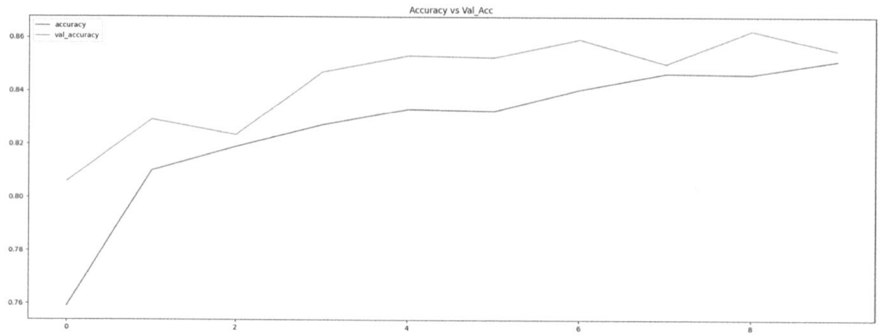

FIGURE 4.12 Training vs Validation Accuracy Graph

############### Classification Report ###############

	precision	recall	f1-score	support
0	0.85	0.77	0.81	1000
1	0.99	0.95	0.97	1000
2	0.74	0.75	0.74	1000
3	0.85	0.83	0.84	1000
4	0.70	0.79	0.75	1000
5	0.96	0.95	0.95	1000
6	0.65	0.65	0.65	1000
7	0.91	0.95	0.93	1000
8	0.95	0.97	0.96	1000
9	0.97	0.94	0.95	1000
accuracy			0.86	10000
macro avg	0.86	0.86	0.86	10000
weighted avg	0.86	0.86	0.86	10000

FIGURE 4.13 Classification report.

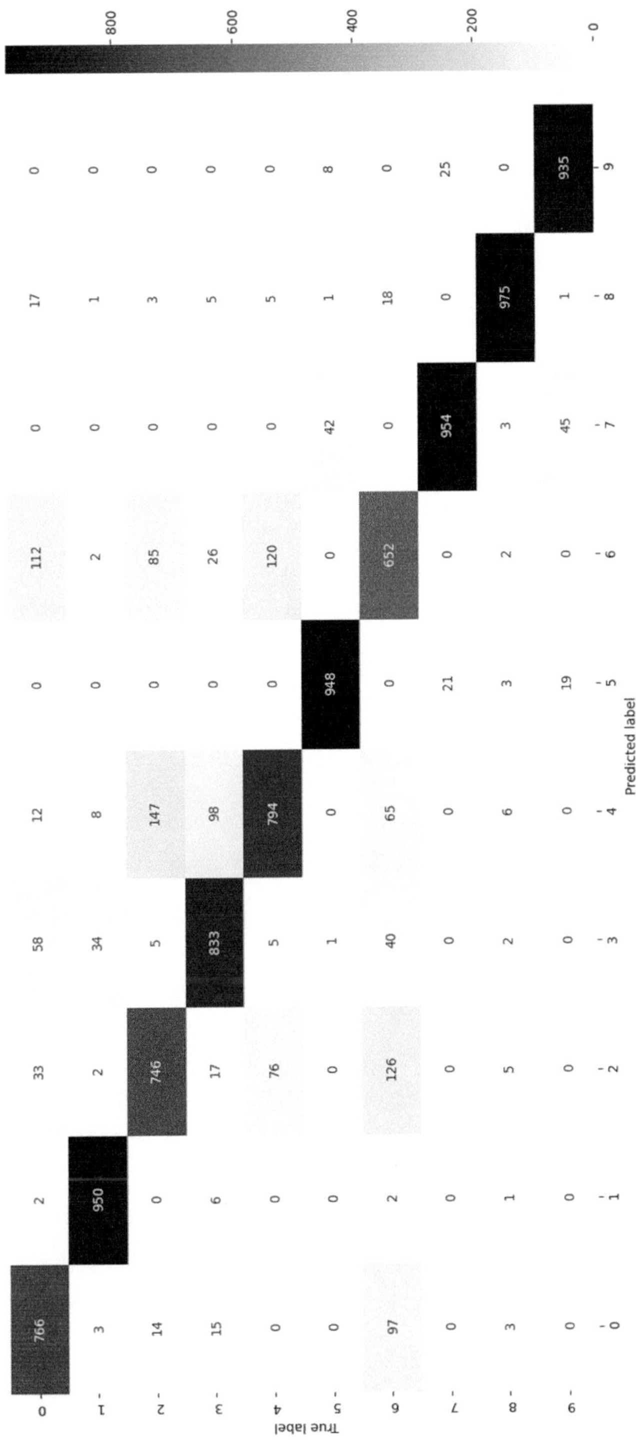

FIGURE 4.14 Confusion matrix: ANN with batch normalization.

```
# ANN structure with Batch Normalization

model = Sequential()
model.add(Flatten(input_shape=[28,28]))

model.add(Dense(128, activation='relu')) ## Layer 1
model.add(Dropout(0.2))
model.add(BatchNormalization())

model.add(Dense(128, activation='relu')) ## Layer 2
model.add(Dropout(0.2))
model.add(BatchNormalization())

model.add(Dense(256, activation='relu')) ## Layer 3
model.add(Dropout(0.2))
model.add(BatchNormalization())

model.add(Dense(10, activation='softmax')) ## Output layer

model.compile(loss='sparse_categorical_crossentropy',
          optimizer='adam',
          metrics=['accuracy'])

model.fit(X_train, y_train,
       epochs=10, batch_size = 32,
       validation_data=(X_test, y_test), callbacks=[early_stop])

losses = pd.DataFrame(model.history.history)
losses[['accuracy','val_accuracy']].plot(figsize = (10,5), title="Accuracy vs
Val_Acc")
```

```
predictions = np.argm ax(model.predict(X_test), axis=-1)

print("############### Classification Report ###############\n\n",
classification_report(y_test, predictions))

plt.figure(figsize=(15,6))
sns.heatmap(confusion_matrix(y_test, predictions),annot=True,cmap="Bl
ues", fmt='g')
plt.ylabel('True label')
plt.xlabel('Predicted label')
plt.title('Confusion matrix - ANN with Batch Normalization')
plt.show()
```

SECTION C: CONVOLUTIONAL NEURAL NETWORKS

The Need for Specialized Architectures in Vision

While feedforward ANNs can approximate any function in theory; in practice, they struggle with high-dimensional inputs like images. Consider an RGB image of size 224 × 224. Flattening it for an ANN results in over **150,000 input features**, losing all spatial relationships like edges, textures, or patterns.

To solve this, we need architectures that:

- Handle spatial data efficiently
- Detect patterns irrespective of position
- Are computationally feasible to train

This gave rise to **CNNs**[10]—models inspired by the animal visual cortex, where neurons respond to overlapping regions of the visual field. A high-level CNN architecture highlighting convolution, pooling, and dense layers is shown in Figure 4.15.

CNN Architecture Overview

A CNN consists of several building blocks:

- **Convolutional layers:** Instead of processing all pixels independently (as in ANN), CNNs slide small filters (also called kernels) across the image. Each filter detects a specific feature, such as an edge, corner, or texture.
  - **Stride** determines how much the filter moves across the image.
  - **Padding** adds extra pixels (usually zeros) around borders to control output size.

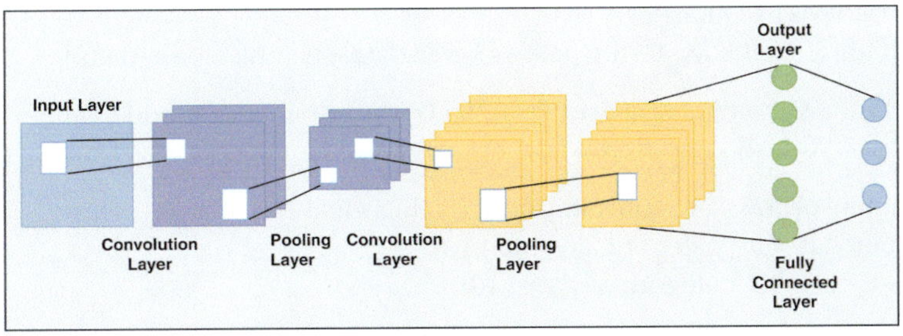

FIGURE 4.15 Basic CNN architecture. (Credits: Image source: https://www.researchgate.net/figure/Basic-architecture-of-CNN_fig3_335086346. Copyright licenses: https://creativecommons.org/licenses/by/4.0/).

- **Activation functions (ReLU):** After the convolution step, we apply a rectified linear unit (ReLU) activation function. ReLU introduces nonlinearity and is computationally efficient.
- **Pooling layers:** Pooling reduces the spatial size of the feature maps, making the network more efficient and translation invariant.
  - **Max pooling** is most common, it retains only the most prominent feature in each region.
- **Fully connected layers (dense layers):** After several convolution + pooling blocks, the output is "flattened" into a 1D vector and passed through fully connected (dense) layers for classification or regression.

Example: CNN with TensorFlow/Keras

```
# Basic CNN model

import pandas as pd
import numpy as np
import tensorflow as tf
from tensorflow import keras
import matplotlib.pyplot as plt
import seaborn as sns

from tensorflow.keras.models import Sequential
from tensorflow.keras.layers import Dense, Conv2D, MaxPool2D, Flatten,
Dropout, Activation
from tensorflow.keras.callbacks import EarlyStopping

import warnings
warnings.filterwarnings('ignore')

%matplotlib inline

## Load Mnist Dataset
(X_train, y_train), (X_test, y_test) = keras.datasets.mnist.load_data()

X_train = X_train[..., np.newaxis] / 255.0  # Normalize and add channel dim
X_test = X_test[..., np.newaxis] / 255.0

from tensorflow.keras.utils import to_categorical
y_train_cat = to_categorical(y_train,10)
y_test_cat = to_categorical(y_test,10)

early_stop = EarlyStopping(monitor='val_accuracy', mode = "max",
patience=7, verbose=1)

## Build the model
model = Sequential()
```

```
## Convolutional layers
model.add(Conv2D(filters=64, kernel_size=(4,4),input_shape=(X_train.
shape[1:]), activation='relu'))
model.add(Conv2D(filters=64, kernel_size=(4,4),input_shape=(X_train.
shape[1:]), activation='relu'))

## Pooling Layers
model.add(MaxPool2D(pool_size=(2, 2)))
model.add(Dropout(0.25))

model.add(Flatten())

model.add(Dense(128, activation='relu'))
model.add(Dropout(0.50))

model.add(Dense(10, activation='softmax')) # Output layer

model.compile(loss='categorical_crossentropy',
          optimizer= 'adam',
          metrics=['accuracy'])

model.fit(X_train, y_train_cat, epochs=10, batch_size = 32,
validation_data=(X_test, y_test_cat),
        callbacks=[early_stop])

losses = pd.DataFrame(model.history.history)
losses[['accuracy','val_accuracy']].plot(figsize=(20,7),
                        title="Train vs Validation Accuracy (Base Model)",
                        xlabel="Epochs",
                        ylabel="Accuracy_Score")
```

Model Evaluation

After training, use accuracy and confusion matrices to evaluate performance. For multi-class problems, **categorical accuracy** is most common. The training dynamics of the CNN are illustrated in Figure 4.16. And, the model's classification performance and error distribution are shown in Figures 4.17 and 4.18.

```
predictions = np.argmax(model.predict(X_test), axis=-1)

from sklearn.metrics import classification_report, confusion_matrix

print("################ Classification Report ################ \n\n",
classification_report(y_test, predictions))
```

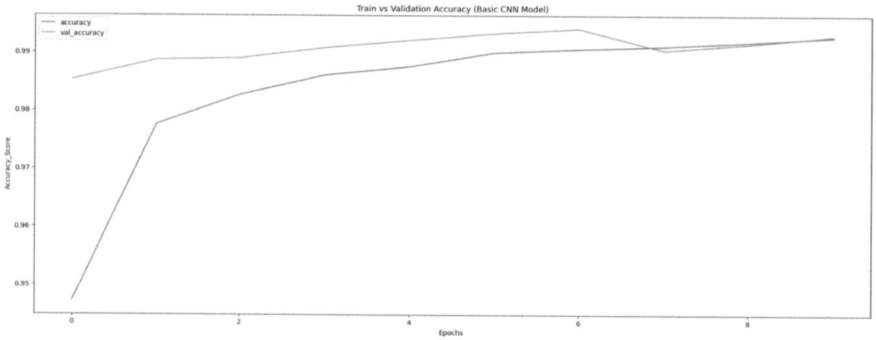

FIGURE 4.16 Training vs. validation accuracy graph.

```
plt.figure(figsize=(15,6))
sns.heatmap(confusion_matrix(y_test, predictions), annot=True,
cmap="Blues", fmt='g')
plt.ylabel('True label')
plt.xlabel('Predicted label')
plt.title('Confusion matrix')
plt.show()
```

Computational Considerations

CNNs are highly parallelizable, benefiting greatly from **GPU**[11] **acceleration.** Training a CNN on a CPU may take **hours**, while GPUs can do the same job in **minutes**.

############## Classification Report ##############

	precision	recall	f1-score	support
0	1.00	0.99	1.00	980
1	0.99	1.00	0.99	1135
2	0.99	0.99	0.99	1032
3	0.99	1.00	0.99	1010
4	0.99	0.99	0.99	982
5	1.00	0.99	0.99	892
6	0.99	0.99	0.99	958
7	0.99	0.99	0.99	1028
8	0.99	0.99	0.99	974
9	0.99	0.99	0.99	1009
accuracy			0.99	10000
macro avg	0.99	0.99	0.99	10000
weighted avg	0.99	0.99	0.99	10000

FIGURE 4.17 Classification report.

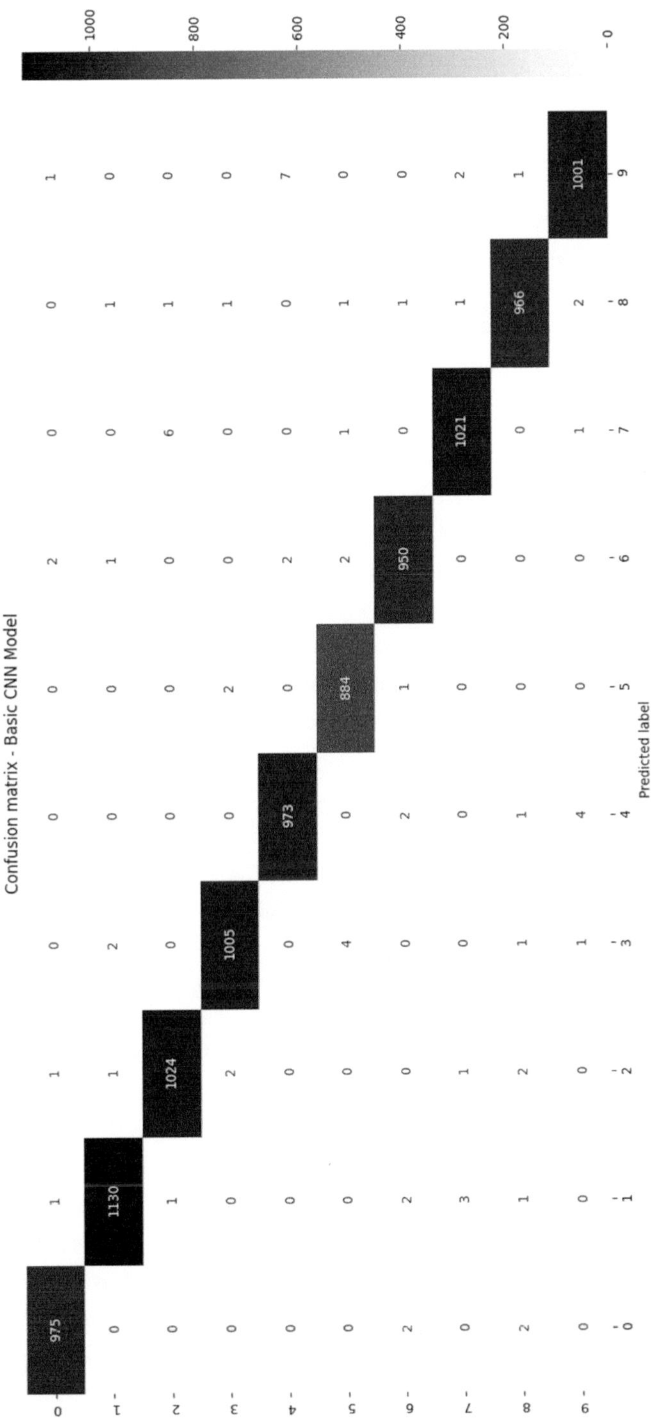

FIGURE 4.18 Confusion matrix.

```
Use tf.config.list_physical_devices('GPU') to verify GPU access.
```

Summary

CNNs are the go-to architecture for spatial data. They've powered advances in medical imaging, autonomous vehicles, facial recognition, document and invoice parsing.

By using weight-sharing (filters), pooling, and nonlinearity, CNNs make deep learning feasible on high-dimensional image data.

SECTION D: RECURRENT NEURAL NETWORKS

The Sequence Challenge: Why NLP Needed a New Architecture

While CNNs performed well in vision, language posed a different challenge. Language is sequential, ambiguous, and contextual, and meaning often depends on words that are far apart—e.g., "bank" can refer to a financial institution or the side of a river.

Traditional machine learning models and even early deep learning architectures like feedforward networks can't model sequence relationships well.

To address this, we need models that can:

- Understand **order and context** in sequences.
- Handle **long-range dependencies**.
- Scale to massive text datasets and tasks.

This journey in natural language processing (NLP)[12] started with **recurrent neural networks (RNNs)**[13], evolved through **long short-term memory (LSTMs)**, and culminated in **transformers** which are now the backbone of large language models (LLMs) like GPT, BERT, and their derivatives.

Recurrent Neural Networks

In traditional machine learning, models assume that all inputs are independent of one another. But in the real world, **sequential data is everywhere**—from transaction histories and customer support transcripts to clinical records and sensor logs. Enter the **RNN**, a foundational architecture in the evolution of deep learning for sequence modeling. The structural difference between feedforward and recurrent networks is illustrated in Figure 4.19.

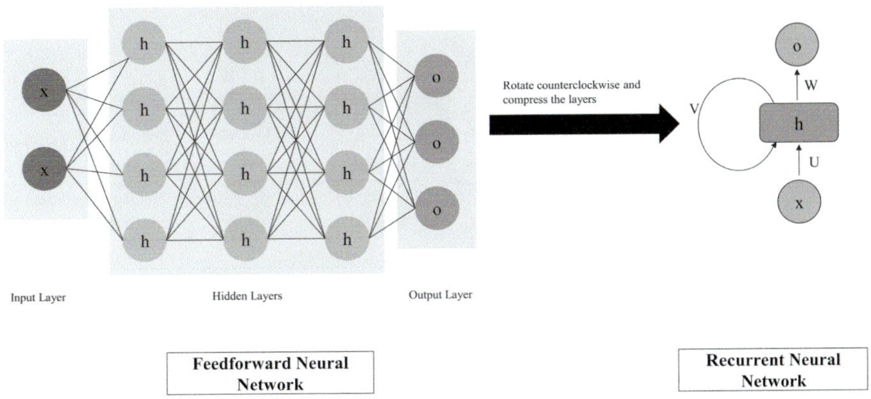

FIGURE 4.19 Feedforward and recurrent neural network.

Early neural models for language used RNNs, where each word's representation depended on the previous word's state. RNNs are designed to handle **time-dependent data**, where current predictions depend on previous inputs. They introduce the concept of **memory** by maintaining a hidden state that's updated at each step of the sequence. Imagine a model reading a sentence word by word—it needs to "remember" earlier words to understand the meaning of the current one.

How RNNs Work

The feedforward network can be transformed into an RNN by rotating the layers counterclockwise and compressing them.

At each time step t, an RNN receives an input x_t and updates a hidden state h_t based on the previous hidden state h_{t-1} and the new input:

$$h_t = tanh(Ux_t + Vh_{t-1} + b_h)$$

where U is input → hidden weight matrix; V is hidden → hidden/recurrent weight matrix; b_h is hidden layer bias.

And the output equation would be:

$$o_t = Wh_t + b_o$$

where W is hidden → output weight matrix and b_o is output layer bias.

This recursive update allows the model to **retain context** over time. An unfolded representation of the RNN across time steps is shown in Figure 4.20.

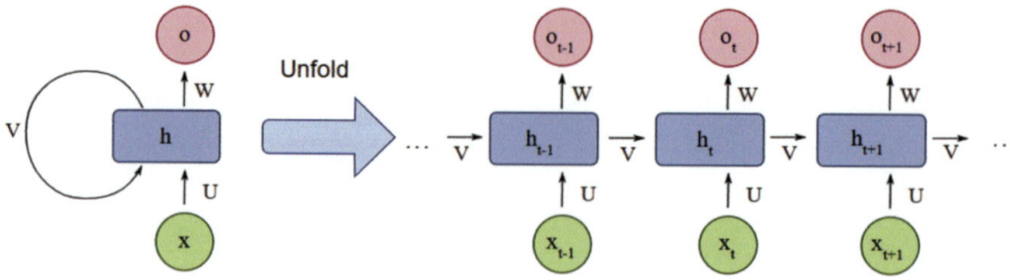

FIGURE 4.20 RNN architecture connector diagram. (Credits: https://commons.wikimedia.org/wiki/File:Recurrent_neural_network_unfold.svg. Copyright licenses: https://creativecommons.org/licenses/by-sa/4.0/).

RNN Code Example

```
import tensorflow as tf
from tensorflow import keras
from tensorflow.keras.models import Sequential
from tensorflow.keras.layers import Embedding, SimpleRNN, Dense
from tensorflow.keras.datasets import imdb

# Load and preprocess data
(x_train, y_train), (x_test, y_test) = imdb.load_data(num_words=10000)
x_train = tf.keras.preprocessing.sequence.pad_sequences(x_train,
maxlen=200)
x_test = tf.keras.preprocessing.sequence.pad_sequences(x_test,
maxlen=200)

# Build RNN model
model = Sequential([
  Embedding(input_dim=10000, output_dim=128, input_length=200),
  SimpleRNN(64),
  Dense(1, activation='sigmoid')
])

model.compile(loss='binary_crossentropy', optimizer='adam',
metrics=['accuracy'])
model.fit(x_train, y_train,
        validation_data=(x_test, y_test),
        epochs=2)
```

However, RNNs were hard to train, slow, and struggled with long-term dependencies. For long sequences, the gradients used in training can become too small (or too large)—a problem known as the **vanishing/exploding gradient**.

This makes it hard for the model to learn long-term dependencies, like remembering the start of a long document when generating a summary at the end. Long short-term memory (LSTM) networks improved this by adding gating mechanisms, but even these struggled with very long texts or parallelization.

Long Short-Term Memory Networks

LSTMs were introduced to address a key shortcoming in RNNs: the **inability to retain information over long distances**. For applications in policy compliance, contract review, or patient risk modeling, this matters a great deal. For example, a legal clause early in a document can influence the interpretation of another clause 500 words later. You need memory that lasts.

How LSTMs Work?

LSTMs introduce a **memory cell** and three **gates** that regulate the flow of information:

1. **Forget gate f_t**: What to discard from memory
2. **Input gate i_t:** What new information to store
3. **Output gate o_t**: What to pass to the next layer or time step

$$
\begin{aligned}
\boldsymbol{f_t} &= \sigma(W_f x_t + U_f h_{t-1} + b_f) \\
\boldsymbol{i_t} &= \sigma(W_i x_t + U_i h_{t-1} + b_i) \\
\boldsymbol{\tilde{c}_t} &= tanh(W_c x_t + U_c h_{t-1} + b_c) \\
\boldsymbol{c_t} &= f_t \cdot c_{t-1} + i_t \cdot \tilde{c} \\
\boldsymbol{o_t} &= \sigma(W_o x_t + U_o\ h_{t-1} + b_o) \\
\boldsymbol{h_t} &= o_t \cdot tanh(c_t)
\end{aligned}
$$

Here, $\boldsymbol{c_t}$ is the memory cell, and $\boldsymbol{h_t}$ is the hidden state—passed to the next time step. The internal gating mechanism of an LSTM cell is illustrated in Figure 4.21.

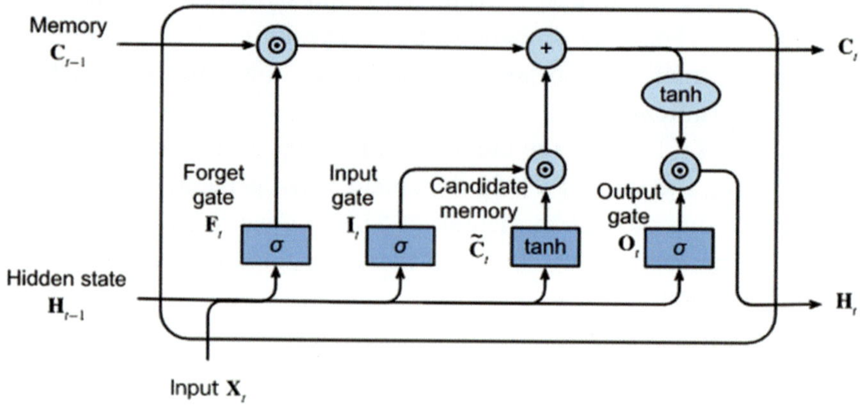

FIGURE 4.21 LSTM architecture. (From Karabas, Ahmet & Aydin, Nizamettin. (2025). Deep Learning Approaches in the Effects of Recession and FOMC Minutes on Oil Prices. IEEE Access. PP. 1-1. 10.1109/ACCESS.2025.3537822. This image is licensed under the Creative Commons Attribution-Share Alike 4.0 International license https://creativecommons.org/licenses/by-sa/4.0/).

LSTM Code Example: Sentiment Classification

```
import tensorflow as tf
from tensorflow import keras
from tensorflow.keras.models import Sequential
from tensorflow.keras.layers import Embedding, LSTM, Dense, Dropout
from tensorflow.keras.callbacks import EarlyStopping
from tensorflow.keras.datasets import imdb

# Load and preprocess data
(X_train, y_train), (X_test, y_test) = imdb.load_data(num_words=10000)
X_train = tf.keras.preprocessing.sequence.pad_sequences(X_train,
maxlen=200)
X_test = tf.keras.preprocessing.sequence.pad_sequences(X_test,
maxlen=200)

# Build an LSTM model with Dropout and Early stopping
model = Sequential()
model.add(Embedding(input_dim=10000, output_dim=128,
input_length=200))
model.add(LSTM(64))
```

```
model.add(Dropout(0.4))
model.add(Dense(1, activation='sigmoid'))

model.compile(loss='binary_crossentropy', optimizer='adam',
metrics=['accuracy'])

# Set up early stopping
early_stop = EarlyStopping(monitor='val_loss', patience=10,
restore_best_weights=False)

model.fit(X_train, y_train,
        validation_data=(X_test, y_test),
        epochs=2, callbacks=[early_stop])

model_loss, model_accuracy = model.evaluate(X_test, y_test)
print(f"\nAccuracy: {model_accuracy*100:.2f}%")

Accuracy: 86.96%
```

Final Thoughts

RNNs laid the groundwork for neural sequence learning. LSTMs carried it forward, powering breakthroughs in **language modeling**, **clinical forecasting**, and **risk modeling**—all with stronger temporal memory. LSTMs remain important where:

- Data is scarce,
- Real-time decisions matter, and
- Interpretability or compactness is required.

In a world where AI increasingly mediates language and time-bound signals, **understanding RNNs and LSTMs is essential**—not just for engineers, but for risk analysts and policymakers tasked with managing these systems responsibly.

Transformers and the Power of Attention

In 2017, a seismic shift occurred.

The paper titled *Attention is All You Need* introduced a new architecture: the transformer.

The core idea behind transformers is the attention mechanism.

Attention allows a model to look at all other words in a sentence and weigh their relevance to a given word. The full encoder–decoder transformer architecture is shown in Figure 4.22.

For instance, in the sentence "The risk analyst read the report because it was urgent," the word "it" could refer to "report." Attention helps the model figure this out.

The Attention Mechanism

At the heart of transformers is the ability to let each word **attend** to others in the input, using a weighted sum of their representations.

$$\text{Attention}(Q, K, V) = \text{softmax}\left(\frac{QK^T}{\sqrt{d_k}}\right)V$$

Where, Q are query vectors, K are key vectors, V are value vectors, and d_k is dimension of keys (for scaling).

Transformers consist of multi-head self-attention layers, feedforward networks, positional encoding, and layer normalization. Rather than processing tokens sequentially like RNNs, transformers process the entire sequence in parallel, making training much faster and more scalable.

Multi-Head Attention

Rather than compute a single attention map, transformers use **multiple heads**:

$$MultiHead(Q, K, V) = Concat(head_1, \ldots, head_h)W^O$$

Each head learns to attend to different linguistic aspects (e.g., syntax, entity reference, etc.).

Two primary types of transformer models emerged:

- **Encoder-only (like BERT)**: Good for classification and extraction tasks.
- **Decoder-only (like GPT)**: Good for generative tasks like writing or summarization.

There are also encoder-decoder models (like T5) that work well for translation and other complex sequence tasks.

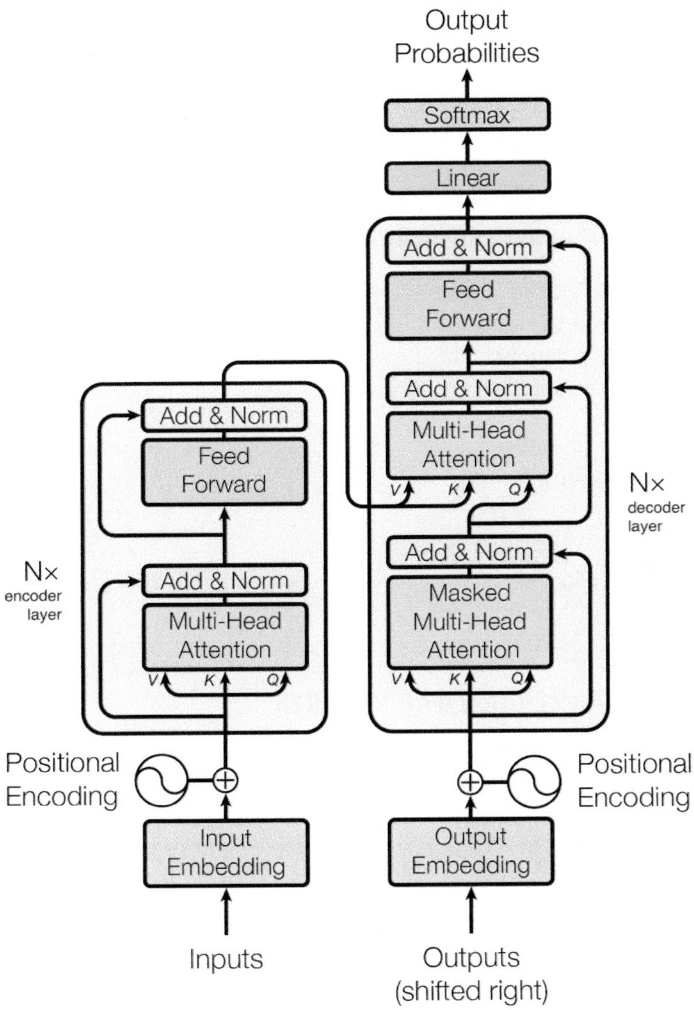

FIGURE 4.22 Transformer model architecture. (From Xi, Hang. (2025). Research on the Application of Speech Recognition Technology Based on Transformer Model. Applied and Computational Engineering. 156. 34-43. 10.54254/2755-2721/2025.CH23276. This image is licensed under the Creative Commons Attribution-Share Alike 4.0 International license (https://creativecommons.org/licenses/by-sa/4.0/). The figure has been modified to include labels for "encoder layer" and "decoder layer" beneath the N× blocks, with minor formatting adjustments for clarity, in accordance with the license requirements.

Transformers scale well, generalize across tasks, and capture long-range dependencies far better than earlier models. As transformer-based models grew larger and were trained on massive corpora, they became foundation models—flexible, general-purpose models that can be fine-tuned or adapted to a wide range of downstream applications.

Sample Code of Transformer Models (DistilBERT and RoBERTa)

Text Classification with DistilBERT

```
from transformers import DistilBertTokenizerFast,
TFDistilBertForSequenceClassification
from transformers import pipeline

tokenizer = DistilBertTokenizerFast.from_pretrained("distilbert-base-uncased")
model = TFDistilBertForSequenceClassification.from_pretrained("distilbert-
base-uncased")

classifier = pipeline("sentiment-analysis", model=model, tokenizer=tokenizer)
print(classifier("This AI book is fascinating!"))
```

Named Entity Recognition with RoBERTa

```
from transformers import pipeline
ner = pipeline("ner", model="roberta-base", grouped_entities=True)
print(ner("In 2023, the European Union passed the AI Act to regulate high-
risk AI applications in sectors like healthcare and finance."))
```

SECTION E: PRACTICAL CASE STUDY OF NLP USING RNN, LSTM, DistilBERT AND RoBERTa

In this hands-on case study, we explore how various deep learning architectures perform on a real-world natural language processing (NLP) task: sentiment classification of IMDB movie reviews. Using a publicly available dataset, we demonstrate the complete machine learning pipeline—from data preprocessing to model evaluation—across traditional RNNs, LSTM networks, and modern transformer-based models such as DistilBERT and RoBERTa.

This case study reinforces key concepts introduced earlier in the chapter, gaining practical intuition behind model choice, architecture behavior, and performance trade-offs.

Step 1: Environment and Library Setup

We begin by installing and importing essential libraries including:

- TensorFlow, Keras for neural architectures (RNN, LSTM)
- Transformers from Hugging Face for BERT-based models
- Textacy, contractions, nltk for advanced text preprocessing

This ensures our environment is well-equipped for both traditional and transformer-based NLP models.

```
!pip install transformers==4.36.0
!pip install --upgrade gensim
!pip install textacy
!pip install contractions

import warnings
with warnings.catch_warnings():
    warnings.simplefilter("ignore")

    # Base
    import numpy as np
    import pandas as pd
    import matplotlib.pyplot as plt
    import seaborn as sns
    import os

    # Model
    import tensorflow as tf
    import transformers
    from tensorflow.keras import layers
    from tensorflow import keras

    from tensorflow.keras.models import Sequential
    from tensorflow.keras.layers import SimpleRNN, Dense, Embedding,
Dropout, LSTM
    from tensorflow.keras.preprocessing.text import Tokenizer
    from tensorflow.keras.preprocessing.sequence import pad_sequences
    from tensorflow.keras.utils import to_categorical
    from tensorflow.keras.losses import SparseCategoricalCrossentropy
    from tensorflow.keras.optimizers import Adam
```

```
from transformers import TFAutoModelForSequenceClassification,
AutoTokenizer

    from sklearn.model_selection import train_test_split
    from tensorflow.keras.callbacks import EarlyStopping
    from sklearn.preprocessing import LabelEncoder

    # Text Pre-Processing
    import re
    import nltk
    from nltk.corpus import stopwords
    from nltk.tokenize import word_tokenize
    from nltk.stem import WordNetLemmatizer
    import textacy
    import textacy.preprocessing as tprep
    import spacy
    import contractions

    # Download required NLTK resources if not already downloaded
    nltk.download('punkt')
    nltk.download('stopwords')
    nltk.download('wordnet')
```

Step 2: Loading Text Source

We utilize the IMDB sentiment dataset (in CSV format, see Figure 4.23), which contains reviews labeled as "positive" or "negative". We split this into training, testing, and validation sets.

```
train = pd.read_csv('Train.csv')
test = pd.read_csv('Test.csv')
valid = pd.read_csv('Valid.csv')
df = pd.read_csv('IMDB_Dataset.csv')
train.head()
```

Step 3: Text Preprocessing

Preprocessing involves:

- Expanding contractions (e.g., "can't" → "cannot")
- Removing special characters, URLs, and stop words
- Tokenization and lemmatization using nltk and spaCy

	text	label
0	I grew up (b. 1965) watching and loving the Th...	0
1	When I put this movie in my DVD player, and sa...	0
2	Why do people who do not know what a particul...	0
3	Even though I have great interest in Biblical ...	0
4	Im a die hard Dads Army fan and nothing will e...	1

FIGURE 4.23 First 5 rows of the dataset with sentiment labels.

This ensures a cleaner input for our models, reducing noise and sparsity in text representation.

```
# Functions to clean and normalize the text
def normalize(text):
    text = tprep.normalize.hyphenated_words(text)
    text = tprep.normalize.quotation_marks(text)
    text = tprep.normalize.unicode(text)
    text = tprep.remove.accents(text)
    text = tprep.replace.phone_numbers(text)
    text = tprep.replace.urls(text)
    text = tprep.replace.emails(text)
    text = tprep.replace.user_handles(text)
    text = tprep.replace.emojis(text)
    text = text.lower()
    return text

def preprocess_text(text):
    # Remove HTML tags
    text = re.sub('<[^>]*>', '', text)

    # Handle contractions (optional but useful)
    text = contractions.fix(text)  # If using contractions module

    # Remove non-alphabetic characters but keep digits
    text = re.sub('[^a-zA-Z0-9]', ' ', text).lower()
```

```
    # Tokenize the text
    words = word_tokenize(text)

    # Remove punctuation
    words = [word for word in words if word.isalnum()]  # Retains alphanu-
meric tokens

    # Remove stopwords but keep negations like "not", "no", "never"
    stop_words = set(stopwords.words('english')) - {'not', 'no', 'never'}
    words = [word for word in words if word not in stop_words]

    # Lemmatize the words
    lemmatizer = WordNetLemmatizer()
    words = [lemmatizer.lemmatize(word) for word in words]

    # Remove extra whitespaces
    return ' '.join(words).strip()

train['processed_text'] = train['text'].apply(normalize)
test['processed_text'] = test['text'].apply(normalize)
valid['processed_text'] = valid['text'].apply(normalize)
df['processed_text'] = df['text'].apply(normalize)

train['processed_text'] = train['processed_text'].apply(preprocess_text)
test['processed_text'] = test['processed_text'].apply(preprocess_text)
valid['processed_text'] = valid['processed_text'].apply(preprocess_text)
df['processed_text'] = df['processed_text'].apply(preprocess_text)
```

Dataset after applying text preprocessing steps such as cleaning, normalization, tokenization, and lemmatization is shown in Figures 4.24.

Step 4: Classical Deep Learning Models: RNN and LSTM

We tokenize the text data and convert it into padded sequences.

```
def prepare_data_for_model(max_words, max_len, df, train, valid, test):

# Label encode the target variable
#le = LabelEncoder()
#df['label'] = le.fit_transform(df['label'])

X_train, X_test, y_train, y_test = train_test_split(df['processed_text'],
df['label'], test_size=0.2, random_state=42)
```

	text	label	processed_text
0	I grew up (b. 1965) watching and loving the Th...	0	i grew up (b. 1965) watching and loving the th...
1	When I put this movie in my DVD player, and sa...	0	when i put this movie in my dvd player, and sa...
2	Why do people who do not know what a particula...	0	why do people who do not know what a particula...
3	Even though I have great interest in Biblical ...	0	even though i have great interest in biblical ...
4	Im a die hard Dads Army fan and nothing will e...	1	im a die hard dads army fan and nothing will e...
...	...	...	...
49995	Man, I loved this movie! This really takes me ...	1	man, i loved this movie! this really takes me ...
49996	Recovery is an incredibly moving piece of work...	1	recovery is an incredibly moving piece of work...
49997	You can take the crook out of the joint, but i...	1	you can take the crook out of the joint, but i...
49998	FUTZ is the only show preserved from the exper...	1	futz is the only show preserved from the exper...
49999	"The Mother" tells of a recently widowed mid-6...	1	"the mother" tells of a recently widowed mid-6...

50000 rows × 3 columns

FIGURE 4.24 Dataset after text preprocessing.

```
X_train, X_valid, y_train, y_valid = train_test_split(X_train, y_train, test_
size=0.2, random_state=42)

tokenizer = Tokenizer(num_words=max_words)
tokenizer.fit_on_texts(X_train)

X_train = tokenizer.texts_to_sequences(X_train)
X_test = tokenizer.texts_to_sequences(X_test)
X_valid = tokenizer.texts_to_sequences(X_valid)

X_train = pad_sequences(X_train, maxlen=max_len)
X_test = pad_sequences(X_test, maxlen=max_len)
X_valid = pad_sequences(X_valid, maxlen=max_len)

y_train = to_categorical(y_train)
y_test = to_categorical(y_test)
y_valid = to_categorical(y_valid)

return X_train, X_valid, X_test, y_train, y_valid, y_test

# Tokenize the data
max_words = 10000
max_len = 100

# Call the function to prepare data
X_train, X_valid, X_test, y_train, y_valid, y_test = prepare_data_for_
model(max_words, max_len, df, train, valid, test)
```

Then we build two Keras models:

- **Simple RNN**: Captures sequential dependencies but struggles with long-term context due to vanishing gradients.

```
# Model with dropout and early stopping
def rnn_model(max_words, max_len, X_train, X_valid, X_test, y_train, y_
test, y_valid):

  model = Sequential()
  model.add(Embedding(max_words, 128, input_length=max_len))
  model.add(SimpleRNN(64))
  model.add(Dropout(0.5))
  model.add(Dense(2, activation='softmax'))

  # Compile the model
  model.compile(optimizer='adam', loss='categorical_crossentropy',
metrics=['accuracy'])

  # Set up early stopping
  early_stop = EarlyStopping(monitor='val_loss', patience=10,
restore_best_weights=True)

  # Train the model
  history = model.fit(X_train, (y_train), validation_data=(X_valid, (y_valid)),
                epochs=25, batch_size=128, callbacks=[early_stop])

return model

rnn_dropout = rnn_model(max_words, max_len, X_train, X_valid, X_test,
y_train, y_test, y_valid)

# Evaluate the model
rnn_dropout_loss, rnn_dropout_accuracy = rnn_dropout.evaluate(X_test,
y_test)
print("Test accuracy:", rnn_dropout_accuracy)
Test accuracy: 0.8702999949455261
```

- **LSTM**: Adds memory gates to handle long-range dependencies better.

```
# Model with dropout and early stopping
def lstm_model_dropout(max_words, max_len, X_train, X_valid, X_test,
y_train, y_test, y_valid):
```

```
    model = Sequential()
    model.add(Embedding(max_words, 128, input_length=max_len))
    model.add(LSTM(64))
    model.add(Dropout(0.5))
    model.add(Dense(2, activation='softmax'))

    # Compile the model
    model.compile(optimizer='adam', loss='categorical_crossentropy',
metrics=['accuracy'])

    # Set up early stopping
    early_stop = EarlyStopping(monitor='val_loss', patience=10,
restore_best_weights=True)

    # Train the model
    history = model.fit(X_train, (y_train), validation_data=(X_valid, (y_valid)),
              epochs=25, batch_size=128, callbacks=[early_stop])

    return model

lstm_dropout = lstm_model_dropout(max_words, max_len, X_train, X_
valid, X_test, y_train, y_test, y_valid)

# Evaluate the model
lstm_dropout_loss, lstm_dropout_accuracy = lstm_dropout.evaluate(X_
test, y_test)
print("Test accuracy:", lstm_dropout_accuracy)
Test accuracy: 0.8851000070571899
```

Both models are trained with early stopping and evaluated using accuracy and loss curves.

Key Observations:

- LSTM consistently outperforms RNN on validation accuracy.
- LSTM shows better generalization and lower overfitting.

STEP 5: TRANSFORMERS: DistilBERT And RoBERTa

Using Hugging Face's transformers library, we fine-tune two pre-trained models:

- **DistilBERT**: A lightweight, distilled version of BERT, ideal for faster inference with comparable accuracy.

- **RoBERTa**: A robustly optimized BERT variant that achieves higher accuracy but requires more compute.

Steps include:

1. Tokenizing the text using model-specific tokenizers,
2. Fine-tuning using *TFAutoModelForSequenceClassification*, and
3. Evaluating using standard classification metrics.

```
# DistilBERT

from transformers import DistilBertTokenizerFast
from transformers import TFDistilBertForSequenceClassification

# Detect TPU and set up distribution strategy
try:
   tpu = tf.distribute.cluster_resolver.TPUClusterResolver()  # TPU detection
   print(f'Running on a TPU w/{tpu.num_accelerators()["TPU"]} cores')
except ValueError:
   raise BaseException('ERROR: Not connected to a TPU runtime; please
see the previous cell in this notebook for instructions!')

tf.config.experimental_connect_to_cluster(tpu)
tf.tpu.experimental.initialize_tpu_system(tpu)
tpu_strategy = tf.distribute.TPUStrategy(tpu)

model_name = 'distilbert-base-uncased'
tokenizer = AutoTokenizer.from_pretrained(model_name)

max_len = 512

# Split into train, test and validation sets
X_train, X_test, y_train, y_test = train_test_split(df['processed_text'],
df['label'], test_size=0.2, random_state=42)
X_train, X_valid, y_train, y_valid = train_test_split(X_train, y_train, test_
size=0.2, random_state=42)

X_train = tokenizer(text=X_train.tolist(), add_special_tokens=True, max_
length=max_len, truncation=True, padding=True, return_tensors='tf')
y_train = y_train.values
```

```
X_train_np = X_train['input_ids'].numpy()
X_train_np, X_val_np, y_train, y_val = train_test_split(X_train_np, y_train,
test_size=0.2, random_state=42)

# Create TensorFlow datasets
train_dataset = tf.data.Dataset.from_tensor_slices((X_train_np, y_train)).
batch(32)
val_dataset = tf.data.Dataset.from_tensor_slices((X_val_np, y_val)).batch(32)

with tpu_strategy.scope():
  model = TFAutoModelForSequenceClassification.from_
pretrained(model_name, num_labels=2)

  optimizer = tf.keras.optimizers.Adam(learning_rate=5e-5)
  loss = tf.keras.losses.SparseCategoricalCrossentropy(from_logits=True)
  model.compile(optimizer=optimizer, loss=loss, metrics=['accuracy'])

# Set up early stopping
early_stop = tf.keras.callbacks.EarlyStopping(monitor='val_loss', patience=3,
restore_best_weights=True)

batch_size = 32
epochs = 10
history = model.fit(train_dataset, epochs=epochs, validation_data=val_
dataset, callbacks=[early_stop])

X_test = tokenizer(text=X_test.tolist(), add_special_tokens=True,
max_length=max_len, truncation=True, padding=True, return_tensors='tf')
y_test = y_test.values

# Convert the test dataset into a TensorFlow dataset
test_dataset = tf.data.Dataset.from_tensor_slices((X_test['input_ids'],
X_test['attention_mask'])).batch(32)

y_pred = model.predict(test_dataset)
y_pred_labels = np.argmax(y_pred.logits, axis=1)
bert_dropout_accuracy = np.sum(y_pred_labels == y_test) / len(y_test)
print(f"Test accuracy: {bert_dropout_accuracy:.2f}")

Test accuracy: 0.91
```

```
# RoBERTa

model_name = 'roberta-base'
tokenizer = AutoTokenizer.from_pretrained(model_name)

max_len = 512
X_train = tokenizer(text=train['text'].tolist(), add_special_tokens=True,
max_length=max_len, truncation=True, padding=True, return_tensors='tf')
y_train = train['label'].values

X_train_np = X_train['input_ids'].numpy()
X_train_np, X_val_np, y_train, y_val = train_test_split(X_train_np, y_train,
test_size=0.2, random_state=42)

# Create TensorFlow datasets
train_dataset = tf.data.Dataset.from_tensor_slices((X_train_np, y_train)).
batch(16)
val_dataset = tf.data.Dataset.from_tensor_slices((X_val_np, y_val)).batch(16)

with tpu_strategy.scope():
  model = TFAutoModelForSequenceClassification.from_
pretrained(model_name, num_labels=2)

  optimizer = tf.keras.optimizers.Adam(learning_rate=2e-6)
  loss = tf.keras.losses.SparseCategoricalCrossentropy(from_logits=True)
  model.compile(optimizer=optimizer, loss=loss, metrics=['accuracy'])

batch_size = 16
epochs = 10

# Add early stopping
early_stopping = tf.keras.callbacks.EarlyStopping(monitor='val_loss',
patience=3, restore_best_weights=True)

history = model.fit(train_dataset, epochs=epochs, validation_data=val_
dataset, callbacks=[early_stopping])

X_test = tokenizer(text=test['text'].tolist(), add_special_tokens=True,
max_length=max_len, truncation=True, padding=True, return_tensors='tf')
y_test = test['label'].values

# Convert the test dataset into a TensorFlow dataset
test_dataset = tf.data.Dataset.from_tensor_slices((X_test['input_ids'],
X_test['attention_mask'])).batch(16)
```

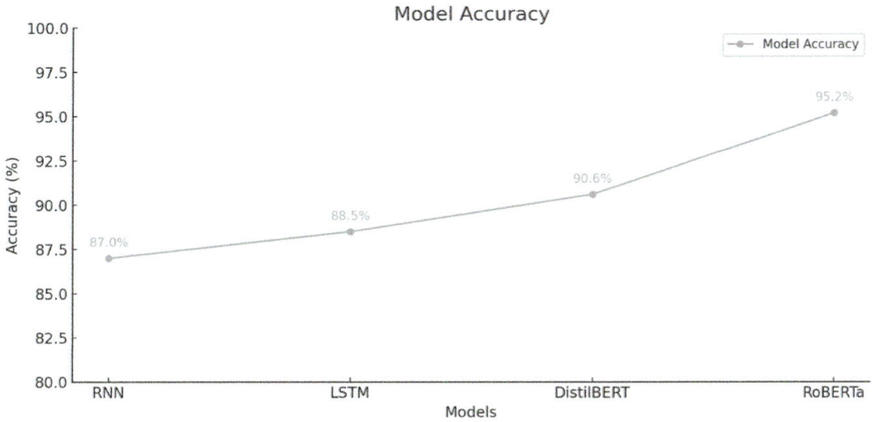

FIGURE 4.25 Accuracy across models.

```
y_pred = model.predict(test_dataset)
y_pred_labels = np.argmax(y_pred.logits, axis=1)
roberta_dropout_accuracy = np.sum(y_pred_labels == y_test) / len(y_test)
print(f"Test accuracy: {roberta_dropout_accuracy:.2f}")

Test accuracy: 0.95
```

A comparative summary of model performance across architectures is presented in Figure 4.25.

Key Observations:

- Transformer models outperform RNNs/LSTMs significantly in both accuracy and inference consistency.
- DistilBERT provides a strong balance between speed and performance.
- RoBERTa is the most accurate but computationally heavier.

NOTES

1. Logistic regression is a simple method that a computer uses to make yes or no decisions. It looks at different pieces of information (e.g., age, income, or symptoms) and gives a score between 0 and 1, like a probability. If the score is closer to 1, it means "yes," and if it's closer to 0, it means "no." It's like how we decide whether to take an umbrella: we think about the clouds, the weather report, and past experience, then make a decision.

2. A decision tree is like playing 20 questions to make a choice. The computer asks a series of yes/no questions (like "Is the temperature high?" or "Is the color red?") and follows the branches of a tree until it reaches an answer. It's just like how we decide what to wear by going step by step—"Is it cold? Yes. Then wear a coat." The computer uses this structure to make predictions or decisions.
3. Support vector machines are like drawing a line (or a wall) to separate two groups of things. Imagine placing apples and oranges on a table and finding the best straight line to divide them. SVMs find the best way to split the groups so future items (like a new fruit) can be placed on the correct side. It's especially good when the groups are tricky to separate.
4. An ANN is a computer system inspired by how our brain works. It is made up of tiny units called "neurons" that are connected together in layers. Each neuron receives information, does a simple calculation, and passes the result to the next layer. By doing this over and over, the network can learn to recognize patterns—like faces in photos or words in speech. It learns by adjusting the strength of the connections between neurons, kind of like how we learn from experience and improve over time.
5. Weights are like tiny volume knobs in a computer's brain that control how much importance to give to each piece of information. When the computer is learning, it adjusts these knobs to decide what matters most—just like we learn to pay more attention to traffic lights than billboards when driving. If a certain detail helps make better predictions, the weight for that gets turned up. If not, it gets turned down. These weights keep changing during learning so the computer gets smarter over time.
6. Backpropagation is a key algorithm used to train neural networks. It works by calculating the error (difference between predicted and actual output) and then propagating this error backward through the network. During this process, it computes the gradient of the loss function with respect to each weight using the chain rule of calculus. These gradients are then used to update the weights (typically via gradient descent) to minimize the error. This step-by-step adjustment allows the model to learn patterns and improve predictions over time. It's used during *training* of a neural network and is part of what makes deep learning possible. Without backpropagation, the model wouldn't know how to improve itself. **In simple words,** backpropagation is how a computer "learns from mistakes" when trying to make predictions—kind of like how a child learns to walk by falling and adjusting each time. It starts with a guess, sees how far off the answer was, then sends that error backwards through the network to adjust each step it took along the way. These tiny adjustments to its "thinking steps" help it get better over time. It does this many times, slowly improving with each try—just like practicing something over and over makes us better.
7. Gradient descent is how a computer learns the best way to improve its answers step by step. Imagine you're trying to find the lowest point in a valley while blindfolded—you take small steps downhill until you can't go any

lower. That's what the computer does: it checks which direction reduces its mistakes the most and keeps adjusting its steps (or weights) until the error is as small as possible. It's a slow and steady path to better answers!

8. TensorFlow serves as a core platform and library for machine learning. TensorFlow's APIs use Keras to allow users to make their own machine learning models. In addition to building and training their model, TensorFlow can also help load the data to train the model, and deploy it using TensorFlow Serving. You can use PyTorch as well.
9. **Adam (Adaptive Moment Estimation)** optimizer combines the advantages of **Momentum** and **RMSprop** techniques to adjust learning rates during training. It works well with large datasets and complex models because it uses memory efficiently and adapts the learning rate for each parameter automatically.
10. CNNs are a special kind of computer brain made to understand pictures. Instead of looking at the whole image at once, they look at small parts—like scanning a photo through a tiny window—to spot patterns like edges, shapes, or colors. These patterns help the computer recognize things, like faces, animals, or letters. It works kind of like how we recognize a friend by noticing their eyes, smile, or hairstyle first. CNNs learn what to look for, layer by layer, to "see" images better and more accurately.
11. Graphics processing unit (GPU) is like a super-fast helper in a computer, originally built to make video games and graphics look good. But now, it also helps with big math problems, especially for training AI. While a regular computer brain (CPU) is good at doing one task at a time, a GPU can do thousands of tiny tasks all at once—like having a big team instead of one worker. This makes it perfect for teaching computers to learn patterns in data, like recognizing faces or translating languages, really quickly.
12. **Natural language processing (NLP)** is how computers learn to understand and talk in human language—like English, Hindi, or any other language we speak. It helps computers read, listen, write, and even have conversations. So when you talk to Alexa, type a message that gets auto-corrected, or ask a chatbot a question, that's NLP at work. It's like teaching a computer how to read a book or understand a joke, so it can interact with us more naturally.
13. **RNNs** are a special kind of computer brain that remembers things over time. They're great for tasks where the order matters—like understanding a sentence, listening to music, or predicting the next word in a message. Unlike regular networks that look at everything one step at a time and forget, RNNs keep a "memory" of what just happened to make smarter guesses about what comes next. It's like how we remember the words in a sentence so we understand the meaning better!

CHAPTER 5

From Generative AI to Context-Aware Intelligence

INTRODUCTION

Generative artificial intelligence (GenAI)[1] represents a shift from analytical machine learning to creative and synthetic intelligence. While classical models focused on predicting numbers, flags, or labels, GenAI is about producing—generating coherent text, images, speech, and code from learned representations.

This transformation was enabled by **large language models (LLMs)**[2]—neural networks trained on vast amounts of text to understand and generate human-like language. But GenAI is not a monolithic concept. It unfolds in stages, each with its own breakthroughs, limitations, and engineering patterns.

LLMs have transformed natural language processing (NLP) by moving beyond symbolic or feature-engineered methods to learned representations that scale with data and compute. The architectural shift from traditional NLP pipelines to large language models integrated within augmented intelligence systems is illustrated in Figure 5.1. In particular, transformer-based architectures have enabled emergent capabilities—including multilingual translation, code generation, and reasoning—with minimal task-specific data.

DOI: 10.1201/9781003607298-5

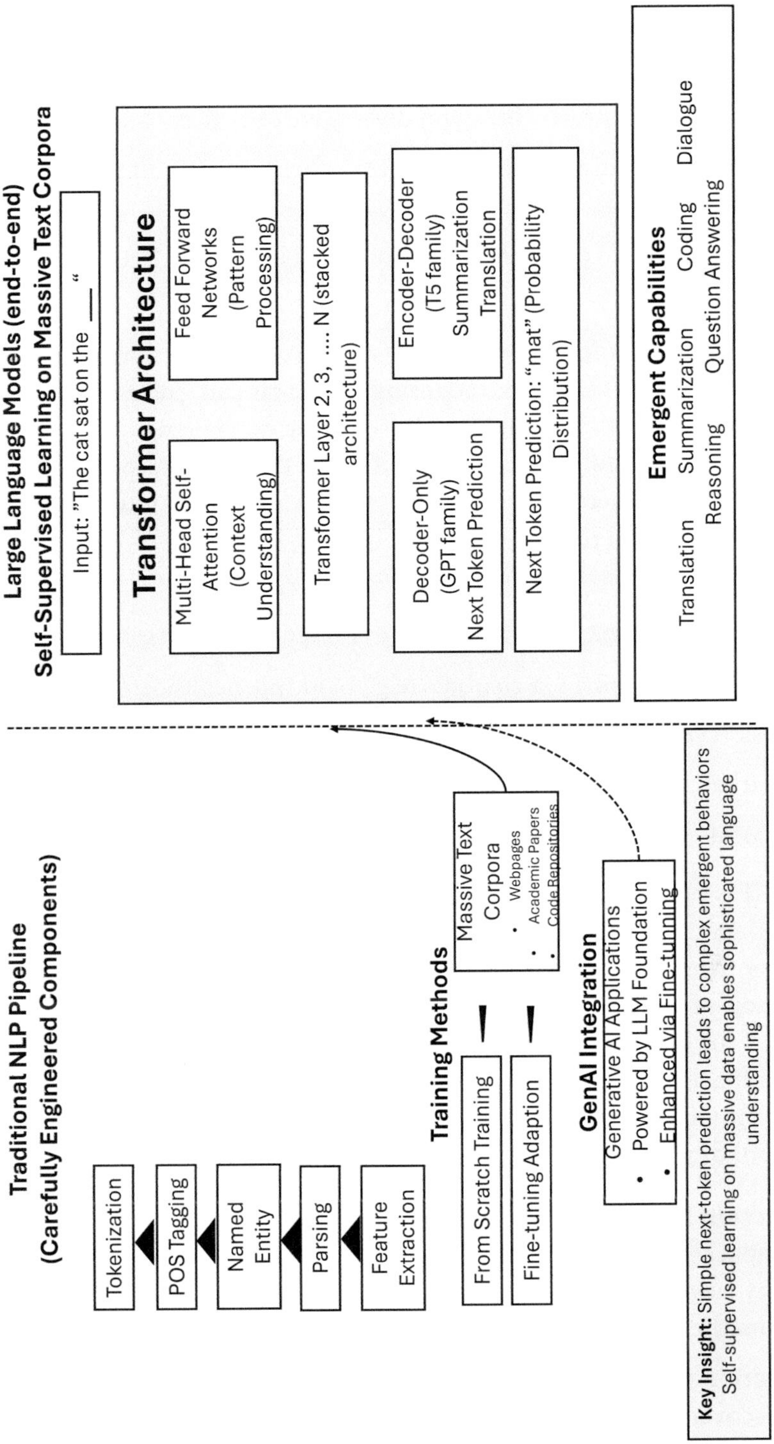

FIGURE 5.1 LLM and augmented intelligence architecture.

One of the major leaps in LLM capability stems from the convergence of three factors:

- **Massive-scale pre-training** on diverse corpora (web, books, code),
- **General-purpose architectures** (transformers with attention-based modeling), and
- **Prompt-based task generalization**, enabling models to be reused across tasks.

This shift has profound implications: GenAI systems now operate as "**zero-shot engines**,"[3] capable of adapting on-the-fly using natural language prompts. However, this flexibility also introduces challenges—especially with **truthfulness**, **staleness**, and **lack of grounding** in enterprise-specific contexts. This is where techniques like **retrieval-augmented generation (RAG)** play a central role.

Real-world use cases

- Text summarization of long legal or policy documents,
- Customer support via chatbots (e.g., banking, healthcare),
- Risk scenario modeling with narrative generation,
- Marketing: ad copywriting, email campaigns, and
- Education: content generation and personalized tutoring.

GenAI is powered by LLMs trained either from scratch or adapted via fine-tuning.

Let us together, embark on a **journey into the heart of GenAI**—an epic fusion of cutting-edge research and real-world impact. This chapter is crafted for everyone: seasoned AI practitioners seeking fresh insights, scholars charting new academic frontiers, and students igniting their passion for tomorrow's technology.

We will dive deep through two illuminating sections:

- **Section A: Large Language Models**
  Unpack the transformative architectures and training innovations that have powered today's state-of-the-art conversational agents, from the birth of the transformer to today's trillion-parameter giants.
- **Section B: Retrieval-Augmented Generation**
  Discover how we blend massive pre-trained models with dynamic knowledge retrieval—enabling AI to answer questions with up-to-the-minute facts, grounded context, and human-level fluency.

Whether you are refining algorithms, exploring new theories, or simply curious, this chapter will equip you with the conceptual clarity and practical depth to unlock the promise—and navigate the challenges—of GenAI.

SECTION A: LARGE LANGUAGE MODELS AND THE ARCHITECTURE OF AUGMENTED INTELLIGENCE

The advent of LLMs marked a leap forward in AI's ability to reason and converse using natural language. Unlike traditional NLP pipelines which depended on carefully engineered components, LLMs are trained end-to-end on a massive corpora of text.

They learn to predict the next token in a sequence—a deceptively simple task that leads to emergent capabilities in translation, summarization, coding, and dialogue.

These models, such as GPT[4] and T5,[5] are built on the transformer architecture. Decoder-only transformers (like GPT) generate text by predicting the next word given previous context, while encoder-decoder models (like T5) excel at tasks such as summarization and translation.

T5[6] reframes all NLP tasks as text-to-text transformations—enabling consistent task handling across translation, summarization, and question answering. This abstraction powers generalization across tasks with a single model interface.

Foundations: Pre-training and Scaling Laws

The key to LLM performance lies in **scale**. As model size, data volume, and training compute increase, performance improves predictably—a pattern formalized in **scaling laws**.[7] GPT-2's 1.5 billion parameters were dwarfed by GPT-3's 175 billion, and now models from Meta, Anthropic, and OpenAI operate at even greater scales.

These **pre-trained foundation models** capture general linguistic structure, facts about the world, and task behaviors—all without labeled data. They are flexible and powerful but come with following limitations:

- **Static**: Trained only once and they don't know your data,
- **Opaque in reasoning**: You can't easily understand how or why they respond, and
- **Limited**: Bound by training cutoff or outdated knowledge and prone to hallucinations.

What Are Scaling Laws?

In simple words, scaling laws are like recipes that show what happens when you give a computer more ingredients, such as more data, more computer power, or a bigger model. Researchers found that when you "scale up" these ingredients, the AI usually gets smarter and makes fewer mistakes. It's like how a child who reads more books and practices more often gets better at school. These laws help scientists predict how much better an AI can get if they keep feeding it more information and increase training time.

Scaling laws provide **empirical evidence** that model performance improves smoothly with more parameters, data, and compute—**but only when all three increase proportionally**. These laws describe how loss decreases as a function of following three key variables:

- **Model parameters**, N
- **Training dataset size**, D
- **Compute cost** (in FLOPs), C

In a seminal paper,[8] OpenAI showed that loss (i.e., model performance) scales predictably as a power-law with respect to:

$$L(N,D,C) = A_1 \cdot N^{-\alpha} + A_2 \cdot D^{-\beta} + A_3 \cdot C^{-\gamma}$$

Where, α, β, γ are empirically derived scaling exponents and A_1, A_2, and A_3 are positive coefficients (constants).

This finding formalized **model scaling as a science** rather than an art—leading to the design of billion-parameter models like GPT-3 and PaLM.

In practice, this means:

- Doubling model size yields noticeable improvement—until data or compute becomes the bottleneck.
- GPT-2 (1.5B) → GPT-3 (175B) followed this law and saw strong zero-shot gains.
- Models like PaLM, Chinchilla, and LLaMA 2 were built by rebalancing compute–data ratios using scaling law estimates.

Limitations remain, however:

- **Data quality vs. quantity**: After a certain point, repeating low-quality data adds little benefit.
- **Model capabilities plateau**: For tasks requiring structured logic or factual precision, scaling alone doesn't help beyond a threshold.

Pre-trained LLMs and Foundation Models

As the scale of training data, model size, and compute has increased, a new class of models has emerged: **foundation models**.[9] These are large pre-trained models trained on broad, diverse corpora that can be adapted—via prompting or fine-tuning—to a wide range of downstream tasks.

Unlike older task-specific models, foundation models are designed to be **general-purpose**. They are trained using self-supervised objectives such as:

- **Causal language modeling** (e.g., GPT-style, predicting the next token)
- **Masked language modeling** (e.g., BERT-style, predicting missing tokens)
- **Span corruption or denoising** (e.g., T5-style)

These objectives help the model learn general linguistic structures, reasoning patterns, and world knowledge without explicit labels. Once pre-trained, these models can be used out-of-the-box or further adapted through prompting or fine-tuning.

- **Decoder-only models** are optimized for continuation and generation tasks—they work well with prompting and are the backbone of most chat-based GenAI systems.
- **Encoder-only models** are bidirectional and good for classification or scoring.
- **Encoder-decoder models** are sequence-to-sequence architectures, ideal for tasks like summarization or translation.

What Makes a Model "Foundational"?

The term "**foundation model**" was formalized by the Stanford CRFM team[10] (Bommasani et al., 2021), which describes these systems as "**models trained on broad data at scale that can be adapted to a wide range of downstream tasks.**"

These models are **not inherently intelligent**, but serve as infrastructure—much like the operating systems or compilers of classical computing.

A model is typically called a foundation model if it is:

- Trained on large-scale, diverse data,
- Capable of generalization across tasks, and
- Adaptable via prompting or fine-tuning.

The most common categories of pre-trained LLM architectures and their typical use cases are summarized in Table 5.1.

TABLE 5.1 Common Types of Pre-trained LLM Architectures

Model Type	Simple Explanation	Example Models	Key Use Cases
Decoder-only	These models are like smart story-tellers. You give them a starting word or sentence, and they guess what comes next—one word at a time. They're great at writing, chatting, or finishing your thoughts. Think of them like a parrot that listens, learns, and then keeps talking!	GPT2, GPT3, GPT4	Text generation, dialogue, code
Encoder-only	These are great at reading and understanding. They don't try to write back but focus on making sense of what you gave them. It's like a wise librarian who reads everything quickly and tells you what it all means, but doesn't write their own stories.	BERT, RoBERTa	Classification, entity recognition
Encoder-decoder	These are like expert translators. One part reads and understands (encoder), and the other part responds or rewrites it in a different form (decoder). For example, they can take English and turn it into French. It's like a person who listens carefully and then speaks clearly in another language!	T5, FLAN-T5, BART	Summarization, translation, QA

Key features of foundation models include:

- **Emergence**: Unpredictable capabilities arise as models scale (e.g., few-shot learning).
- **Homogenization**: The same model can support search, classification, summarization, coding, and dialogue—reducing system complexity.

Examples include:

- **GPT-3.5/GPT-4** (OpenAI)
- **FLAN-T5** (Google)
- **LLaMA 2** (Meta)
- **PaLM** (Google DeepMind)
- **Claude** (Anthropic)

Foundation models **reduce the need for task-specific models**. Instead, you can:

- Use zero-shot or few-shot prompts
- Apply instruction tuning or LoRA adapters
- Embed them in retrieval-augmented generation (RAG) pipelines

This shift has enabled rapid development of generalist AI systems, such as ChatGPT, that can perform translation, summarization, and reasoning—all from a single pre-trained base.

Prompting and In-context Learning: Teaching Without Changing Weights

In-context learning (ICL) refers to the ability of pre-trained LLMs to perform new tasks simply by observing examples provided in the prompt—without updating any of the model's parameters. This behavior was one of the most surprising and valuable emergent capabilities of transformer-based LLMs.

For instance, consider this prompt:

```
Translate English to French:

English: Hello
French: Bonjour

English: Thank you
French:
```

This process, known as **in-context learning**,[11]—no weights are changed. Despite not being trained explicitly for translation, an LLM like GPT-3 can infer the pattern and output "Merci"—because it generalizes the task from the examples provided in the context.

Prompt Engineering: Talking to LLMs Intelligently

Prompt engineering builds on the foundation of in-context learning by optimizing how we communicate tasks to the model. Instead of retraining the model, we **guide its behavior through careful phrasing, formatting, and structuring** of the input prompt. LLMs like GPT-3 surprised researchers with their ability to learn from a handful of examples. This is called few-shot learning. By adding examples directly into the prompt, the model can generalize to new tasks. Zero-shot prompting, in which only a task description is given, is also remarkably effective.

Prompt engineering is one of the most effective tools for adapting and guiding LLMs without modifying their weights or requiring fine-tuning. With a well-structured prompt, you can transform a general-purpose LLM into a summarizer, translator, sentiment detector, legal assistant, or coding tutor—all by example and instruction.

This section covers the main prompting styles: **zero-shot**, **one-shot**, **few-shot**, and **chain-of-thought (CoT)**.

Zero-Shot Prompting

Zero-shot prompting provides only a task instruction and no examples. The LLM relies entirely on pre-training to interpret and execute the request.

In simple words, zero-shot prompting is when you ask a smart computer to do something *without* showing it any examples first. You just give it clear instructions in plain language, and it tries to figure it out based on what it already learned. It's like asking a well-read person, "Can you write a poem about sunflowers?"—even if they've never written one before, they'll give it a good try using what they know. No practice needed, just the prompt!

```
Prompt:

Classify the following message as spam or not spam:
"You've won a free cruise to the Bahamas! Click here now."

Expected Output:
Spam
```

While zero-shot prompting is the fastest and requires almost no training or setup, it may be brittle if the task isn't common or the instruction is vague.

One-Shot Prompting This includes a single example alongside the task instruction. This gives the LLM a format reference but little generalization.

```
Prompt:
Classify messages as spam or not spam.

Message: "Get your free trial today!" → Spam
Message: "Meeting moved to 3 PM." →
```

The model infers the label format and can continue in that pattern.

In simple words, one-shot prompting is when you show the computer *one* example of what you want before asking it to do the task. It learns from that single sample and then tries to copy the pattern. It's like showing your grandchild how to fold a napkin just once, and then asking them to fold the next one the same way. One good example helps it understand what to do!

Few-Shot Prompting Few-shot prompting provides **multiple examples** in the prompt. This helps the LLM pick up patterns, output format, and edge cases.

```
Prompt:
Classify the following messages.
Message: "Win a free phone now!" → Spam
Message: "Project due on Monday." → Not Spam
Message: "You've been selected for a prize!" →
```

Few-shot prompting is powerful for tasks like classification, entity extraction, or instruction-following. But it increases token cost and latency due to prompt size.

Chain-of-Thought Prompting Some tasks—especially arithmetic or logic reasoning—benefit from **step-by-step explanations**. CoT prompting teaches the model to reason explicitly, improving performance on multi-step problems.

```
Prompt:
Q: Lily has 3 packs of markers. Each pack contains 4 markers. She gives 5
markers to her friend. How many markers does Lily have left?
A: First, 3 packs × 4 markers = 12 markers.
She gives away 5, so 12 – 5 = 7.
Answer: 7
```

CoT is especially useful for models ≥100B parameters. It improves **logical and reasoning accuracy** and **math capabilities**, where the inductive bias for multistep thinking emerges more clearly.

Tips for effectiveness:

- Be **explicit** about the task.
- Match **format** and **terminology** to target domain.
- Try **role prompting** (e.g., "You are a tax auditor…").
- Keep prompts **short** when possible—long prompts reduce token budget for response.

Sample Prompt Playground (Using OpenAI API)

```
import openai

openai.api_key = <your_openai_key>

prompt = """You are a helpful assistant. Answer the question with reasoning.

Q: A store sells pencils in packs of 3. If you buy 4 packs and give away 2
pencils, how many do you have?
```

```
A:"""

response = openai.ChatCompletion.create (
    model="gpt-4",
    messages=[{"role": "user", "content": prompt}],
    temperature=0.3
)

print(response.choices[0].message["content"])
```

Prompt Sensitivity: Why Prompt Framing Matters

Prompt engineering directly impacts LLM performance. Even subtle wording changes can alter the outcome.

In other words, prompt sensitivity means that the computer's answers can change a lot depending on how you ask a question. Even small changes in wording can lead to very different replies. It's like talking to someone who gives a different answer if you say "What's for dinner?" versus "Is there anything to eat?" The meaning is similar, but the response can vary. So, choosing your words carefully helps the computer give better answers!

Compare:

```
Q: What are the risks of AI?
vs.
Q: As a risk manager, list three business risks associated with deploying AI
models in production.
```

The second is more grounded, specific, and role-aware—leading to more relevant output. This sensitivity requires rigorous **prompt testing** during model development.

You can evaluate prompt quality by comparing:

- Output length and fluency
- Presence of hallucinated facts
- Task accuracy
- Prompt transferability (does it generalize to similar queries?)

However, prompting has limitations: it's fragile and hard to optimize. This led to instruction tuning—training LLMs on thousands of prompts and instructions to improve usability. ChatGPT and Claude are fine-tuned in this way to respond more helpfully and safely.

Instruction Tuning: Aligning Models with Task Goals

LLMs such as GPT-3, T5, and FLAN-T5 have demonstrated remarkable capabilities, but their ability to generalize effectively often depends on how they are adapted for specific tasks. One of the most effective adaptation strategies—particularly for enabling general-purpose usability—is **instruction tuning.**[12]

Instruction tuning refers to the process of fine-tuning a pre-trained model on a diverse collection of tasks, where each training example includes a natural language instruction, an optional input, and the expected output. The goal is not to specialize the model in a single domain, but to teach it **how to generalize across many tasks** when guided by clear instructions.

For example, the training data may include examples like:

```
{
   "instruction": "Summarize the paragraph",
   "input": "Machine learning is a field of artificial intelligence...",
   "output": "A brief summary of machine learning as part of AI."
}
```

Unlike in-context learning, where the model adapts during inference via examples in the prompt, instruction tuning **updates the model's weights** to align it more closely with human-style task framing. This makes the model more robust to ambiguous prompts, reduces the need for prompt engineering, and enables **zero-shot generalization**—the ability to follow new instructions it has never seen before.

FLAN-T5: A Case Study in Instruction-Tuned LLMs

One of the most widely used instruction-tuned models is Fine-tuned Language Net with T5 (**FLAN-T5**), which is developed by Google. It builds on the original T5 (Text-to-Text Transfer Transformer) architecture but is fine-tuned on over 1,800 NLP tasks, spanning summarization, translation, classification, question answering, and reasoning.

This fine-tuning allows FLAN-T5 to understand prompts like:

- "Translate this sentence to French"
- "Summarize the following article"
- "Classify the sentiment of this tweet"
- "Answer the question based on the context"

and respond accordingly, even for instructions that weren't in the training data—a key benefit of its broad task mixture.

Example: FLAN-T5 for Summarization

```
from transformers import AutoTokenizer, TFAutoModelForSeq2SeqLM

model = TFAutoModelForSeq2SeqLM.from_pretrained("google/
flan-t5-base")
tokenizer = AutoTokenizer.from_pretrained("google/flan-t5-base")

inputs = tokenizer("Summarize: The EU AI Act regulates high-risk
systems...", return_tensors="tf")
outputs = model.generate(**inputs)
print(tokenizer.decode(outputs[0], skip_special_tokens=True))
```

This shows how the model uses a plain English instruction to identify the task, extract meaning, and generate a task-specific output—all without needing hand-crafted prompts or few-shot examples. Practical guidance on when instruction-tuned models are most appropriate is provided in Table 5.2.

Datasets Behind Instruction Tuning

Popular datasets used in instruction tuning include:

- **Natural Instructions (NI)**: A collection of real-world tasks written in plain English.

TABLE 5.2 When to Use Instruction-Tuned Models

Scenario	Recommended?	Why
General-purpose assistant	Yes	Handles many tasks with just a prompt
Domain-specific language or vocabulary	Partial	May require additional fine-tuning or LoRA layers
Fully custom, non-natural instruction format	No	May perform poorly if prompt doesn't match training

- **FLAN Collection**: The curated dataset used to train FLAN-T5, covering translation, classification, QA, and more.
- **Self-Instruct**: A meta-learning technique where models generate their own instructions and outputs.

These datasets have proven effective in enabling LLMs to generalize not just across tasks, but also across task formats and phrasing styles.

Fine-Tuning LLMs

LLMs are powerful out-of-the-box, but real-world applications that often require customization. Fine-tuning lets us adapt pre-trained models to specific tasks, data, or tone. This section explores **full fine-tuning, parameter-efficient tuning techniques** like **LoRA** and **QLoRA**, and provides practical examples to get started.

Full Fine-Tuning: Retraining All Parameters

This requires retraining the **entire model** using your labeled dataset. It is effective, but expensive and computationally intensive.

In full fine-tuning, **every parameter** of the model is updated using task-specific labeled data. This yields highly adapted models, but at great cost:

- **Requires massive GPU memory**
- **High compute time**
- Risk of **catastrophic forgetting** (losing pre-training knowledge)
- Not feasible for billion-parameter models unless using specialized infrastructure

Still, full-tuning is the most flexible. For example, you might use it when building a **medical chatbot** from GPT-2, trained on a corpus of radiology reports.

```
from transformers import TFAutoModelForCausalLM, AutoTokenizer

model = TFAutoModelForCausalLM.from_pretrained("gpt2")
tokenizer = AutoTokenizer.from_pretrained("gpt2")
```

```
inputs = tokenizer("Input text", return_tensors="tf")
labels = tokenizer("Expected output", return_tensors="tf").input_ids

model.compile(optimizer="adam", loss=model.compute_loss)
model.fit(inputs["input_ids"], labels, epochs=3)
```

Parameter-Efficient Fine-Tuning

To make fine-tuning more accessible, researchers introduced **parameter-efficient fine-tuning (PEFT)** methods such as **Low-Rank Adaptation (LoRA)** and **Quantized LoRA (QLoRA)**.

LoRA: Low-Rank Adaptation of Weight Matrices: To reduce compute, LoRA freezes the original model weights and injects small, trainable low-rank matrices into the transformer (attention) layers. This drastically reduces the number of trainable parameters—often by more than 90%. Instead of updating weight matrix $W \in \mathbb{R}^{dxd}$ (original frozen weight matrix), we train two smaller matrices:

$$W' = W + AB$$

Where, $A \in \mathbb{R}^{dxr}$, $B \in \mathbb{R}^{rxd}$ are the **low-rank adapters,** r is a small rank (e.g., 8), original weights are untouched, **only a few million parameters are trained**, saving cost and time.

Benefits:

- Minimal memory overhead
- Compatible with existing weights
- Ideal for multi-task or personalized LLMs

Example: LoRA with Hugging Face *PEFT*

```
from peft import LoraConfig, get_peft_model
from transformers import AutoModelForCausalLM

base_model = AutoModelForCausalLM.from pretrained("tiiuae/falcon-7b")

config = LoraConfig (
   r=8,
   lora_alpha=32,
   target_modules=["q_proj", "v_proj"],
   task_type="CAUSAL_LM"
)
model = get_peft_model(base_model, config)
```

With LoRA, training is faster, cheaper, and easy to swap across use cases.

QLoRA: Quantized LoRA for Even Lower Cost: **QLoRA** combines **4-bit quantization** with **LoRA**, enabling even larger models to run on a single GPU.

Quantization compresses model weights into smaller numeric representations (e.g., 4-bit ints), significantly reducing memory usage. Combined with LoRA, we can now fine-tune models like **LLaMA-13B** on consumer hardware.

Key Components:

- 4-bit quantized base model
- LoRA adapters for tuning
- BitsAndBytes for quantization-aware training

Example: QLoRA with Hugging Face *bitsandbytes*

```
from transformers import BitsAndBytesConfig, AutoModelForCausalLM

quant_config = BitsAndBytesConfig(load_in_4bit=True,
bnb_4bit_compute_dtype="float16")

model = AutoModelForCausalLM.from_pretrained(
  "meta-llama/Llama-2-7b-hf",
  quantization_config=quant_config
)
```

QLoRA enables accessible fine-tuning at scale—particularly useful for **domain-specific retrieval tasks** like medical summaries, financial reports, or regulatory guidance. A comparative overview of full fine-tuning, LoRA, and QLoRA is presented in Table 5.3.

TABLE 5.3 Comparison Table

Method	Trainable Params	Hardware Needed	Customization Quality	Speed	Use Case
Full fine-tuning	100%	Multi-GPU	High	Slow	Rare, high-budget applications
LoRA	~1–2%	Single GPU	Medium–High	Fast	Chatbot tuning, personalization
QLoRA	~1–2%	Single GPU (4-bit)	Medium	Very fast	Large model on budget devices

TABLE 5.4 When to Fine-Tune vs. Prompt

Goal	Recommended Strategy
Simple task, fast iteration	Prompt engineering
Custom domain language	LoRA or QLoRA
Full behavior change or tone shift	Full fine-tuning (if budget allows)

Fine-Tuning: When and How

When your task is highly structured (e.g., legal clause classification) or your prompts become unwieldy, fine-tuning becomes attractive.

Fine-tuning makes sense when:

- You need consistent outputs across inputs.
- Your documents have a specific format or domain (e.g., contracts, logs).
- You want to reduce prompt length and latency.

Still, fine-tuning requires care: managing drift, versioning, and model governance. Table 5.4 summarizes decision criteria for choosing between prompting, parameter-efficient tuning, and full fine-tuning. For most applications including RAG, prompt engineering plus embedding retrievers is enough.

Reinforcement Learning with Human Feedback

Simply put, RLHF is a way of teaching a computer by having humans guide it when it's learning. The computer tries different answers, and people give a thumbs up or down to show what's good or bad. The computer then learns to do more of what people like. It's just like training a pet—you reward good behavior, and over time, it gets better at doing what you want. This helps AI become more helpful, safe, and human-friendly.

Unlike LoRA or full fine-tuning, RLHF introduces human preference modeling as part of the objective function.

RLHF addresses alignment—the challenge of making LLMs output helpful, safe, and truthful responses. It begins with supervised instruction tuning and then uses human preferences to train a reward model. That reward model is used to fine-tune the LLM using reinforcement learning, most often via proximal policy optimization (PPO).

This method was crucial to models like **InstructGPT** and **ChatGPT**. While too costly for most users to replicate, understanding RLHF helps practitioners choose models trained with it and design workflows that build on top of them.

How RLHF Works: From Human Judgments to Model Fine-Tuning

Reinforcement learning with human feedback (RLHF) is used to align LLMs with human preferences—especially in open-ended tasks where there is no single "correct" answer.

It begins with a **base LLM** that has already been instruction-tuned. This model is used to generate multiple responses to a prompt. Then, **human annotators rank** those responses from best to worst. These rankings are used to train a **reward model**, which predicts how preferable a response is given a prompt.

Once trained, the reward model becomes part of a reinforcement learning loop, where the original language model is further fine-tuned using a policy optimization algorithm—usually **PPO**.[13]

While RLHF is computationally expensive and rarely done from scratch outside of large research labs, its benefits are widely felt in consumer-facing models like ChatGPT, Claude, and Gemini.

Evaluating LLMs: Metrics, Sampling Strategies

As LLMs grow more powerful, evaluating their responses becomes more important and more nuanced.

> Evaluation is not a one-size-fits-all task.

Some use cases prioritize factual accuracy; others prioritize fluency, creativity, or reasoning ability.

In this section, we explore key methods for **evaluating** LLM performance—including **generation control** (e.g., temperature, top-k/p), and **output quality metrics** such as BLEU, and ROUGE.

Controlling Model Output

Controlling Model Output helps us influence how a language model generates its responses—whether we want concise, reliable outputs or more creative, exploratory ones. Controlling LLM output involves adjusting parameters like: Temperature, Top-k, and Top-p sampling to influence randomness, and using prompt engineering techniques to provide clear instructions and structure.

Controlling model output is like adjusting a storyteller's creativity—how wild or careful the computer is when picking what to say next. **Temperature**

is like turning up or down the "spice" of the computer's answers. A low temperature means it plays it safe and gives predictable answers. A high temperature makes it more adventurous and creative—but sometimes a bit silly! **Top-k Sampling:** Here, the computer looks at the *top k* best word choices (like picking from the five best options), then randomly picks one. It's like picking dinner from your top five favorite dishes instead of the whole menu. Top-p Sampling (also called nucleus sampling) is similar, but instead of choosing a fixed number of options, it picks from the smallest set of words whose combined probability mass is above a certain threshold (like 90%). This makes it more adaptive than top-k, balancing both diversity and coherence.

Generative models don't always produce the same answer—nor should they. When generating tokens, LLMs sample from a **probability distribution** over the vocabulary. This distribution can be shaped by two core parameters:

Temperature: The **temperature** parameter (T) controls how "sharp" or "random" the sampling is.

- **Low temperature (e.g., 0.2)** → more deterministic, focuses on high-probability tokens
- **High temperature (e.g., 0.9)** → more diverse, exploratory output

Mathematically, it modifies the softmax function:

$$P(x_i) = \frac{e^{z_i/T}}{\Sigma_j e^{z_j/T}}$$

Where:

- z_i is the logit score for token i
- T is the temperature parameter:
  - $T < 1$: sharper, more deterministic distribution
  - $T > 1$: flatter, more random distribution
  - At $T = 1$, this reduces to the standard softmax function.

Lowering T increases the gap between probabilities, making top tokens more likely.

Top-k Sampling: With **top-k**, only the k most likely tokens are considered for sampling. The model generates output from a truncated distribution:

- **k = 5** → sample from the top 5 predicted tokens only
- Reduces risk of rare or off-topic outputs

Top-p Sampling (Nucleus Sampling): **Top-p** selects the smallest set of tokens whose **cumulative probability** ≥ **p** (e.g., p = 0.9). This dynamically adapts the candidate set size.

- Example: If the top 3 tokens have cumulative probability 0.91, only those are sampled from.
- Balances diversity and coherence better than fixed-k.

Quantitative Evaluation Metrics

BLEU[14] (Bilingual Evaluation Understudy): Used primarily in translation tasks, BLEU compares n-grams in the generated output to a reference output.

- **BLEU-1**: unigram overlap
- **BLEU-4**: up to 4-gram overlap

$$\text{BLEU} = \text{BP} \cdot \exp\left(\sum_{n=1}^{N} w_n \cdot log\ p_n\right)$$

Where, p_n is the precision of n-grams and *BP* is a brevity penalty.

$$\text{BP} = \left\{ \begin{array}{ll} 1, & if\ c > r \\ e^{(1-r/c)}, & if\ c \leq r \end{array} \right\}$$

ROUGE (Recall-Oriented Understudy for Gisting Evaluation): **ROUGE** is a score that checks how good a computer is at summarizing or generating text—like writing short news stories or summaries. It compares the computer's version with a human-written one and sees how many matching words or phrases there are. The more overlap, the better the score. It's like having two people summarize a story and seeing how much they agree. ROUGE helps tell if the computer "got the gist" of what it was supposed to say.

Common in summarization, ROUGE measures overlap with a reference, focusing on recall.

- **ROUGE-1**: unigram recall
- **ROUGE-L**: evaluates the quality of a generated sequence based on the **longest common subsequence (LCS)** with a reference.

Given:

- X = reference sequence
- Y = generated sequence
- $LCS(X, Y)$ = length of the longest common subsequence

Then:

- Precision, $P = \frac{LCS(X,Y)}{|Y|}$
- Recall, $R = \frac{LCS(X,Y)}{|X|}$
- F1 Score, ROUGE-$L_F = \frac{(1+\beta^2)\cdot P\cdot R}{R+\beta^2\cdot P}$

Typically, $\beta = 1$, so F1 gives equal weight to precision and recall.

Longest common subsequence (LCS) is a way to compare two pieces of text by finding the longest set of words or letters that appear in both, in the same order (but not necessarily right next to each other). It helps measure how similar two sentences are. Think of it like comparing two family recipes and finding the longest list of ingredients they have in common, in the same order. The more matches, the more alike they are!

Perplexity measures the fluency or confidence of a language model. It is defined as the exponentiation of the cross-entropy loss:

$$\text{Perplexity} = \exp\left(-\frac{1}{N}\sum_{i=1}^{N} \log P(x_i)\right)$$

Where, N is the number of tokens in the sequence and $P(x_i)$ *is the predicted probability of token* x_i.

Lower perplexity implies more fluent or confident output.

Cosine Similarity (for Embedding Comparison): Used to measure semantic similarity between two sentence or document embeddings. Given two vectors $\vec{a}$ and $\vec{b}$:

$$\cos\_\text{sim}\left(\vec{a}, \vec{b}\right) = \frac{\vec{a} \cdot \vec{b}}{||\vec{a}|| \cdot ||\vec{b}||}$$

Values range from −1 (opposite direction) to +1 (identical direction), with values >0.7 typically indicating high similarity in NLP.

Simply put, **Cosine Similarity** is a way for the computer to measure how similar two pieces of text are—not by exact words, but by meaning. It turns each sentence into numbers (called *embeddings*) and then checks the angle between them. If the angle is small, the sentences are very similar—just like two arrows pointing in the same direction. It's like asking, "Are these two thoughts going the same way?" The closer they point, the more alike they are in meaning!

Real-World Evaluation: Combining Metrics

In production settings, you might combine:

- **Automatic metrics** (ROUGE, BLEU, perplexity)
- **Human ratings** (fluency, factuality, safety)
- **Task-specific tests** (e.g., retrieval precision, summarization fidelity)

For RAG systems, you might also evaluate:

- **Context relevance** (retrieved docs vs. query)
- **Answer grounding** (is the answer based on retrieved chunks?)
- **Latency and cost** (response time, API tokens used)

Example: Evaluating Prompt Temperature

```
from transformers import pipeline, set_seed

generator = pipeline("text-generation", model="gpt2")
set_seed(42)
```

```
# Temperature = 0.2 (more deterministic)
print(generator("The future of AI in medicine is", max_length=30,
temperature=0.2))

# Temperature = 0.9 (more creative)
print(generator("The future of AI in medicine is", max_length=30,
temperature=0.9))
```

This example shows how changing the temperature can shift the tone and creativity of the output—a useful method for prompt optimization.

SECTION B: RETRIEVAL-AUGMENTED GENERATION

Despite their prowess, LLMs still face a foundational limitation: they are static, pre-trained systems. No matter how large the model or how diverse the dataset, a pre-trained LLM[15] cannot "know" real-time information unless it was explicitly included in its training corpus.

They also suffer from hallucination, making up facts not present in training data. This gap poses serious limitations for use cases in compliance, finance, healthcare, and policy, where trust and timeliness are essential.

Enter retrieval-augmented generation (RAG).

Retrieval-augmented generation (RAG) is a technique that enhances the outputs of LLMs by integrating them with external knowledge sources. RAG works by retrieving relevant information from these external sources (like databases or documents) and using it to augment the LLM's response generation. The end-to-end retrieval-augmented generation workflow is illustrated in Figure 5.2. This results in more accurate, contextually relevant, and up-to-date answers.

In simple words, RAG is like giving a computer both a smart brain *and* a library card. When you ask it a question, it first looks up helpful information from trusted sources (like flipping through books), and then uses that info to write a better, more accurate answer. It doesn't just guess from memory—it actually "retrieves" facts before speaking. It's like a student who checks notes before answering a test question, so the reply is smarter and more reliable!

It is a framework that bridges this gap. Rather than asking an LLM to answer questions purely from memory, RAG augments the input prompt with **relevant context** retrieved from a custom knowledge base. In essence,

RAG systems separate knowledge from reasoning, as shown conceptually in Figure 5.2: the retriever finds supporting documents; the generator crafts a fluent answer.

Where classical question-answering pipelines relied on structured databases or keyword-based search, RAG uses **dense vector retrieval**[16]—leveraging embedding models like Sentence-BERT to represent documents and queries in a shared semantic space. This allows the system to surface the most relevant chunks of text from a document corpus, even when the user's query doesn't contain exact keyword matches.

This way, the model doesn't need to memorize everything—it simply accesses the right information at the right time. RAG provides several benefits:

- Reduced hallucination, since responses are grounded in real documents.
- Custom knowledge integration, like company policies or risk manuals.
- Efficient updates, since adding documents is faster than fine-tuning.

How RAG Works: Conceptual Pipeline

The RAG Advantage

RAG mitigates the risks (like training cutoffs, hallucinations, opaque reasoning) by combining LLMs with retrieval engines, providing the model

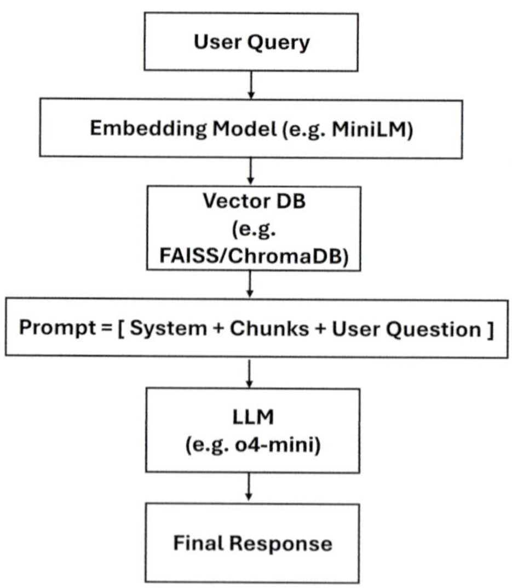

FIGURE 5.2 In a RAG pipeline, the LLM becomes a reasoning engine guided by up-to-date, traceable context.

with dynamic, external knowledge. This architecture offers three major benefits for enterprise-grade AI systems:

- **Real-time access to evolving and proprietary knowledge**
  RAG enables LLMs to respond using live data from internal systems (e.g., knowledge bases, intranets, databases), making it suitable for domains where knowledge updates frequently or must remain confidential.
- **Improved transparency and explainability**
  By surfacing the documents or sources that informed the response, RAG supports **traceable decision-making**, facilitating compliance with AI governance frameworks like the NIST AI RMF or EU AI Act.
- **Model reusability without retraining**
  Enterprises can **update the retrieval layer independently of the model**, minimizing downtime and infrastructure costs. This makes RAG particularly advantageous in dynamic environments where retraining LLMs is impractical due to scale, cost, or latency.

Why RAG Is Critical for Enterprises

RAG is not just a technical innovation—it is a paradigm shift in how AI systems integrate with enterprise intelligence. A side-by-side comparison of traditional LLMs and RAG-augmented systems across key enterprise criteria is provided in Table 5.5.

TABLE 5.5 Comparison Table: Traditional LLM versus RAG-Augmented LLM

Key Feature	Traditional LLM	RAG
Knowledge freshness	Static (based on training)	Dynamic (retrieves latest content)
Hallucination risk	High	Lower (answers grounded in retrieved docs)
Explainability	Low	High (can cite sources)
Custom domain adaptation	Requires fine-tuning	Uses retriever to inject domain knowledge
Compliance fit	Limited	High (traceable sources, updatable corpora)
Use in regulated industries	Risk-prone	Relatively less Risk-prone

> **For risk leaders, RAG offers a rare combination: agility without compromise**, innovation without increased exposure. In the age of regulatory scrutiny and rising AI accountability, RAG architectures may become the backbone of trustworthy, explainable, and operationally sound AI deployments.

LLMs are limited by their training cutoff and prone to hallucinations when they lack enough grounding. For enterprises that must provide **auditable**, **fact-based**, and **real-time** answers, these limitations are deal-breakers.

RAG addresses them by:

- Giving the model access to **up-to-date** or **proprietary** information.
- Improving **explainability** by citing retrieved content.
- Allowing for **model reuse** without retraining (change the database, not the model).

Technical Building Blocks

- **Embedding model**: Converts queries and documents into high-dimensional vectors. Models like *all-MiniLM-L6-v2* are fast and effective for RAG pipelines.
- **Vector store**: Efficiently indexes and searches embeddings. Popular tools include **ChromaDB**, **FAISS**, and **Weaviate**.
- **Retriever logic**: Given a query vector, retrieves the top-k most similar document chunks.
- **Prompt assembly**: Constructs a final message to the LLM, often including:
  - A system message ("Use the following context to answer …")
  - The retrieved content
  - The user's original question
- **LLM generator**: Produces the final output. The LLM is now grounded with fresh, relevant information even though its weights remain unchanged.

Building a Lightweight RAG Prototype with FAISS[17] and Evaluation

This section presents a lightweight, notebook-based prototype. It demonstrates how you can build and test a RAG workflow with minimal setup—especially useful for experimentation, debugging, or small-scale pilots.

This example uses **FAISS** for vector indexing and integrates OpenAI or Hugging Face models to generate context-aware answers. It also includes **BLEU**[18] and **ROUGE**[19] scores to evaluate how well the model responds, which is a critical step in responsible LLM development.

Use Case: Summarize Regulatory Guidance from Document Chunks

Suppose you're working with regulatory compliance documents and want to answer questions like:

"What does the EU AI Act say about high-risk systems?"

Your knowledge base is a set of chunked paragraphs extracted from PDF documents. You'll embed them, build a FAISS index, retrieve the top-k chunks for a query, and use a generation model to produce an answer.

Step 1: Install and Import Required Libraries

```
!pip install faiss-cpu
!pip install sentence-transformers
!pip install PyPDF2
!pip install pdf2image
!pip install pytesseract
!pip install rouge-score
!pip install transformers
!pip install nltk
!pip install openai==0.28

import os
import json
import faiss
import numpy as np
import PyPDF2
from sentence_transformers import SentenceTransformer, util
import nltk
from nltk.translate.bleu_score import sentence_bleu, SmoothingFunction
from rouge_score import rouge_scorer
import openai

nltk.download('punkt')
```

Step 2: Extract Text from PDF Files

```
def extract_text_from_pdf(file_path):

text = ""
try:
  with open(file_path, "rb") as f:
    reader = PyPDF2.PdfReader(f)
    for page in reader.pages:
      page_text = page.extract_text()
      if page_text:
        text += page_text + "\n"

except Exception as e:
  print(f"PyPDF2 error for {file_path}: {e}")

return text.strip()
```

Step 3: Load and Preprocess Text Data

```
def load_dataset(data_dir="data"):

  texts = []
  for file_name in os.listdir(data_dir):
    file_path = os.path.join(data_dir, file_name)

    if file_name.lower().endswith(".pdf"):
      extracted_text = extract_text_from_pdf(file_path)

      if extracted_text:
        texts.append(extracted_text)

      else:
        print(f"No text extracted from {file_name}.")

  return texts

def clean_text(text):
  return text.strip()

# Load and preprocess documents.
documents = load_dataset(data_dir="/content")
documents = [doc.strip() for doc in documents if doc.strip()]
print(f"Loaded {len(documents)} documents.")
```

Step 4: Generate Embeddings for the Documents and Build FAISS Index

```
embedding_model = SentenceTransformer("all-MiniLM-L6-v2")
embeddings = embedding_model.encode(documents, show_progress_
bar=True).astype("float32")

index = faiss.IndexFlatL2(embeddings.shape[1])
index.add(embeddings)

print(f"FAISS index built with {index.ntotal} documents.")
```

Step 5: Prompt Engineering with Few-Shot and CoT Options

```
few_shot_examples = [
  {"question": "What does GDPR stand for?", "answer": "General Data
Protection Regulation."},
  {"question": "What is the purpose of HIPAA?", "answer": "To protect the
privacy and security of patients' health information while also making it
easier to maintain health insurance coverage and reduce healthcare admin-
istrative costs."}
]

def build_prompt(query, context, few_shot=few_shot_examples,
chain_of_thought=False):

  prompt = "You are an expert on AI risk policies and regulations.\n\n"

  if few_shot:
    prompt += "Few-shot examples:\n"
    for example in few_shot:
    prompt += f"Q: {example['question']}\nA: {example['answer']}\n\n"

if chain_of_thought:
  prompt += ("When answering, think step-by-step to reason through the
context and guidelines, "
        "then provide a concise answer.\n\n")

  prompt += "Relevant Context:\n" + context + "\n\n"
  prompt += "Q: " + query + "\nA:"

return prompt
```

Step 6: Truncate Context Tokens to Fit Model Limit

```
from transformers import GPT2TokenizerFast
tokenizer = GPT2TokenizerFast.from_pretrained("gpt2")

def truncate_text(text, max_tokens):

    tokens = tokenizer.encode(text)
    if len(tokens) > max_tokens:
        tokens = tokens[:max_tokens]
        return tokenizer.decode(tokens)

return text
```

Step 7: Generate Answer Using ChatGPT-4

```
openai.api_key = <your_openai_key>

def generate_response_chatgpt(context, query, chain_of_thought=False):

    max_context_tokens = 3000 # Adjust this value as needed.
    context = truncate_text(context, max_context_tokens)
    prompt = build_prompt(query, context, chain_of_thought=chain_
of_thought)

try:
    response = openai.ChatCompletion.create(
        model="gpt-4",
        messages=[
            {"role": "system", "content": "You are an expert on AI risk policies and
regulations."},
            {"role": "user", "content": prompt}
        ]
    )

        # Extract and return the response text
    generated_text = response.choices[0].message['content']

except Exception as e:
    print("Error during OpenAI API call:", e)
    generated_text = ""

return generated_text
```

Step 8: Define the RAG-Based Chatbot Function

```
def chatbot(query, top_k=3, chain_of_thought=False):

    # Generate embedding for the query.
    query_embedding = embedding_model.encode([query]).astype("float32")
    distances, indices = index.search(query_embedding, top_k)
    retrieved_contexts = [documents[idx] for idx in indices[0] if idx <
len(documents)]
    context = "\n\n".join(retrieved_contexts)
    answer = generate_response_chatgpt(context, query,
chain_of_thought=chain_of_thought)

    return answer
```

Step 9: Evaluate the Chatbot with BLEU, ROUGE, and Similarity

```
def evaluate_chatbot(test_cases, chain_of_thought=False):

    smoothing_function = SmoothingFunction().method1
    rouge_evaluator = rouge_scorer.RougeScorer(['rouge1', 'rougeL'],
use_stemmer=True)
    results = []

    for case in test_cases:
        query = case["query"]
        expected = case["expected"]
        response = chatbot(query, chain_of_thought=chain_of_thought)

        bleu_score = sentence_bleu([expected.split()], response.split(),
smoothing_function=smoothing_function)
        rouge_scores = rouge_evaluator.score(expected, response)

        response_embedding = embedding_model.encode(response,
convert_to_tensor=True)
        expected_embedding = embedding_model.encode(expected,
convert_to_tensor=True)
        similarity = util.cos_sim(response_embedding, expected_embedding).
item()

        result = {
            "query": query,
            "response": response,
            "expected": expected,
```

```
            "semantic_similarity": similarity,
            "bleu_score": bleu_score,
            "rouge_scores": rouge_scores
        }
        results.append(result)

        print(f"Query: {query}\n")
        print(f"Response: {response}\n")
        print(f"Expected: {expected}\n")
        print(f"Semantic Similarity: {similarity:.3f}")
        print(f"BLEU Score: {bleu_score:.3f}")
        print(f"ROUGE Scores: {rouge_scores}")
        print("-" * 80)

    return results
```

Example Usage

```
# Example usage:
user_query = "What does GDPR stand for?"
response = chatbot(user_query, chain_of_thought=True)
print("Chatbot Response:")
print(response)

# Example evaluation using test cases
test_cases = [
    {
        "query": "What does GDPR stand for?",
        "expected": "General Data Protection Regulation."
    },
    {
        "query": "What is the purpose of HIPAA?",
        "expected": "To protect the privacy and security of patients' health
information while also making it easier to maintain health insurance
coverage and reduce healthcare administrative costs."
    },
    {
        "query": "What guidelines exist for AI risk management in the EU?",
        "expected": "They include a set of rules and guidelines as per the EU
AI Act and related policies."
    }
]

evaluation_results = evaluate_chatbot(test_cases, chain_of_thought=True)
```

Output

```
Query: What does GDPR stand for?

Response: General Data Protection Regulation.

Expected: General Data Protection Regulation.

Semantic Similarity: 1.000

BLEU Score: 1.000

ROUGE Scores: {'rouge1': Score(precision=1.0, recall=1.0, fmeasure=1.0),
'rougeL': Score(precision=1.0, recall=1.0, fmeasure=1.0)}

--------------------------------------------------------------------------------

Query: What is the purpose of HIPAA?

Response: The purpose of HIPAA (Health Insurance Portability and
Accountability Act) is to ensure the confidentiality, integrity, and availability
of protected health information (PHI). It establishes national standards for
electronic healthcare transactions and addresses the security and privacy
of patients' health data. Its goal is to protect the privacy and security of
patients' health information while also making it easier to maintain health
insurance coverage and reduce healthcare administrative costs.

Expected: To protect the privacy and security of patients' health informa-
tion while also making it easier to maintain health insurance coverage and
reduce healthcare administrative costs.

Semantic Similarity: 0.595

BLEU Score: 0.333

ROUGE Scores: {'rouge1': Score(precision=0.36231884057971014,
recall=1.0, fmeasure=0.5319148936170213),

'rougeL': Score(precision=0.36231884057971014, recall=1.0,
fmeasure=0.5319148936170213)}

--------------------------------------------------------------------------------

Query: What guidelines exist for AI risk management in the EU?

Response: The EU has established several guidelines for AI risk management.
One primary set of regulations is the General Data Protection Regulation
(GDPR), which addresses AI's handling of personal data. Additionally, a
document titled "Ethics Guidelines For Trustworthy AI" was released by the
EU's High-Level Expert Group on AI. This guideline stresses human over-
sight, technical robustness and safety, privacy and data governance, trans-
parency, and several other factors to ensure AI's trustworthy and ethical
```

use. Moreover, the European Commission published a proposal for a legal framework on AI in April 2021, aiming to address AI risks and their potential impact on fundamental rights and safety, thus marking a significant legislative step in AI risk management in the EU.

Expected: They include a set of rules and guidelines as per the EU AI Act and related policies.

Semantic Similarity: 0.677

BLEU Score: 0.005

ROUGE Scores: {'rouge1': Score(precision=0.075, recall=0.5294117647058824, fmeasure=0.13138686131386862),

'rougeL': Score(precision=0.058333333333333334, recall=0.4117647058823529, fmeasure=0.10218978102189781)}

Summary: When and Why to Use This Prototype

This RAG notebook gives you:

- A quick and flexible testbed for evaluating **retrieval quality**
- The ability to run RAG logic **without Docker or backend setup**
- Reproducible BLEU/ROUGE metrics for comparing models or prompts

It's not meant to replace a production deployment, but it **complements it**—ideal for testing new prompts, models, or document preprocessing strategies before committing to a full stack like the one shown in the final chapter.

NOTES

1. **Generative AI (GenAI)** refers to a type of AI that can create new content—such as text, images, music, code, or videos—based on patterns it has learned from large datasets. Unlike traditional AI, which is often limited to recognizing or classifying data, Gen AI can **generate original outputs**, often resembling human creativity. Tools like ChatGPT, DALL·E, and Midjourney are examples of GenAI in action. These systems use advanced models like transformers to understand context and produce coherent, realistic, and contextually relevant content. GenAI is transforming industries by enabling faster content creation, personalized experiences, and intelligent automation.

2. LLM is a type of AI model trained on vast amounts of text data to understand, generate, and respond in human-like language. LLMs, such as generative pre-trained transformer (GPT), use deep learning—specifically transformer architectures—to recognize patterns in language, summarize information, answer questions, translate text, and even write code. What makes LLMs powerful is their ability to generalize across topics and adapt to various tasks without task-specific training. They are widely used in chatbots, search engines, content creation, and decision-support systems, making them a foundational technology in modern AI.
3. See also: Brown et al., 2020 (GPT-3)—Language Models are Few-Shot Learners, https://arxiv.org/abs/2005.14165
4. GPT is a type of large language model developed by OpenAI that uses deep learning to understand and generate human-like text. "Generative" means it can create content; "pre-trained" refers to its training on vast amounts of text data before being fine-tuned for specific tasks; and "transformer" is the neural network architecture it uses to understand language context and relationships. GPT models can write essays, answer questions, summarize documents, generate code, and carry on conversations. They are designed to predict the next word in a sentence, enabling them to produce coherent and context-aware text.
5. T5 (Text-To-Text Transfer Transformer) is a large language model developed by Google that frames every natural language processing (NLP) task as a text-to-text problem. Whether it's translation, summarization, question answering, or classification, T5 takes in text as input and generates text as output. Built on the Transformer architecture, T5 was trained on a massive dataset called the "Colossal Clean Crawled Corpus" (C4) and fine-tuned for multiple tasks using a unified format. This makes it highly flexible and effective across a wide range of NLP applications. Its text-to-text approach simplifies model design and promotes transfer learning across diverse language tasks.
6. See also: Raffel et al., 2020—Exploring the Limits of Transfer Learning with a Unified Text-to-Text Transformer https://arxiv.org/abs/1910.10683
7. Scaling laws are like recipes that show what happens when you give a computer more ingredients—like more data, more computer power, or a bigger model. Researchers found that when you "scale up" these ingredients, the AI usually gets smarter and makes fewer mistakes. It's like how a child who reads more books and practices more often gets better at school. These laws help scientists predict how much better an AI can get if they keep feeding it more information and training time.
8. See also: Kaplan et al., 2020—Scaling Laws for Neural Language Models https://arxiv.org/abs/2001.08361
9. Foundation models are big, smart computer brains that are trained on a huge variety of information—like books, websites, and conversations—so they can do many different tasks. Once trained, they can be fine-tuned to do specific jobs, like writing stories, answering questions, or translating languages. It's like baking a big plain cake (the foundation) that you can

decorate in different ways depending on the occasion—birthday, wedding, or tea party. One strong base, many possibilities!

10. Reference: Bommasani et al., 2021—On the Opportunities and Risks of Foundation Models https://arxiv.org/abs/2108.07258
11. In-context learning is a feature of LLMs where the AI learns to perform a task just by seeing a few examples in the prompt—without needing retraining. Instead of changing the model's internal settings, it uses the context provided during the conversation or input to figure out what to do. For example, if you show it a few math problems with answers, it can solve a new one using the same pattern. It's like teaching someone a rule by showing examples on the spot, rather than training them in advance.
12. Instruction tuning is like teaching a computer to follow directions better. After learning a lot from books and data, the computer is given special training where it's shown examples like: "If someone says this, you should reply like that." This helps it understand and respond more politely, clearly, or helpfully—depending on what's asked. It's like teaching a child not just facts, but also *how* to answer nicely when someone asks a question.
13. Proximal policy optimization (PPO) is widely used across research and industry for training reinforcement learning agents due to its balance of performance, stability, and simplicity. Example: OpenAI used PPO to train a robotic hand to solve a Rubik's cube autonomously. It most likely ensure safe, interpretable updates in high-stakes environments. In summary, PPO is the go-to algorithm when you need a powerful yet stable reinforcement learning method that works out-of-the-box in complex, high-dimensional, or sensitive domains.
14. BLEU is a score that tells how good a computer is at translating from one language to another. It compares the computer's translation to a human-made one and checks how many words and phrases match. The more matches, the higher the score. It's like a teacher grading a student's translated sentence by seeing how close it is to the correct answer. BLEU doesn't understand meaning, but it's a quick way to see if the computer is "speaking" the new language well.
15. Pre-trained LLMs are advanced AI models trained on vast amounts of text data to understand and generate human-like language. Before being applied to specific tasks, these models—such as GPT, BERT, or LLaMA—undergo extensive unsupervised training on diverse datasets like books, websites, and articles. This pre-training enables them to learn grammar, context, reasoning patterns, and world knowledge. Once pre-trained, LLMs can be fine-tuned for targeted applications like chatbots, legal analysis, or medical summaries. Their versatility and linguistic intelligence make them foundational tools in modern natural language processing and AI-powered solutions.
16. **Dense vector retrieval** is how a computer finds the most relevant information—not by looking for exact words, but by comparing *meanings*. It turns questions and documents into special number lists called **dense vectors**, which capture the overall idea. Then it compares those number lists to find

the closest match—kind of like finding the puzzle piece that best fits. It's smarter than simple keyword search because it looks for things that *mean* the same, even if the words are different!

17. **FAISS** (Facebook AI Similarity Search) is a tool that helps computers quickly find things that are *similar*—especially when dealing with huge amounts of information. Imagine you're looking for a photo in a giant album that "looks like this one." FAISS helps the computer search through millions of items in seconds by comparing their meaning (as numbers) and finding the closest match. It's like a super-fast librarian who doesn't just find books with the same words, but books with the same *idea*!
18. **BLEU (Bilingual Evaluation Understudy)** is a score that tells how good a computer is at translating from one language to another. It compares the computer's translation to a human-made one and checks how many words and phrases match. The more matches, the higher the score. It's like a teacher grading a student's translated sentence by seeing how close it is to the correct answer. BLEU doesn't understand the meaning, but it's a quick way to see if the computer is "speaking" the new language well.
19. **ROUGE** (Recall-Oriented Understudy for Gisting Evaluation) is a score that checks how good a computer is at summarizing or generating text—like writing short news stories or summaries. It compares the computer's version with a human-written one and sees how many matching words or phrases there are. The more overlap, the better the score. It's like having two people summarize a story and seeing how much they agree. ROUGE helps tell if the computer "got the gist" of what it was supposed to say.

CHAPTER 6

Role of Artificial Intelligence in Risk Management and Vice Versa

"Questions drive revolution, if followed by right process".

Ian Goodfellow,[1] widely regarded as the pioneer of adversarial machine learning, emphasized in his seminal work that adversarial examples reveal serious vulnerabilities in artificial intelligence (AI) systems.[2] His research highlighted that building robust and secure models must be considered a foundational requirement, not an afterthought.

The integration of AI into risk management signifies a seismic shift from traditional methodologies toward a future characterized by predictive precision, adaptive intelligence, and dynamic governance. Historically, risk managers navigated uncertainty with tools and frameworks built upon known risks and predictable outcomes. Today, we stand amidst **a paradigm shift where intelligent algorithms do not simply react to risk—they foresee it, create it, and shape its trajectory.**

DOI: 10.1201/9781003607298-6

AI's emergence as a central force in risk management has been profoundly illuminated by seminal research. For instance,

> **Floridi et al. (2018)** presented a compelling perspective in their paper, "**AI4People—An Ethical Framework for a Good AI Society,**" highlighting the necessity for a robust ethical and governance framework to harness AI effectively.
>
> They argue that AI can indeed reduce risks by enhancing decision-making accuracy but concurrently introduces significant ethical and governance challenges, such as bias and transparency issues. This nuanced perspective resonates directly with our **book's mission of balancing technological advancement and risk vigilance.**
>
> Floridi and his collaborators (2018) put it simply: AI can help us make smarter, more accurate decisions, but without careful ethical guardrails, it may also magnify risks like bias and opacity. Their work, AI4People—An Ethical Framework for a Good AI Society, captures the very balance this book seeks to explore—leveraging technology while staying vigilant to its consequences.
>
> We recommend reading the full work (which has open access) on https://link.springer.com/article/10.1007/s11023-018-9482-5
>
> **Geoffrey Hinton,**[3] famously known as the "Godfather of AI," highlighted in his keynote address at NeurIPS (2018) the dual nature of AI's potential, remarking, "**AI is not merely about automation; it is fundamentally reshaping human decision-making, ethics, and control mechanisms.**" His groundbreaking insights underline the essential intersection where AI reshapes risk management strategies and where effective governance profoundly impacts AI deployment. Hinton's pioneering thoughts compel us to ask: How must risk management evolve to responsibly harness this technological revolution?
>
> Moreover, **Nobel laureate Daniel Kahneman,**[4] known for his influential work on behavioral economics, provided a critical cognitive lens in his book *Noise: A Flaw in Human Judgment* (2021). Kahneman emphasizes AI's capability to reduce the "noise" in human decision-making, significantly enhancing precision and consistency. However, he cautions that reliance on AI also

introduces new, unprecedented risks related to algorithmic transparency and accountability—precisely the ethical dilemmas this chapter scrutinizes.

In our opinion, the findings from these studies demonstrate the mutual influence of AI and risk management practices.

The application of AI and generative AI (gen AI) transforms traditional risk management frameworks while strong risk management practices guide ethical AI usage and its sustainability.

This chapter utilizes detailed research alongside real-world examples and practical guidance to provide professionals in finance, healthcare, technology, and academia with necessary frameworks and tools to manage this complex and dynamic intersection.

As readers journey through this chapter, **key questions will guide their exploration: How can AI enhance existing risk frameworks? Which approaches can be implemented to maintain transparency and ethical standards while holding AI systems accountable?**

Traditional risk management principles[5] influence the development, governance, and regulation of AI. This chapter aims to deliver essential information while motivating readers to engage in meaningful discussions.

Risk managers[6] as well as AI specialists,[7] executives and students who are yet to start their professional journey should all engage with the following content through deep critical thinking and passionate involvement.

The journey ahead will transform your understanding of intelligent risk mastery and enable you to capitalize on intelligent opportunities during a time when AI shapes risk along with informing it.

SECTION A: ROLE OF AI IN MANAGING RISK

AI plays a transformative role in risk management by *enhancing the ability of organizations* to identify, assess, and mitigate risks more efficiently and effectively.

Below is an overview of how AI contributes to risk management across various domains.

Enhanced Risk Identification

AI systems are adept at identifying risks that are too complex, fast-evolving, or subtle for traditional methods. By leveraging machine learning, natural language processing (NLP), and real-time data analytics, AI enables **early warning systems** that can detect emerging patterns, anomalies, or vulnerabilities—often **before they manifest into actual threats**.

Why Early Identification Matters

Early identification of risk is critical for reducing the **impact, cost, and spread** of potential disruptions. When risks are caught early, organizations can shift from reactive damage control to **proactive risk mitigation**, preserving reputation, stakeholder trust, and operational continuity.

How Early Risk Detection Works?

- **Predictive modeling**: AI can forecast risk scenarios using historical trends, market signals, and behavioral indicators.
- **Real-time monitoring**: AI algorithms scan financial transactions, system logs, or social media to flag early indicators of fraud, outages, or compliance breaches.
- **Unstructured data analysis**: NLP-enabled tools can process emails, contracts, news, and internal documents to reveal hidden risks.
- **Scenario simulations**: Generative AI and agent-based models can simulate complex environments, stress test strategies, and highlight cascading failure points.

How to Enable Yourself for Early Detection

- **Invest in data infrastructure** that allows continuous ingestion and analysis of diverse internal and external data sources.
- **Develop AI literacy** among risk teams to understand model outputs, anomaly detection thresholds, and explainability.
- **Collaborate cross-functionally** with IT, data science, and operations to co-create early detection workflows.
- **Adopt AI-powered tools** that integrate with your ERM systems to provide real-time dashboards and predictive alerts.

From Detection to Decision

Imagine your car's dashboard shows a blinking engine warning light. Early identification is great—but if you don't quickly decide to pull over or head to a mechanic, the problem could escalate into a breakdown, accident, or expensive repair. In contrast, responding immediately allows for a minor fix, avoids further damage, and keeps your journey on track. Similarly, in AI, spotting a bias or vulnerability early is only useful if you act quickly to correct it—ensuring the system stays safe, reliable, and aligned with your goals.

> AI doesn't just identify risks—it prioritizes them. Intelligent systems can assess **likelihood, severity, and interdependencies**, enabling leaders to allocate resources where they matter most. Coupled with human judgment and governance frameworks, AI enhances the **speed, accuracy, and relevance** of decision-making.

Once a risk is identified, the real differentiator lies in how quickly and accurately an organization responds. Timely decision-making is critical to scaling transformation in the right direction—especially when developing robust and safe AI models. A delayed or misinformed response can allow risks to evolve into system failures, legal liabilities, or ethical breaches. For AI, where models continuously learn and adapt, real-time decisions ensure that risks like bias, drift, or unintended consequences are mitigated before causing harm. Swift action not only protects the integrity of the AI system but also reinforces trust, accountability, and long-term value creation.

To make quick, effective decisions once a risk is identified—but before it materializes—requires a combination of **preparedness, clarity, and empowerment**. Here's how one can enable themselves and their organization to act swiftly and wisely:

1. **Establish clear risk thresholds and triggers**
   Define what constitutes a tolerable vs. intolerable risk. Pre-set thresholds (e.g., model accuracy drops below 85%, or a bias score exceeds a defined limit) act as automatic signals to initiate response protocols—eliminating indecision.

2. **Create decision frameworks in advance**
   Use structured decision trees, playbooks, or scenario templates to guide actions. These frameworks clarify roles, escalation paths, and fallback options, reducing cognitive load during high-pressure moments.

3. **Enable real-time data access and visualization**
   Equip teams with real-time dashboards, anomaly alerts, and explainable AI insights. Fast decisions require visibility—not just of the problem, but of its context and potential consequences.

4. **Empower cross-functional teams**
   Ensure the right people (risk, data science, legal, operations) are connected and authorized to make decisions without bottlenecks. Agile response requires breaking down silos and distributing decision rights.

5. **Run simulations and drills**
   Just like fire drills, risk response simulations improve reflexes and reveal blind spots. Practicing how to respond before a real risk hits increase speed and confidence in action.

6. **Cultivate risk-aware culture**
   Speedy decisions come more easily in organizations that trust their data, processes, and people. Educating teams on risk impacts, and fostering a "fail-fast, fix-faster" mindset, reduces hesitation and fear of accountability.

In essence, **speedy decisions aren't reactive—they're pre-enabled**. The best organizations don't wait for risks to explode; they prepare to neutralize them the moment they spark.

Improved Risk Assessment with AI

Traditional risk assessment methods often rely on static models, periodic reviews, and human judgment grounded in historical data. While useful, these approaches can fall short in today's fast-moving, hyperconnected, and data-saturated environment. **AI transforms risk assessment** by enabling dynamic, real-time, and more granular analysis. AI systems not only process complex and voluminous datasets quickly—they also **learn and adapt**, improving over time with new information.

Why AI-Driven Risk Assessment Matters Today

Modern risks—cyber threats, misinformation, algorithmic failures, ESG violations—are **multi-dimensional, fast-evolving, and context-dependent**. AI's ability to process high-frequency, high-volume, and high-variety data gives it a unique edge in surfacing hidden threats and forecasting risk events before they escalate.

If organizations continue to rely solely on traditional assessments:

- **Emerging threats may go undetected** until damage is already done.
- **Response times lag**, exposing businesses to reputational, regulatory, and financial consequences.
- **Opportunity costs rise**, as leaders miss insights that could drive innovation and resilience.

AI makes risk assessment **predictive, personalized, and continuous**—a key shift from reactive governance to intelligent, proactive management.

How AI Enhances Risk Assessment

1. **Quantitative risk assessment**
   AI systems leverage machine learning algorithms to assess **probability, impact, and interdependencies** of various risks:

   - **Bayesian models**, decision trees, and neural networks process multi-source data (financial, operational, behavioral).
   - These models help **quantify uncertainty** and simulate multiple risk scenarios with varying inputs.

   Example: Insurance companies now use AI to evaluate customer risk profiles with greater precision, incorporating dynamic data such as driving behavior (via telematics), location trends, and real-time events alongside traditional credit and claims history.

2. **Sentiment and external risk analysis**
   NLP allows AI to monitor and interpret **unstructured data**—like social media, customer reviews, and news articles:

   - This helps assess **reputational risks**, regulatory sentiment, or geopolitical signals early.
   - AI can quantify public sentiment and detect patterns that may precede a crisis.

Example: A global consumer brand can use AI sentiment analysis to flag rising social unrest or negative consumer perception in a region, enabling early response to protect brand equity and stakeholder trust.

3. **Cyber and IT risk detection**
   AI can scan system logs, network traffic, and user behavior in real time to identify vulnerabilities and anomalies:
   - AI-enhanced threat intelligence platforms can **prioritize risks** based on potential damage and exploitability.
   - Predictive models forecast attack vectors and recommend pre-emptive patches or isolation protocols.

   Example: Cybersecurity teams deploy AI to detect unusual login patterns, unauthorized access, or latent vulnerabilities—allowing immediate mitigation before breaches occur.

How to Implement AI-Enhanced Risk Assessment

1. **Integrate AI into existing risk frameworks**
   - Use AI to **augment—not replace—existing ERM processes.**
   - Embed AI scoring models within risk registers, heat maps, or dashboards.
2. **Invest in diverse and high-quality data**
   - AI performance hinges on input data. Ensure **broad coverage** (internal + external) and **bias mitigation**.
   - Include **real-time sources** (sensor data, transaction logs, market signals) for up-to-date assessments.
3. **Establish feedback loops**
   - Continuously validate model outputs with human experts.
   - Use model performance metrics (precision, recall, drift) to retrain and refine models regularly.
4. **Train risk and business teams**
   - Empower risk managers and domain experts with **AI literacy** so they can interpret outputs, challenge assumptions, and build trust in AI-led insights.

5. **Monitor for unintended consequences**
    - Assess whether AI-driven decisions introduce new risks (e.g., unfair pricing, discriminatory profiling).
    - Ensure interpretability and regulatory compliance, especially in high-impact sectors like finance and healthcare.

FROM ACCURACY TO ACTION

Ultimately, AI does more than improve accuracy—it **enables action at speed and scale**. With adaptive models, real-time insights, and scenario-based projections, organizations can **prioritize, personalize, and preemptively address risks**. In a world defined by uncertainty, AI-powered risk assessment becomes not just a competitive edge—but a foundational capability for resilient, ethical, and data-driven decision-making.

> *"AI transforms risk from a lagging indicator to a leading compass—guiding organizations safely into the future."*

Proactive Risk Mitigation

AI enables organizations to take proactive measures to mitigate risks by identifying their root causes and suggesting actionable strategies.

Key Features:

- **Scenario planning**: AI simulates various risk scenarios and their potential impacts, helping organizations prepare for contingencies.
- **Automation**: AI-driven systems can automatically trigger mitigation strategies, such as isolating affected systems during a cyberattack.
- **Examples**:
    - AI in healthcare predicts patient health risks, allowing for early intervention and preventive care.
    - In project management, AI identifies potential delays and resource constraints, enabling teams to adjust plans.

Continuous Risk Monitoring

AI excels in continuously monitoring risks, ensuring that organizations stay vigilant in rapidly changing environments.

Key Features:

- **Anomaly detection**: AI identifies unusual activities that deviate from normal patterns, such as fraudulent financial transactions or security breaches.
- **Key risk indicators (KRIs)**: AI systems automatically update KRIs and send alerts when thresholds are crossed.
- **Examples**:
  - Banks use AI to monitor compliance with regulations, reducing the risk of penalties.
  - AI in manufacturing tracks equipment performance to prevent breakdowns and downtime.

AI in Regulatory Compliance

As regulatory landscapes grow increasingly complex and dynamic, organizations face mounting pressure to ensure continuous compliance across jurisdictions, sectors, and functions. **AI** is transforming compliance from a resource-intensive, manual process into an intelligent, scalable, and proactive discipline. By leveraging machine learning and NLP, AI not only interprets regulatory changes in real time but also helps operationalize compliance efficiently and accurately across the enterprise.

Why AI-Driven Compliance Is Critical Today

Regulatory requirements—from **anti-money laundering (AML)** and **data privacy laws** to **sustainability disclosures** and **AI governance rules**—are expanding in scope, volume, and velocity. Traditional compliance methods often rely on static policies, reactive audits, and spreadsheet-based tracking—tools that struggle to keep pace.

If AI is not embedded into compliance systems:

- Organizations risk **noncompliance penalties**, legal actions, or license revocations.
- Manual errors and audit delays can **amplify exposure to operational and reputational risk**.
- A compliance culture based on checkbox behavior persists, instead of dynamic accountability.

AI enables **continuous, intelligent compliance**—shifting the role of compliance from a regulatory burden to a competitive differentiator.

How AI Enhances Regulatory Compliance

1. **Regulatory text analysis**
   AI-powered NLP tools can ingest and interpret large volumes of legal and regulatory texts across jurisdictions and languages. These tools:

   - Map relevant clauses to internal policies and operational controls.
   - Detect policy misalignments or missing procedural safeguards.
   - Highlight regulatory overlaps or conflicts across frameworks.

   Example: A global bank uses AI to scan updates from over 200 global regulatory bodies and instantly map new AML guidelines to its internal KYC workflows—avoiding months of manual gap analysis.

2. **Audit automation and real-time monitoring**
   AI can streamline internal audits by:

   - Continuously monitoring system logs, transactions, and policy adherence.
   - Automatically flagging anomalies, inconsistencies, or deviations from regulatory rules.
   - Generating real-time compliance reports with traceable audit trails.

   Example: A fintech company uses AI to automate audit cycles, reducing audit prep time by 70% while ensuring 24/7 coverage of high-risk areas like customer verification and payment monitoring.

3. **Data privacy and consent management**
   AI systems help organizations:

   - Detect and classify personally identifiable information (PII) across unstructured datasets.
   - Monitor data flows to ensure lawful basis for processing under GDPR (General Data Protection Regulation), which is a European

Union law that protects the data of individuals in the EU, and CCPA (California Consumer Privacy Act), which is a California state law that protects the data of California residents, and similar laws.

- Provide real-time alerts for unauthorized access or policy breaches.

Example: A health-tech firm uses AI to scan internal servers and detect unprotected health records, automatically alerting data stewards and enforcing encryption policies.

How to Implement AI-Driven Compliance Practically

1. **Deploy regulatory intelligence platforms**
   - Use tools like Ascent, ComplyAdvantage, or Ayasdi to map regulatory texts to business controls in real time.
   - Leverage open datasets and AI regulators' APIs for cross-border compliance alignment.
2. **Automate policy audits and testing**
   - Build AI-driven controls into internal audit programs that auto-check documentation, process adherence, and evidence logs.
   - Apply AI models to test the effectiveness of controls based on transactional behavior.
3. **Invest in consent-aware data architecture**
   - Use AI tools to label and track data usage based on consent levels and jurisdiction-specific rules.
   - Enable dashboards that show compliance status by department or region in real time.
4. **Train cross-functional teams in AI compliance**
   - Ensure that compliance officers understand how AI models make decisions, and how to validate, explain, and challenge them.
   - Introduce joint training for legal, IT, and data science teams to create a shared language around responsible AI compliance.

FROM OBLIGATION TO OPPORTUNITY

With the rise of **AI-specific regulations** such as the EU AI Act and the NIST AI RMF, compliance itself is becoming a space for innovation. Organizations that embed AI into their compliance strategy will:

- Reduce costs and audit fatigue.
- Increase speed and precision in implementing legal requirements.
- Strengthen stakeholder confidence through demonstrable accountability.

"AI doesn't just automate compliance—it elevates it from reactive checklists to predictive, intelligent governance."

Ethical AI in Risk Management

As organizations increasingly embed AI into decision-making and risk management systems, **ethical AI is no longer a choice—it's a necessity.** Ensuring fairness, transparency, and accountability is critical to building trustworthy AI systems that align with societal values, legal frameworks, and organizational missions.

Why Ethical AI Is Crucial Today

In a world where AI influences decisions on hiring, lending, healthcare, security, and public services, the **ethical integrity of algorithms has real-life consequences.** Bias in training data, opacity in decision-making, and lack of human oversight can lead to unjust outcomes—such as discriminatory hiring, unfair loan rejections, or amplified misinformation.

If ethical AI is not prioritized:

- **Inequities become automated** and scaled rapidly.
- **Public trust erodes**, affecting adoption and innovation.
- Organizations face **legal liabilities**, reputational damage, and regulatory penalties.
- Long-term AI advancements risk being derailed by societal backlash and fear.

Ethical lapses may not always be intentional—but in AI, **"unconscious code" becomes policy.** That's why **risk managers, developers, and decision-makers** must go beyond compliance to embed ethical thinking by design.

WHY PRIORITIZE ETHICAL AI BEYOND RULES

Regulations are essential—but **they are reactive, often lagging behind innovation**. Ethical risk management demands **proactive responsibility**. As a:

- **Developer**: You shape how machines "think." Embedding bias checks, fairness constraints, and interpretability into your code can prevent harm.
- **Risk manager**: You must assess not only operational risk, but **societal and reputational risk** arising from model behavior.
- **Decision-maker**: Your leadership sets the tone. Ethical prioritization builds a culture of integrity, future-proof strategies, and attracts conscious investors and consumers.

How to Implement Ethical AI Practically

1. **Bias detection and mitigation**
    - You can use tools like IBM AI Fairness 360, Google's What-If Tool, or Microsoft's Fairlearn.
    - Example: In credit scoring, monitor demographic parity and remove variables that proxy for protected classes (e.g., zip code for race).
2. **Model explainability**
    - You can adopt explainable AI (XAI) techniques such as LIME, SHAP, or integrated gradients to make decisions auditable and understandable.
    - Example: In fraud detection, offer transparent reasons for a flagged transaction instead of just denying service.
3. **Ethics checklists and responsible AI frameworks**
    - We highly recommend implementing structured ethical reviews at each phase of the model lifecycle—data collection, training, deployment, and monitoring.
    - Use frameworks from NIST AI RMF (Figure 6.1), OECD AI principles, or EU AI Act as a baseline.
4. **Human-in-the-loop systems**
    - Ensure critical decisions (e.g., healthcare triage, surveillance, criminal justice) involve human oversight to balance automated outcomes with contextual judgment.

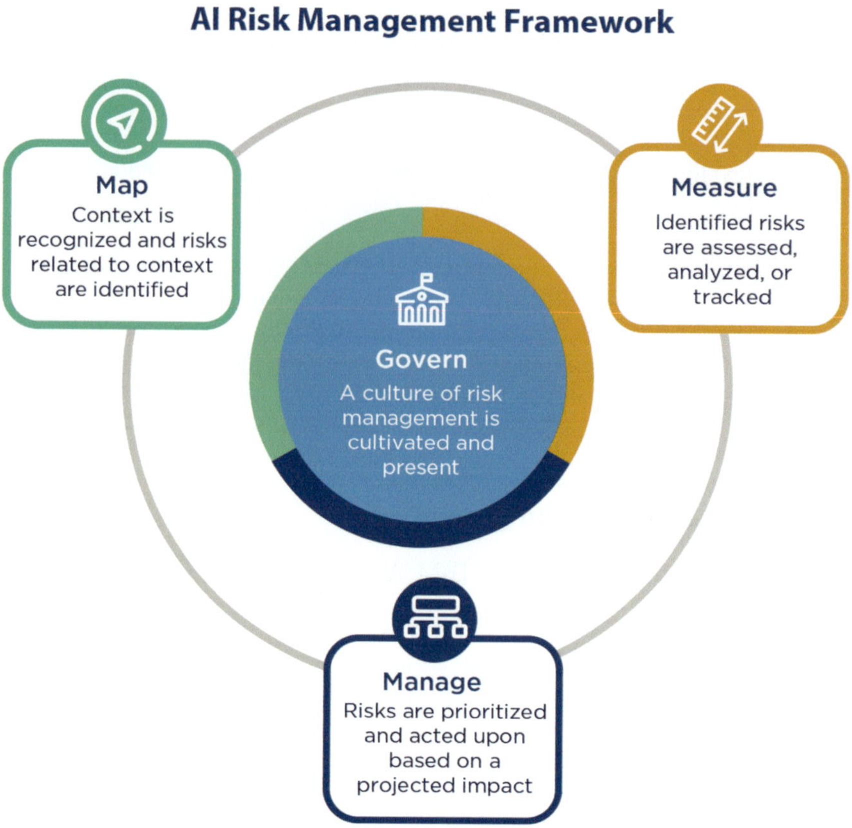

FIGURE 6.1 NIST AI risk management framework. (The NIST Trustworthy and Responsible Artificial Intelligence Resource Center (AIRC) is a platform to support people and organizations in government, industry, and academia—both in the U.S. and internationally—driving technical and scientific innovation in AI. The AIRC is developed to support and operationalize the NIST AI Risk Management Framework (AI RMF 1.0) and its accompanying playbook which can be found on the following link: https://airc.nist.gov/airmf-resources/airmf/. The AI RMF is voluntary guidance to improve the ability to incorporate trustworthiness considerations into the design, development, use, and evaluation of AI products, services, and systems.)

5. **Inclusive design and testing**

   - Involve diverse teams in data labeling, model evaluation, and user testing to catch blind spots early.
   - Example: Before deploying an AI-driven HR screening tool, simulate outcomes across gender, age, and ethnicity to ensure equity.

6. **Mindset shift through training**
    - Train cross-functional teams in AI ethics, bias literacy, and responsible innovation.
    - Embed ethical questions into everyday sprints: *"Who might this harm?" "What data is missing?" "Would I trust this decision if I were the subject?"*

FROM MINDSET TO MANDATE

Ethical AI is not just a technical fix—it's a **cultural and strategic shift**. It begins with the belief that every AI-enabled decision reflects **organizational intent and societal impact**. When risk professionals and technologists co-own this responsibility, AI evolves not just as a tool for efficiency, but as a **force for good**.

> *"Ethical AI is not about slowing down progress—it's about ensuring that the progress we make is one we can stand behind."*

Industry-Specific Applications

AI's role in risk management varies across industries, addressing unique challenges and requirements. For example:

- **Financial services**: Fraud detection, credit risk assessment, and regulatory compliance.
- **Healthcare**: Predictive analytics for patient care and supply chain optimization.
- **Manufacturing**: Monitoring equipment risks and ensuring workplace safety.
- **Energy and utilities**: Managing climate risks and optimizing asset performance.

Summary

There are many benefits of using AI in risk management.

AI is revolutionizing risk management by making it more dynamic, data-driven, and proactive. Its ability to analyze complex data, predict future scenarios, and automate mitigation processes empowers organizations to navigate uncertainty with confidence.

As AI continues to evolve, its role in managing risks will become even more integral to organizational success and resilience.

1. **Accuracy**: AI improves the precision of risk assessments by processing complex datasets without human error.
2. **Efficiency**: Automated processes save time and resources, allowing teams to focus on high-priority tasks.
3. **Scalability**: AI systems can handle large-scale data and operations across global enterprises.
4. **Proactivity**: Predictive capabilities allow organizations to address risks before they materialize.

SECTION B: FUTURE OF RISK MANAGEMENT IN THE RAPIDLY EVOLVING WORLD OF AI

Ethical considerations in AI development must transcend regulatory compliance. Practitioners should embed **ethical ethos in daily coding** practices, using rigorous quantitative and qualitative methods to ensure responsible, equitable, and transparent AI technologies.

The widespread integration of AI into different sectors shows that we need sophisticated risk management strategies tailored to each model. Present evaluation approaches require more specificity which demands explicit evaluation metrics for AI models including faithfulness (fidelity), accuracy (precision, recall, F1-score), and robust validation methods. A critical approach to AI model management involves implementing regulatory limitations on model parameters alongside interpretability techniques[8] such as LRP, SHAP, and LIME to manage complexity.

In high-risk scenarios robust safety measures like robustness testing along with kill-switch mechanisms and anomaly detection will become essential components.

Future trends will encompass real-time monitoring systems together with continuous learning frameworks and mandatory bias detection while measuring ethical compliance through standardized metrics and building collaborative networks to share industry best practices. A forward-looking, integrated view of these emerging practices is presented in the recommended Future AI Risk Management Framework shown in Figure 6.2. The development of regulatory guidelines will lead to standardized thresholds and procedures that ensure transparency and accountability.

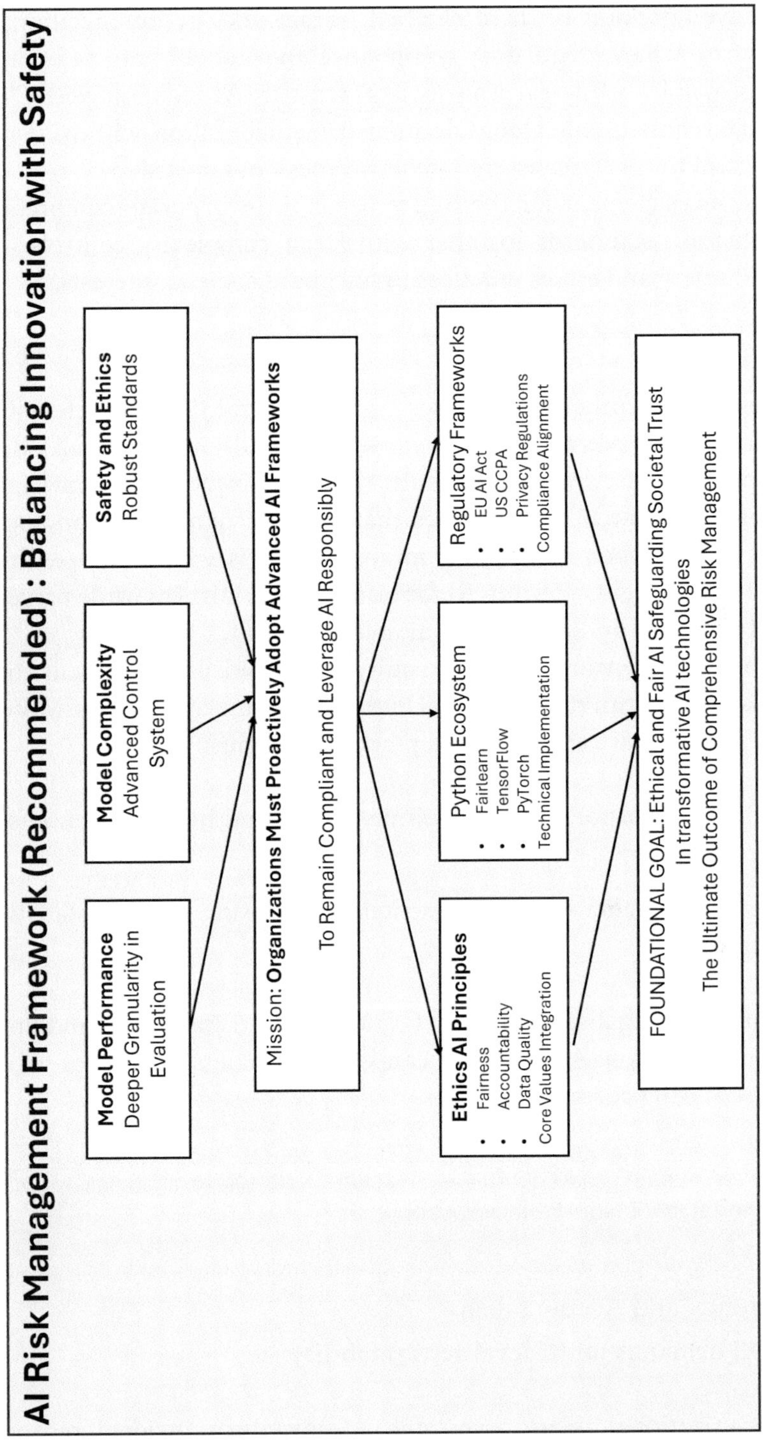

FIGURE 6.2 Future of AI Risk Management Framework (Recommended).

Proactive adoption of these detailed frameworks by organizations is necessary to achieve regulatory compliance and uphold both safety and ethical principles while earning societal trust in AI technologies. Clear regulatory requirements alongside industry collaboration will drive risk management toward greater comprehensiveness and precision.

AI risk management for the future needs to incorporate comprehensive evaluation standards together with strict complexity controls and advanced safety and ethics practices to safeguard societal interests.

Bias and Fairness

AI systems inherently absorb biases from their training datasets which reproduce societal prejudices and historical inequalities. Biases in AI algorithms produce discriminatory results that negatively impact marginalized groups. Research demonstrates that facial recognition technologies perform poorly when identifying minority groups which can result in breaches of civil rights. Testing AI for bias achieves fairness while preventing legal problems and ensuring equitable treatment.

AI bias testing ensures fairness, equity, and avoids legal repercussions. Unchecked biases can result in social harm and financial penalties. Moreso in today's progressive environment, practitioners must:

- Actively incorporate bias assessment tools and inclusive datasets in their workflows, and
- Regularly evaluate data representativeness using relevant statistical measures.

For example, using disparate impact ratios (DIR) to ensure fair and unbiased hiring selection: A DIR significantly lower than 0.8 indicates potential bias requiring corrective actions.

> Disparate Impact Ratio (DIR) = (Selection Rate of Protected Group)/(Selection Rate of Non-Protected Group)

Transparency and Accountability

Ethical AI demands **multi-level accountability**:

- Organizational (board oversight, AI inventory, incident response plans)

- Legal (compliance with nondiscrimination, data protection laws)
- Social (public trust, community engagement)

The **NIST Playbook**[9] provides actionable policies across the AI lifecycle, including change management, whistleblower channels, and third-party auditing mechanisms.

AI systems often operate as "black boxes" with hidden decision-making processes that create major accountability issues. Transparent AI models build user trust while making regulatory compliance easier and establishing clear accountability.

When unintended consequences occur, the absence of transparency leads to diminished public trust and complex accountability issues.

For example, integrate *explainability techniques*, such as Local Interpretable Model-agnostic Explanations (LIME) and SHapley Additive exPlanations (SHAP), into regular coding practices.

Developers can test the interpretability of their models using:

$$\text{SHAP value for feature } i = \Sigma_{S \subseteq N\{i\}} \left(|S|!(n-|S|-1)!/n!\right) [f\_x(S \cup \{i\}) - f\_x(S)]$$

This mathematical framework helps quantify each feature's contribution to the final output, enhancing model transparency.

Privacy and Security

The dependency of AI systems on extensive datasets filled with confidential information creates major privacy issues. When unauthorized parties gain access to data disclosure it results in significant privacy violations and damage to reputation.

Relevance: Data privacy compliance with GDPR regulations maintains public trust.

Implementation: Utilize privacy-enhancing methods like differential privacy to maintain data utility while protecting individual privacy:

$$\text{Differential Privacy Definition: } \Pr[K(D1) \in S] \leq \exp(\varepsilon) \times \Pr[K(D2) \in S] + \delta$$

Here, ε denotes the privacy loss parameter and δ represents the probability of exceeding privacy loss ε, guiding practitioners on maintaining privacy thresholds.

Job Displacement and Societal Impact

AI automation brings disruption to labor markets through job displacement while expanding socioeconomic disparities. Ethical AI requires careful evaluation of socioeconomic consequences while encouraging workforce flexibility and advancing social fairness.

Organizations need to include social impact evaluations when developing their AI deployment plans.

Developers need to perform regular job impact evaluations through econometric models like the Elasticity of Substitution:

Elasticity of Substitution (σ) = % change in Labor Demand/% change in Relative Wage

This helps assess automation's potential effects on employment and inform reskilling initiatives.

Ethical AI Development Frameworks

Embedding ethics throughout the AI lifecycle—from inception to deployment—is essential. Standards like the NIST AI Risk Management Framework as illustrated in Figure 6.1 and OECD principles emphasize AI system trustworthiness.

Ethical standards guide developers toward robust, compliant, and trustworthy AI systems. Adhere to structured frameworks, ensuring AI models undergo rigorous validation:

Model Validation Equation: Error = Actual Output – Predicted Output MSE = $\Sigma(\text{Error}^2)$ N

Regular validation ensures model robustness, accuracy, and compliance with ethical standards.

Ethical by Design

Ethical AI demands accountability at organizational, legal, and social levels, encompassing clear roles, responsibilities, and stakeholder engagement.

Multi-level accountability enhances **trust**, **legal compliance**, and **ethical governance**. Maintain detailed documentation and clear incident-response plans. Implement quantitative risk assessment:

Risk = Probability × Impact

Regularly assess AI system risks, integrating feedback loops and real-time monitoring to adaptively manage ethical implications.

BONUS SECTION: RECOMMENDED RESEARCH PAPERS FOR DEEPER EXPLORATION

1. **Sociotechnical Safety Evaluation of Generative AI Systems**
   Authors: Weidinger et al., Google DeepMind (2023)
   Read here: arXiv:2310.11986 (PDF)
   Why recommended: Offers a three-layered framework (capabilities, human interaction, and systemic impact) for evaluating generative AI safety—essential for readers who want to move beyond technical testing and understand societal implications.

2. **Preventing Repeated Real World AI Failures by Cataloging Incidents: The AI Incident Database**
   Author: Sean McGregor (XPRIZE Foundation, Partnership on AI, Syntiant Corp.)
   Read here: arXiv:2011.08512
   Why recommended: Introduces the AI Incident Database, a growing repository of 1,000+ real-world AI harms. A must-read for practitioners seeking to avoid repeated mistakes by learning from past failures.

3. **Stop Explaining Black Box Machine Learning Models for High Stakes Decisions and Use Interpretable Models Instead**
   Author: Cynthia Rudin, Duke University
   Read here: arXiv:1811.10154 (PDF) https://arxiv.org/pdf/1811.10154
   Why recommended: A seminal critique of explainable AI, arguing that interpretable models—not "explanations" of black boxes—should guide high-stakes decisions in healthcare, justice, and finance.

4. **Beyond the Black Box: Interpretability of LLMs in Finance**
   Authors: Hariom Tatsat & Ariye Shater

Read here: SSRN #5263803
Why recommended: One of the pioneers and recent finance-focused study on mechanistic interpretability of LLMs. Especially relevant for auditors, risk managers in financial services, showing how to meet regulatory expectations while unlocking LLM potential.

5. **The AI Risk Repository: A Comprehensive Meta-Review, Database, and Taxonomy of Risks from Artificial Intelligence**
   Authors: Peter Slattery et al., MIT FutureTech (2024)
   Why recommended: Compiles 777 distinct AI risks into a unified taxonomy and database. A practical tool for policymakers, auditors, and researchers to benchmark, prioritize, and monitor evolving AI risks.

6. **Training Compute Thresholds: Features and Functions in AI Regulation**
   Authors: Lennart Heim & Leonie Koessler, Centre for the Governance of AI (Oxford, 2024)
   Why recommended: Explains how regulators (EU AI Act, US Executive Order) use compute thresholds to identify "frontier AI" models needing extra scrutiny. Useful for readers tracking the regulatory landscape.

7. **Use Case Cards: A Reporting Framework Inspired by the European AI Act**
   Authors: Isabelle Hupont et al., European Commission Joint Research Centre (2024)
   Why recommended: Provides a structured "use case card" format aligned with the EU AI Act—valuable for documenting intended use, risk level, and regulatory requirements.

8. **NIST AI Risk Management Framework (AI RMF 1.0)**
   Authors: National Institute of Standards and Technology (2023)
   Why recommended: The leading U.S. framework for AI risk governance, built on the four functions—Govern, Map, Measure, Manage. Foundational for practitioners integrating risk management into AI development.

Together, these works complement the themes of this book, offering a roadmap for responsible, risk-aware, and innovative engagement with AI.

CONCLUSION

Future AI risk management will involve significantly deeper granularity in evaluating model performance, controlling model complexity, and ensuring robust safety and ethical standards. Organizations must proactively adopt these advanced frameworks to remain compliant and leverage AI responsibly, safeguarding societal trust in these transformative technologies.

To foster ethical AI and mitigate emerging risks, organizations must:

- **Incorporate ethical AI principles**: Develop AI systems with fairness, accountability, and transparency.
- **Leverage Python's ecosystem**: Use libraries like Fairlearn, TensorFlow, and PyTorch for risk management.
- **Adopt regulatory frameworks**: Align with guidelines such as the EU's AI Act and U.S. privacy regulations like CCPA.

NOTES

1. Ian J. Goodfellow (born 1987[1]) is an American computer scientist, engineer, and executive, most noted for his work on artificial neural networks and deep learning. As per public details available on Wikipedia, he is a research scientist at Google DeepMind, was previously employed as a research scientist at Google Brain and director of machine learning at Apple as well as one of the first employees at OpenAI, and has made several important contributions to the field of deep learning, including the invention of the generative adversarial network (GANs). Goodfellow co-wrote, as the first author, the textbook *Deep Learning* (2016) and wrote the chapter on deep learning in the authoritative textbook of the field of artificial intelligence, *Artificial Intelligence: A Modern Approach* (used in more than 1,500 universities in 135 countries). We encourage our readers to read his published work for a complete understanding on the topic briefly cited here in this chapter.
2. Goodfellow, I. J., Shlens, J., & Szegedy, C. (2014). *Explaining and Harnessing Adversarial Examples*. arXiv preprint arXiv:1412.6572. https://arxiv.org/abs/1412.6572
3. Geoffrey Hinton, often called the "Godfather of AI," is a pioneering figure in deep learning and neural networks. He popularized the backpropagation algorithm, co-invented Boltzmann machines, and helped lay the foundation for modern AI. A co-recipient of the 2018 Turing Award and the 2024 Nobel Prize in Physics, Hinton has influenced both academia and industry. In 2023, he left Google to openly voice concerns about AI risks, becoming a

leading advocate for AI safety. His work continues to shape advancements in image recognition, natural language processing, and ethical AI development across the globe.

4. Daniel Kahneman (1934–2024), Nobel laureate and psychologist, transformed economics by revealing how cognitive biases and heuristics shape human decisions. With Amos Tversky, he developed Prospect Theory, showing that people are more loss-averse than gain-seeking. His book *Thinking, Fast and Slow* introduced the dual-system theory of thinking: intuitive (System 1) and analytical (System 2). Kahneman's work laid the foundation for behavioral economics, challenging the notion of human rationality and influencing fields from finance to public policy. His insights continue to shape how we understand risk, judgment, and decision-making.
5. Traditional risk management principles are rooted in identifying, assessing, and mitigating risks through structured, often linear frameworks based on historical data and human judgment. These principles have long guided organizations in managing financial, operational, and compliance risks. However, in today's era of AI and generative AI, static models and retrospective analysis fall short. Rapidly evolving technologies demand adaptive, real-time, and model-specific risk strategies that account for algorithmic bias, data drift, and ethical concerns. To remain effective, risk management must evolve from reactive control to dynamic, AI-informed governance.
6. Risk managers are professionals responsible for identifying, assessing, and mitigating potential threats that could impact an organization's assets, operations, or reputation. They analyze financial, operational, technological, and regulatory risks, develop mitigation strategies, and ensure compliance with governance standards. In today's complex and data-driven environment, their role is critical to enabling informed decision-making, maintaining business continuity, and fostering resilience. As AI and emerging technologies reshape risk landscapes, risk managers play a pivotal role in bridging technical, ethical, and strategic considerations to safeguard organizational trust and long-term value.
7. AI specialists are experts who design, develop, and optimize artificial intelligence systems, including machine learning models, natural language processors, and neural networks. They translate complex data into intelligent solutions that automate tasks, enhance decision-making, and drive innovation. Their work spans industries—from healthcare and finance to cybersecurity and robotics. As AI systems become more integrated into critical operations, AI specialists play a key role in ensuring models are not only powerful but also explainable, ethical, and aligned with organizational goals. They are essential to building trustworthy, scalable, and responsible AI in an increasingly digital world.
8. Interpretability Techniques for AI Models
   To manage complexity and ensure transparency in AI models, interpretability techniques like LRP (Layer-wise Relevance Propagation), SHAP

(SHapley Additive exPlanations), and LIME (Local Interpretable Model-agnostic Explanations) are widely used.

- LRP traces a model's predictions backward through its layers to highlight which features contributed most.
- SHAP uses game theory to quantify each feature's contribution to the output.
- LIME approximates the model locally with simpler, interpretable models to explain individual predictions.

These tools help developers and risk managers ensure AI decisions are explainable, fair, and regulatory compliant.

9. The NIST AI RMF Playbook provides suggested actions for achieving the outcomes laid out in the AI Risk Management Framework (AI RMF) Core (Tables 1–4 in AI RMF 1.0). Suggestions are aligned to each sub-category within the four AI RMF functions (Govern, Map, Measure, Manage). The Playbook is neither a checklist nor set of steps to be followed in its entirety. Playbook suggestions are voluntary. Organizations may utilize this information by borrowing as many—or as few—suggestions as apply to their industry use case or interests. Read the details on the US Department of Commerce NIST official website: https://airc.nist.gov/airmf-resources/airmf/

CHAPTER 7

Managing Emerging Risks Using Python

Your Detailed Guide on How to Enable Ethical AI for Better Data Risk Governance

INTRODUCTION

The current data-centric environment combined with global connectivity exposes organizations to new and unparalleled levels of risk. Traditional governance frameworks have become inadequate due to the exponential growth of data combined with advanced system sophistication. Managing emerging risks has reached a critical juncture because of data breaches that threaten sensitive information together with algorithmic biases that continue societal inequities.

Building on the foundational principles of risk management explored in **Chapter 1**, where we defined the frameworks and strategies essential for identifying and mitigating traditional and emerging risks, and the deep dive into **artificial intelligence (AI) concepts** in **Chapter 2** which dissected the intricacies of AI models and their role in organizational transformation, this chapter aims to bridge these two critical areas. It provides a hands-on approach to embedding ethical AI principles into robust risk governance practices.

DOI: 10.1201/9781003607298-7

AI goes beyond being a technological breakthrough by acting as a transformative power that changes the framework of risk management. The combination of Python's computational power with AI establishes AI as an essential element for managing complex risks. The strong capabilities of AI necessitate ethical usage to maintain trust and fairness while ensuring transparency.

Emerging risks[1] in AI are not just technological challenges—they are ethical imperatives. Algorithmic biases threaten equality, privacy breaches erode individual freedoms, and unchecked systems compromise accountability. These multifaceted risks require a forward-thinking approach that blends technical precision with moral responsibility.

Python,[2] as a versatile and accessible programming language, has become an indispensable ally in this mission. Its vast ecosystem of libraries and frameworks empowers organizations to identify, assess, and mitigate risks while embedding ethical AI principles into every layer of their operations.

This chapter builds on the risk management theories introduced earlier and the AI deep dives to showcase how **Python can be harnessed to build ethical AI systems and fortify data risk governance**.

By blending mathematical rigor with practical, actionable insights, we demonstrate how organizations can transition from reactive to proactive risk management. Through real-world Python applications and ethical governance frameworks, this chapter offers a comprehensive guide to managing emerging risks with precision, accountability, and innovation.

EMERGING RISKS IN AI AND ETHICAL GOVERNANCE

Algorithmic Bias

This refers to systematic and unfair discrimination embedded in AI systems due to biased data, flawed assumptions, or skewed model design. These biases can lead to unequal outcomes—such as favoring one gender, race, or group over another—often unintentionally. Algorithmic bias can emerge from training data that reflects historical inequalities, underrepresentation of certain groups, or feedback loops in model retraining. If not detected and mitigated, it can compromise fairness, trust, and ethical integrity in AI applications across hiring, lending, healthcare, and law enforcement. Addressing algorithmic bias is essential for building responsible and inclusive AI systems.

Algorithmic bias occurs when AI systems reinforce or amplify existing inequalities present in the data. For example, an AI-powered hiring tool might favor male candidates due to historically biased training data.

Example: Bias in Hiring Systems: A major tech company in 2018 scrapped its AI-based recruitment tool after discovering that it discriminated against female candidates. Python tools like Fairlearn and Aequitas can be used to audit such models.

Python Implementation: Bias Detection

This example (Figure 7.1) demonstrates how to measure model fairness across demographic groups and highlights disparities that need mitigation.

Privacy Risks

Privacy risks refer to the potential harm that arises from the unauthorized access, misuse, or disclosure of personal data. In traditional risk management, privacy risks are typically assessed within the boundaries of known threats—such as data breaches, unauthorized sharing, or noncompliance with established regulations like HIPAA, GDPR, EU AI Act,[3] or CCPA.[4] Organizations manage these risks by implementing policies such as access controls, encryption, consent management, and audit trails. The focus has historically been on **compliance**, **incident response**, and protecting data **at rest and in transit**.

Python Implementation: Bias Detection

```
from sklearn.metrics import confusion_matrix
from fairlearn.metrics import MetricFrame

# Confusion matrix for gender groups
cm_male = confusion_matrix(y_true[gender == 'Male'], y_pred[gender == 'Male'])
cm_female = confusion_matrix(y_true[gender == 'Female'], y_pred[gender == 'Female']

# Fairness metrics
metric_frame = MetricFrame(metrics={"accuracy": accuracy_score},
                           y_true=y_true, y_pred=y_pred,
                           sensitive_features=gender)

print(metric_frame.by_group)
```

This example demonstrates how to measure model fairness across demographic groups and highlights disparities that need mitigation.

FIGURE 7.1 Bias detection.

However, in the context of **emerging risks**, privacy risks have become far more complex, diffuse, and dynamic. As technologies like AI, Internet of Things (IoT),[5] biometric systems, and large-scale behavioral analytics evolve, privacy risks are no longer confined to explicit identifiers (like names or email addresses). Instead, AI can infer sensitive traits—such as political beliefs, health conditions, or personality types—from seemingly innocuous data like location, browsing patterns, or voice tone. These **inferred risks** are harder to detect and regulate.

Moreover, in a hyper-connected digital world, privacy breaches may occur **without a traditional breach**—through algorithmic surveillance, opaque data processing, or data aggregation across platforms. Emerging privacy risks challenge conventional safeguards and require **adaptive governance**, **ethical AI use**, **continuous data monitoring**, and **cross-disciplinary oversight** to protect individual rights in a data-centric economy.

> Privacy risks in AI arise when sensitive data is exposed or misused. Techniques like differential privacy and federated learning have emerged as solutions.

Example: Healthcare Privacy with Federated Learning: In 2020, Google Health implemented federated learning to train diagnostic AI without centralizing sensitive patient data. This reduced the risk of data breaches while maintaining model performance.

This method (illustrated in Figure 7.2) enables privacy-preserving AI in applications like medical diagnostics and financial analytics.

Adversarial Attacks: Manipulating Inputs to Deceive AI Systems

Adversarial attacks are deliberate attempts to fool AI systems by subtly altering input data in ways that are often imperceptible to humans but highly misleading to machines. These attacks exploit the mathematical sensitivity of AI models—particularly deep learning algorithms—by introducing small, strategically crafted perturbations into input data that can significantly skew the model's output.

For example, a common illustration of an adversarial attack is the case of a **sticker placed on a stop sign**. To a human, the stop sign remains clearly recognizable. However, an AI-powered computer

Python Implementation: Federated Learning

```
import tensorflow as tf
from tensorflow.keras import layers

# Define a federated model
def create_model():
    return tf.keras.Sequential([
        layers.Dense(128, activation='relu'),
        layers.Dense(10, activation='softmax')
    ])

# Simulated federated training
federated_data = simulation.datasets.emnist.load_data()
model = create_model()
model.compile(optimizer='adam', loss='categorical_crossentropy', metrics=['accuracy
```

This method enables privacy-preserving AI in applications like medical diagnostics and financial analytics.

FIGURE 7.2 Privacy risk detection.

vision system in an autonomous vehicle might misclassify it as a **speed limit sign**—potentially leading to unsafe driving decisions. This misclassification happens because the model's pattern recognition mechanisms are overly reliant on pixel-level features which can be easily manipulated.

Adversarial attacks pose serious concerns in critical sectors like autonomous transportation, healthcare diagnostics, fraud detection, and cybersecurity. These vulnerabilities can be exploited for malicious purposes, causing AI systems to misdiagnose a disease, bypass facial recognition, or approve fraudulent transactions.

Defending against adversarial attacks requires robust strategies such as adversarial training (exposing models to adversarial examples during training), input sanitization, model interpretability tools, and continuous threat monitoring. As AI becomes more embedded in daily life, **securing AI against adversarial manipulation is essential for building trustworthy and safe intelligent systems.**

Another example: Autopilot Cars Adversarial Vulnerabilities: Based on publicly available news and details, in 2022, researchers demonstrated how minor visual alterations could mislead autopilot AI. Such incidents highlight the importance of robust adversarial defenses.

Python Implementation: Adversarial Training

```
import torch
import torch.nn as nn
import torch.optim as optim

# Define adversarial loss function
def adversarial_loss(model, inputs, targets):
    adv_inputs = inputs + 0.01 * torch.sign(torch.randn(inputs.shape))
    outputs = model(adv_inputs)
    return nn.CrossEntropyLoss()(outputs, targets)

# Train model with adversarial examples
optimizer = optim.Adam(model.parameters(), lr=0.001)
loss = adversarial_loss(model, inputs, targets)
loss.backward()
optimizer.step()
```

Adversarial training improves model robustness against malicious inputs, making it essential for high-stakes applications like autonomous driving.

FIGURE 7.3 Python implementation: Adversarial training.

Python Implementation: Adversarial Training

A Python-based implementation of adversarial training designed to improve model robustness is shown in Figure 7.3.

CASE STUDIES OF ETHICAL AI AND PROFITABILITY

Google's Federated Learning Initiative

Source[6]: Federated Learning of Gboard Language Models with Differential Privacy, Google - https://arxiv.org/pdf/2305.18465

Google has been generally considered as at the forefront of implementing federated learning (FL)[7] to enhance user privacy while maintaining high-quality services. A notable application is in Gboard, Google's virtual keyboard app, which utilizes FL to improve language models without compromising user data.

Implementation Details:

- **Federated learning**: FL enables Gboard to train language models directly on users' devices. This decentralized approach ensures that personal data remains on the device, aligning with privacy concerns. The aggregated model updates are then used to enhance the overall language model without accessing individual user data. FL enhances security and scalability, but it also introduces challenges like communication overhead, inconsistent data quality across participants, and vulnerabilities to model poisoning or adversarial updates. Despite these challenges, FL represents a promising step toward **privacy-preserving AI** and decentralized intelligence.

- **Differential privacy (DP)—Protecting individual user data:** DP is a mathematical framework that ensures **individual user data cannot be reverse-engineered or identified**, even from aggregated model updates. In Google's implementation for Gboard, DP is used to **inject controlled statistical noise** into model updates during the training process. This noise makes it mathematically impossible to determine whether any single user's data was part of the training dataset, even with full access to the model's parameters. This is crucial in federated settings where **on-device data is sensitive** (e.g., typed messages, search history). By adding this layer of privacy, Google ensures compliance with stringent privacy expectations while still benefiting from decentralized learning.
- **Differentially private follow-the-regularized-leader (DP-FTRL): Enabling practical privacy guarantees:** To achieve formal differential privacy in practice, Google developed and deployed the **DP-FTRL algorithm**—a variant of the classic follow-the-regularized-leader optimization method. Unlike many traditional DP methods that rely on **uniform client sampling** (i.e., every device having equal chance of being selected), DP-FTRL is designed to work under the **nonuniform, real-world device availability** conditions common in mobile environments.

  Key benefits of DP-FTRL:

  - **Scalability**: Efficient in large-scale, real-world deployments like Gboard, involving millions of devices.
  - **Utility preservation**: Achieves strong privacy guarantees while minimizing the degradation of model quality.
  - **Client-level DP**: Ensures privacy at the user level, not just at the data point level.

Together, **FL + DP-FTRL** allow Gboard to **learn better language models without ever seeing users' raw text**, setting a high standard for privacy-preserving AI at scale.

Outcomes:

- **Enhanced user experience**: The integration of FL and DP in Gboard has led to significant improvements in next-word prediction, auto-correction, and other language-related features, thereby enhancing the overall user experience.
- **Privacy assurance**: By keeping data on-device and applying differential privacy, Google ensures that user data is not exposed, building greater trust among users.

Mastercard's AI Governance Framework

Source: IMD-7-2288 Case Study[8]: Mastercard's ethical approach to governing AI by Öykü Işık and Lisa Simone Duke

Mastercard has established itself as a leader in implementing ethical AI practices, particularly in fraud detection and prevention. The company's AI Governance Framework ensures that AI technologies are developed and deployed responsibly, balancing innovation with ethical considerations.

Implementation Details:

- **AI Governance Council**: Established in 2018, the council comprises senior leaders, including the Chief Privacy Officer, Chief Data Officer, Chief Security Officer, and EVP of Artificial Intelligence. This body oversees AI initiatives, ensuring they align with ethical standards and regulatory requirements.
- **Ethical guidelines**: Mastercard has developed strict ethical guidelines that govern data usage, model development, and deployment. These guidelines emphasize fairness, transparency, and accountability in AI systems.
- **Regular audits and fairness metrics**: The framework incorporates regular audits and the application of fairness metrics to monitor AI systems continuously. This proactive approach helps in identifying and mitigating biases, ensuring equitable treatment of all customers.

Outcomes:

- **Improved fraud detection**: The ethical AI framework has enhanced the accuracy of fraud detection systems, reducing false positives and ensuring legitimate transactions are not erroneously declined.

- **Increased customer trust**: By prioritizing ethical considerations, Mastercard has strengthened customer trust, which is crucial for sustained business success.
- **Profitability growth:** The implementation of responsible AI practices has not only improved operational efficiency but also contributed to profitability. While specific figures are proprietary, the positive impact on the company's bottom line is evident.

These case studies[9] illustrate how integrating ethical considerations into AI development and deployment can lead to enhanced performance, increased user trust, and improved profitability.

NOTES

1. Emerging risks are newly developing or rapidly evolving threats that are difficult to predict and not yet fully understood. They often arise from technological advancements, regulatory changes, environmental shifts, or societal trends. Unlike traditional risks, emerging risks typically lack historical data, making them harder to quantify and manage using standard frameworks. Examples include risks related to AI, climate change, cybersecurity, and digital misinformation. Early identification and monitoring of emerging risks are critical for organizations to remain resilient, adaptive, and competitive in a fast-changing world. Addressing these risks requires agility, foresight, and innovative risk management approaches.
2. Python is a high-level, versatile programming language known for its simplicity, readability, and wide applicability. It supports multiple programming paradigms—such as procedural, object-oriented, and functional programming—and is widely used in fields like data science, machine learning, web development, automation, and AI. Python's extensive libraries (e.g., NumPy, pandas, TensorFlow) and strong community support make it a popular choice for both beginners and professionals. Its clean syntax and ease of integration allow developers to build powerful applications quickly, making Python a foundational tool in modern technology and AI-driven risk management.
3. European Union. (2021). *Proposal for a Regulation Laying Down Harmonized Rules on Artificial Intelligence (Artificial Intelligence Act)*. A comprehensive framework aiming to regulate AI applications across Europe.
4. California Consumer Privacy Act (CCPA). (2018). Landmark legislation enhancing consumer rights and data privacy protections in the U.S.
5. Internet of Things (IoT) refers to a network of physical devices—like smart home appliances, wearable fitness trackers, industrial machines, or connected cars—that are embedded with sensors, software, and internet connectivity. These devices collect and share data in real time, enabling smarter

decisions, automation, and remote control. IoT helps improve efficiency, safety, and convenience in daily life and business operations. From turning off lights with your phone to monitoring equipment in factories, IoT connects the physical and digital worlds, making everyday objects "smart" and interactive.

6. Paper by Xu, Z., Zhang, Y., Andrew, G., Choquette-Choo, C. A., Kairouz, P., McMahan, H. B., Rosenstock, J., & Zhang, Y. (2023). *Federated Learning of Gboard Language Models with Differential Privacy.* arXiv preprint arXiv:2305.18465.
7. Federated learning (FL) is a machine learning technique that enables multiple devices or organizations to collaboratively train an AI model without sharing their raw data. Instead of sending data to a central server, each participant (such as a smartphone, hospital, or company) trains the model locally on its own data and sends only the model updates (like gradients or weights) back to a central server, which aggregates them to improve the global model. This approach helps preserve data privacy, reduce data transfer costs, and support compliance with data protection laws like GDPR. FL is especially useful in industries like healthcare and finance, where sensitive information cannot be easily shared. For example, hospitals can jointly train a disease prediction model without ever exchanging patient records.
8. IMD Business School. (n.d.). *Mastercard's ethical approach to governing AI.* Retrieved from IMDb.
9. Few additional and insightful case studies that were considered in shaping this chapter are listed below. We recommend reading them from the original source (links below) to gain deeper understanding on the topics of Risk of AI and enhancing governance:
    1. Buolamwini, J., & Gebru, T. (2018). *Gender Shades: Intersectional Accuracy Disparities in Commercial Gender Classification.* Proceedings of the ACM on Human-Computer Interaction. Cited over 3,000 times, this paper underscores disparities in AI systems' performance across demographics.
    2. Goodfellow, I., Shlens, J., & Szegedy, C. (2014). *Explaining and Harnessing Adversarial Examples.* arXiv preprint.This seminal work on adversarial attacks has over 12,000 citations and remains foundational in AI security.
    3. Abadi, M., et al. (2016). *Deep Learning with Differential Privacy.* Proceedings on Privacy Enhancing Technologies.With over 2,500 citations, this paper introduced differential privacy techniques critical for data governance.

CHAPTER 8

Asking the Right Question

Bridge the Gap Between Risk and Artificial Intelligence

"Decision-making related to mapping, measuring, and managing AI risks throughout the lifecycle must be informed by a diverse team—spanning demographics, disciplines, experience, expertise, and backgrounds."

—NIST AI RISK MANAGEMENT FRAMEWORK (AI RMF PLAYBOOK, 2023)

INTRODUCTION

Dynamic field where artificial intelligence (AI) meets risk management faces a vital challenge represented by the disconnect between AI specialists and risk management professionals. The two essential groups who work in separate silos need to establish mutual understanding to effectively apply AI solutions while sustaining strong risk management controls.

DOI: 10.1201/9781003607298-8

The integration between AI specialists and risk management professionals has become essential because AI now touches all areas of business operations. This chapter provides practical guidance through strategies and tools that combine AI functionalities with risk management protocols to create necessary collaboration between teams for innovation and safety.

Successful integration requires recognizing how different viewpoints can unify to achieve organizational objectives.

1. AI experts focus their efforts on developing new solutions through quick iterations and maintaining exceptional model accuracy and efficiency.
2. Risk management teams prioritize strict regulatory compliance while maintaining transparency and accountability to identify and mitigate all possible risks.

The fundamental differences between teams lead to obstacles in communication alongside misunderstandings and reduced operational efficiency. When organizations work intentionally to bridge their operational divides they achieve significant advantages which encompass better compliance adherence as well as minimized risk exposure together with boosted innovation capabilities and superior AI system application.

In this chapter, we will learn about how AI and risk are two sides of one coin.

- **The AI-infused risk manager**
  - Core competencies required in a hybrid world
  - Building AI literacy for risk professionals
- **Programming for risk**
  - Practical applications of Python in risk management
  - Automation and predictive analytics for risk
- **Case studies: Real-world applications**
  - Lessons learned from AI-related risk incidents
  - Success stories in AI-powered risk transformation
  - Technical code using Python to illustrate with a real-life example

SECTION 1: UNDERSTANDING THE COMMUNICATION DIVIDE

Origins and Implications

AI experts and risk professionals experience communication challenges because their technical vocabulary and operational priorities do not match.

- AI teams focus their efforts on technological developments, creative solutions, and fast progress achieved through experimental work and iterative improvement cycles.
- Risk professionals focus on building strong compliance frameworks together with strict control environments while ensuring regulatory transparency and safeguarding the organization's reputation.

The significant differences in objectives and language between teams create major communication obstacles which affect operational efficiency as well as strategic alignment. The integration challenges and interaction points between AI development and risk management functions are illustrated in Figure 8.1. AI technologies develop at such a fast pace that risk teams struggle to keep up with the necessary adaptations and comprehensive understanding.

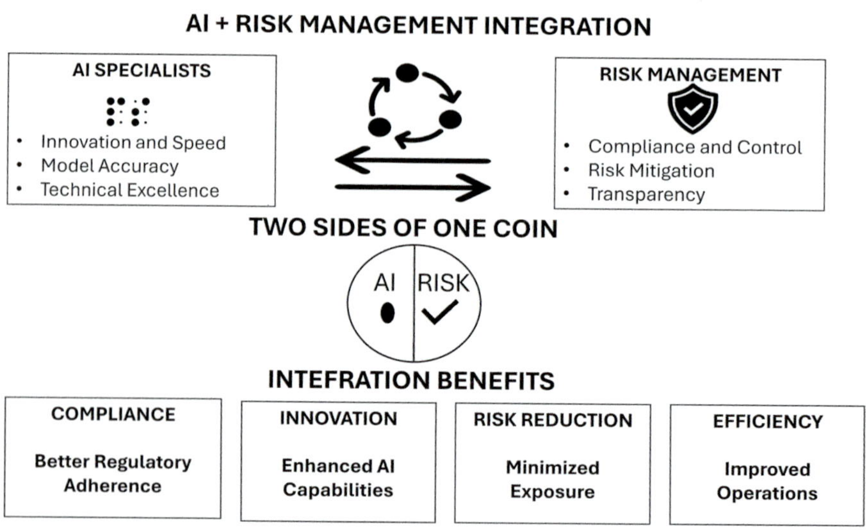

FIGURE 8.1 AI + risk management integration.

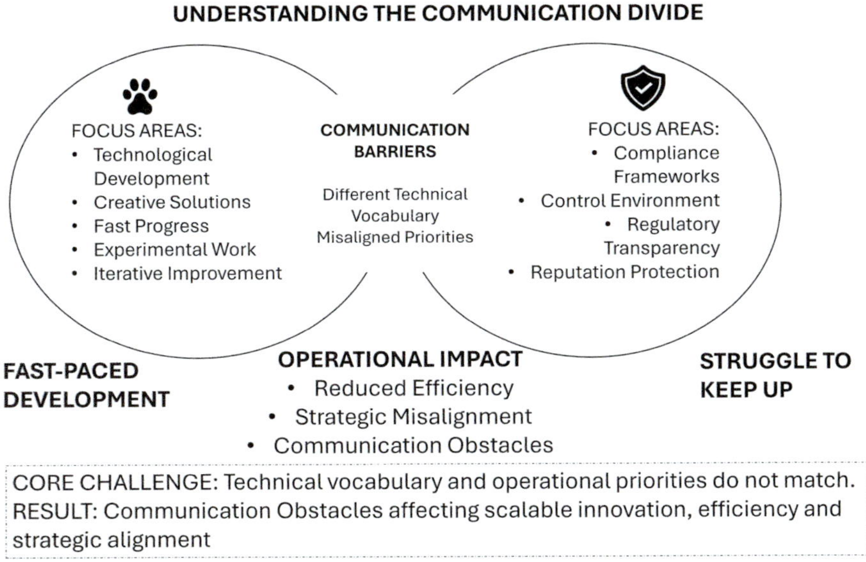

FIGURE 8.2 AI vs. risk management objectives.

Impact of Misalignment

The lack of coordination between AI developers and risk managers often results in expensive errors as well as regulatory penalties along with reputational harm and a reduction in organizational trust. Figure 8.2 contrasts the primary objectives and priorities of AI teams and risk management functions. Many researches have elaborated the risk of AI errors. One of the research from Raji et al. (2020)[1] highlights major difficulties in ensuring algorithmic accountability because of inadequate communication and coordination. Organizations face both unintentional regulatory violations and significant economic damage while losing customer confidence.

Ineffective communication prevents innovation because it causes unnecessary difficulties throughout AI project execution. Organizational delays and inefficiencies restrict competitive positioning while halting technological progress that would have delivered substantial advantages.

SECTION 2: BUILDING COMMON GROUND

Establishing a Shared Language

Creating a shared vocabulary and understanding of key terms is pivotal. Concepts such as "bias," "model drift," and "explainability" need to be universally recognized and understood by both AI experts and risk managers. Equally, risk terminology like "compliance," "ERM,"[2] and "GDPR"[3] must be clearly understood by technologists.

Providing foundational AI training to risk professionals can bridge knowledge gaps, while simultaneously educating AI teams on risk management fundamentals ensures alignment with regulatory expectations.

Cross-functional Teams and Workshops

Bringing together risk specialists and AI experts into cross-functional teams helps create strong mutual understanding and boosts teamwork. Through structured interactions including regular workshops and hackathons along with scenario simulations teams can deeply explore practical challenges and collaborate on effective solutions.

Real-world scenario simulations within workshops enable teams to grasp operational details while identifying compliance challenges and uncovering innovative possibilities. These exercises enable better communication and learning between team members which leads to stronger team dynamics and more effective integration of AI with risk management strategies.

Example: Figure 8.3 explains AI Model Drift Detection:

```
import numpy as np
import pandas as pd
from sklearn.metrics import accuracy_score

def detect_model_drift(old_predictions, new_
  predictions, threshold=0.05).threshold=0.05):)
    drift = np.abs(np.mean(new_predictions) -
    np.mean(old_predictions))
    if drift > threshold:
       return "Model drift detected"
    else: return "No significant drift"
# Example usage
old_preds = np.random.rand(1000)
new_preds = np.random.rand(1000) * 1.2
print(detect_model_drift(old_preds,new_preds)
```

FIGURE 8.3 AI detection Python code.

SECTION 3: IMPLEMENTING INTEGRATED AI-RISK FRAMEWORKS

Framework for AI Governance

Effective AI governance frameworks integrate risk assessment directly into AI development lifecycles, ensuring compliance, transparency, and innovation. Like risks for other types of technology, AI risks can emerge in a variety of ways and can be characterized as long- or short-term, high- or low-probability, systemic or localized, and high- or low-impact.

AI risk management is a key component of responsible development and use of AI systems. Responsible AI practices can help align the decisions about AI system design, development, and uses with intended aim and values. Core concepts in responsible AI emphasize human centricity, social responsibility, and sustainability. AI risk management can drive responsible uses and practices by prompting organizations and their internal teams who design, develop, and deploy AI to think more critically about context and potential or unexpected negative and positive impacts. Understanding and managing the risks of AI systems will help to enhance trustworthiness, and in turn, cultivate public trust.

NIST[4] AI Risk Management Framework (AI RMF), for instance, provides structured guidance for organizations aiming to manage AI-related risks comprehensively.

The AI RMF refers to an AI system as an engineered or machine-based system that can, for a given set of objectives, generate outputs such as predictions, recommendations, or decisions influencing real or virtual environments. AI systems are designed to operate with varying levels of autonomy (Adapted from: OECD Recommendation on AI:2019; iso/iec 22989:2022).

The Framework is designed to **equip** organizations and individuals—referred to here as AI actors—with approaches that increase the trustworthiness of AI systems, and **to help foster the responsible design, development, deployment, and use of AI systems over time**.

AI actors are defined by the Organisation for Economic Co-operation and Development (OECD) as "those who play an active role in the AI system lifecycle, including organizations and individuals that deploy or operate AI" [OECD (2019) Artificial Intelligence in Society| OECD iLibrary]

The lifecycle stages and key dimensions of an AI system as defined in the NIST AI Risk Management Framework are illustrated in Figure 8.4. The Framework is divided into two parts:

Part 1 discusses how organizations can frame the risks related to AI and describes the intended audience. Next, AI risks and trustworthiness

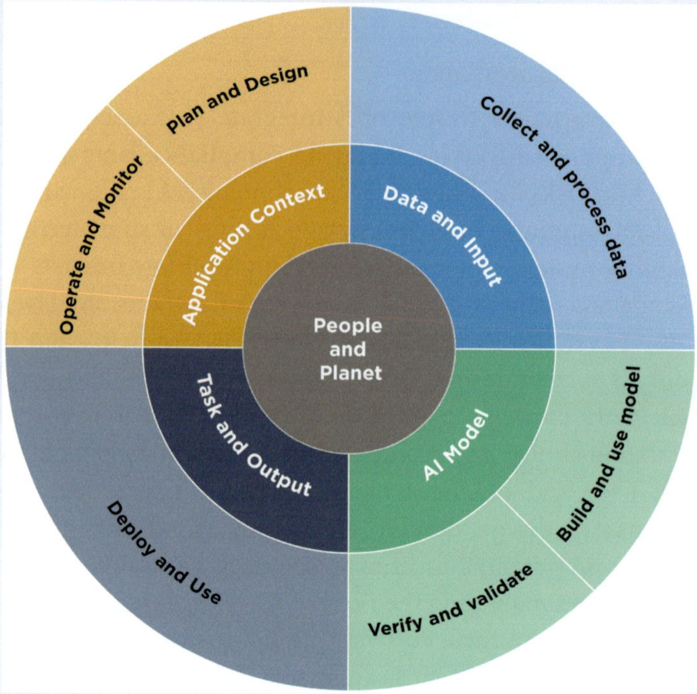

FIGURE 8.4 Lifecycle and key dimensions of an AI system. (From Artificial Intelligence Risk Management Framework (AI RMF 1.0), modified from OECD (2022) OECD Framework for the Classification of AI systems | OECD Digital Economy Papers). The two inner circles show AI systems' key dimensions and the outer circle.

are analyzed, outlining the characteristics of trustworthy AI systems, which include valid and reliable, safe, secure and resilient, accountable and transparent, explainable and interpretable, privacy enhanced, and fair with their harmful biases managed.

Part 2 comprises the "Core" of the Framework. It describes four specific functions to help organizations address the risks of AI systems in practice. These functions – govern, map, measure, and manage—are broken down further into categories and subcategories. While govern applies to all stages of organizations' AI risk management processes and procedures, the map, measure, and manage functions can be applied in AI system-specific contexts and at specific stages of the AI lifecycle.

Additional resources related to this framework are included in the AI RMF playbook, which is available via the NIST AI RMF website: https://www.nist.gov/itl/ai-risk-management-framework.

```
import shap
from sklearn.ensemble import RandomForestClassifier
from sklearn.datasets import load_iris

# Load data
X, y = load_iris(return_X_y=True)
model = RandomForestClassifier().fit(X, y)

# SHAP analysis for explainability
def audit_model_explainability(model, data):
    explainer = shap.TreeExplainer(model)
    shap_values = explainer.shap_values(data)
    shap.summary_plot(shap_values, data)

# Audit example
audit_model_explainability(model, X)
```

FIGURE 8.5 Python code: AI model auditing.

Continuous Risk Monitoring and AI Model Audits

Ongoing monitoring and regular audits ensure models align consistently with ethical standards and regulatory expectations. Automation, particularly through Python-based tools, streamlines model auditing processes, improving transparency and efficiency.

Python Example: Figure 8.5 illustrates Automated AI Model Auditing:

Case Study: Integration in Financial Services

A leading global bank successfully integrated AI and risk management practices by embedding risk professionals within AI development teams. This proactive collaboration streamlined compliance processes, reduced model deployment times by 30%, significantly enhanced transparency, and markedly decreased compliance-related incidents (World Bank, 2022[5]). Such real-world examples underscore the practical benefits of bridging the gap between AI and risk management functions.

CONCLUSION

Bridging the gap between risk and AI experts is crucial for organizations aiming to excel in an AI-driven landscape. Achieving meaningful integration requires structural, procedural, and cultural shifts toward collaboration, continuous education, and shared accountability. Through focused efforts in mutual understanding and integrated governance frameworks, organizations can confidently navigate AI innovation and robust risk management, setting a standard for industry best practices.

NOTES

1. Raji, I. D., et al. (2020). Closing the AI accountability gap: Defining an end-to-end framework for internal algorithmic auditing. In Proceedings of the 2020 Conference on Fairness, Accountability, and Transparency (pp. 33–44).
2. Enterprise Risk Management (ERM) is a structured and proactive approach to identifying, assessing, managing, and monitoring all types of risks—strategic, operational, financial, compliance, and reputational—across an entire organization. Unlike siloed risk practices, ERM integrates risk awareness into decision-making at all levels, aligning with the organization's goals and risk appetite. It helps businesses anticipate uncertainties, reduce losses, seize opportunities, and build long-term resilience. ERM frameworks, like COSO or ISO 31000, provide guidance for creating consistent, transparent, and effective risk practices across departments and functions.
3. General Data Protection Regulation (GDPR) is a European Union law that governs how organizations collect, use, and protect personal data. It grants individuals rights over their data and imposes strict rules on transparency, consent, and data security, with significant penalties for noncompliance.
4. National Institute of Standards and Technology (NIST) is a U.S. government agency that develops cybersecurity, privacy, and technology standards, including widely adopted frameworks like the NIST Cybersecurity Framework and NIST AI Risk Management Framework, to help organizations manage risk, ensure compliance, and promote trust in digital systems.
5. World Bank. (2022). Global Financial Development Report: AI Governance in Financial Services.

## CHAPTER 9

Case Study: Your Practical and Stepwise Guide to Build a RAG-Powered AI Assistant

BUILDING AN RAG CHATBOT FOR RISK AND COMPLIANCE AT SCALE

This chapter puts theory into practice. We walk through the exact architecture of a real-world chatbot designed to allow users to ask questions about PDF documents—policies, transcripts, or audit logs—and get trustworthy, explainable responses. An example of a user querying the AI assistant on an AI risk policy is shown in Figure 9.1.

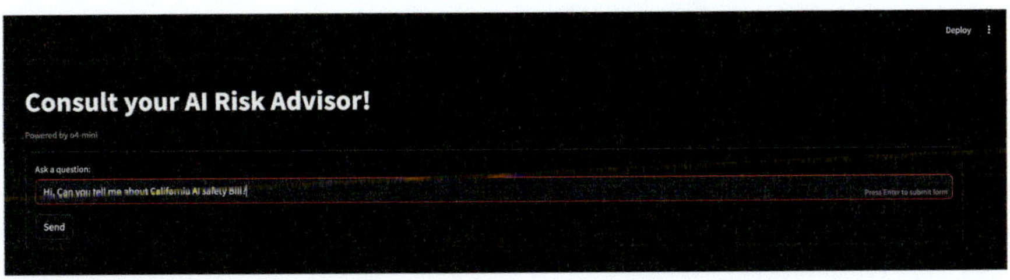

FIGURE 9.1 Ask AI assistant query about AI risk policy.

DOI: 10.1201/9781003607298-9

FIGURE 9.2 AI assistant query about AI risk policy.

Problem Statement

Imagine a compliance officer at a global bank. They're reviewing policy documents to answer: *What are the retention requirements for GDPR-affected data?* Normally, they'd skim 100+ pages. Instead, we built a chatbot that reads the PDFs for them and answers questions grounded in those documents. Figure 9.2 illustrates a real-world compliance query issued to the RAG-powered assistant.

Document Ingestion and Chunking

Our first challenge: parsing PDFs. Using the *pypdf* library, we extract text and break it into sentences using *nltk*. Then we chunk those sentences using a sliding window (e.g., 5 sentences per chunk, with 2-sentence overlap). This preserves context while avoiding token overflow.

We tokenize using *tiktoken*, so each chunk stays within the max token limit.

The output is a set of well-structured, context-rich text snippets.

```
def chunk_sentences(sentences, size=5, overlap=2):
  for i in range(0, len(sentences), size - overlap):
    yield " ".join(sentences[i:i+size])
```

Embedding and Indexing

Each chunk is embedded using *SentenceTransformer("all-MiniLM-L6-v2")* and stored in a ChromaDB vector store. Each vector includes metadata: chunk ID, document name, and page number.

ChromaDB supports fast similarity search using cosine distance. At runtime, we embed the query, retrieve the top-k chunks, and pass them to the large language model (LLM).

```
query_vec = embed_model.encode([user_input])[0]
results = chroma.query(query_vec, top_k=5)
```

Backend: FastAPI Endpoint

Our backend exposes a */chat* endpoint. On each call:

1. The last user message is embedded.
2. Relevant chunks are retrieved from Chroma.
3. A new prompt is built with context prepended.
4. The LLM (e.g., o4-mini) is called with this prompt.

```
prompt = f"You are an assistant. Use the context below to answer the question:\n{context}"
```

The final response includes both the generated answer and a citation list so that users can inspect sources.

Frontend: Streamlit Interface

The frontend, built in Streamlit, includes:

- A chat input box and a send button
- Persistent conversation history (*st.session_state*)
- An expandable section for "Sources Used"

Upon submission, the frontend sends the entire chat history to the backend and renders both the response and the sources in one go. A sample detailed response generated by the AI assistant for a compliance-related query is shown in Figure 9.3. Figure 9.4 demonstrates how the AI assistant exposes its source documents, enabling transparency, traceability, and user trust.

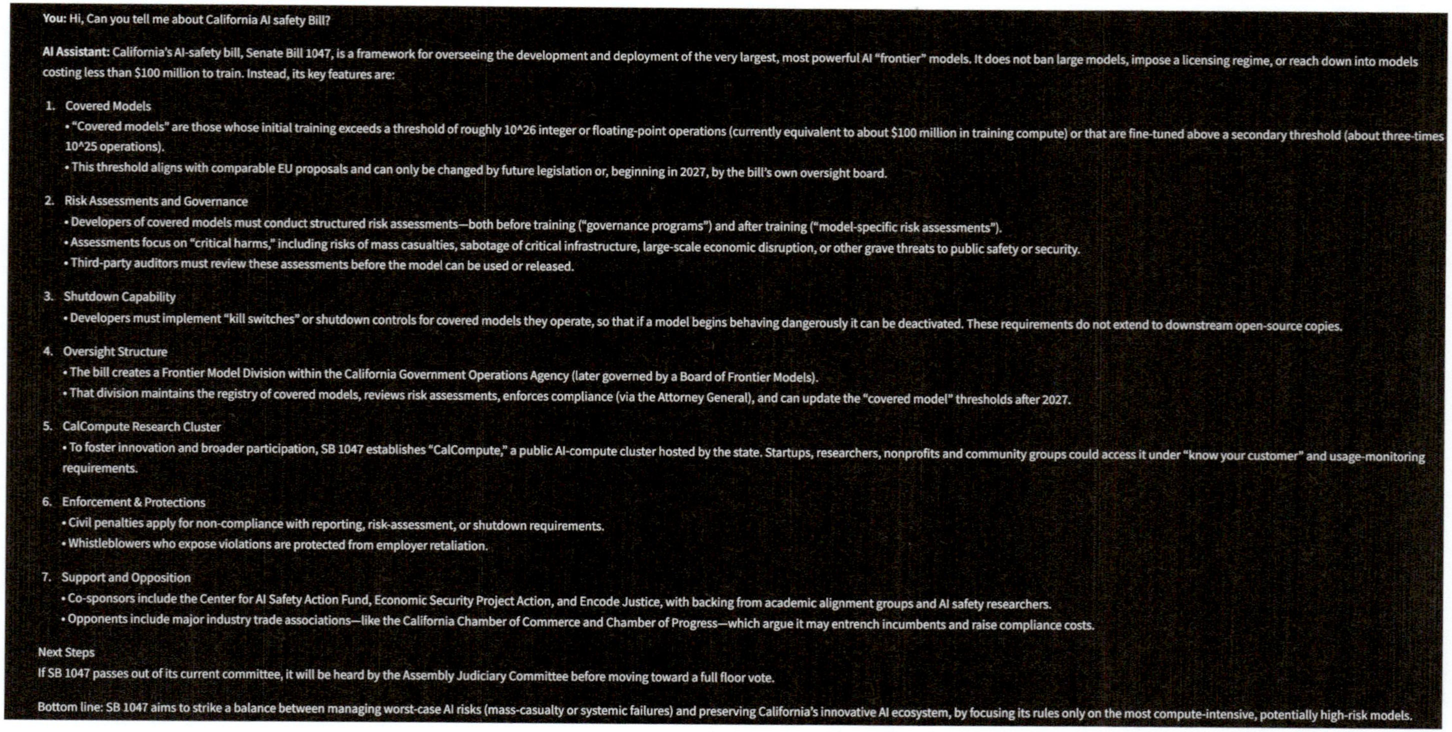

You: Hi, Can you tell me about California AI safety Bill?

AI Assistant: California's AI-safety bill, Senate Bill 1047, is a framework for overseeing the development and deployment of the very largest, most powerful AI "frontier" models. It does not ban large models, impose a licensing regime, or reach down into models costing less than $100 million to train. Instead, its key features are:

1. Covered Models
   • "Covered models" are those whose initial training exceeds a threshold of roughly 10^26 integer or floating-point operations (currently equivalent to about $100 million in training compute) or that are fine-tuned above a secondary threshold (about three-times 10^25 operations).
   • This threshold aligns with comparable EU proposals and can only be changed by future legislation or, beginning in 2027, by the bill's own oversight board.

2. Risk Assessments and Governance
   • Developers of covered models must conduct structured risk assessments—both before training ("governance programs") and after training ("model-specific risk assessments").
   • Assessments focus on "critical harms," including risks of mass casualties, sabotage of critical infrastructure, large-scale economic disruption, or other grave threats to public safety or security.
   • Third-party auditors must review these assessments before the model can be used or released.

3. Shutdown Capability
   • Developers must implement "kill switches" or shutdown controls for covered models they operate, so that if a model begins behaving dangerously it can be deactivated. These requirements do not extend to downstream open-source copies.

4. Oversight Structure
   • The bill creates a Frontier Model Division within the California Government Operations Agency (later governed by a Board of Frontier Models).
   • That division maintains the registry of covered models, reviews risk assessments, enforces compliance (via the Attorney General), and can update the "covered model" thresholds after 2027.

5. CalCompute Research Cluster
   • To foster innovation and broader participation, SB 1047 establishes "CalCompute," a public AI-compute cluster hosted by the state. Startups, researchers, nonprofits and community groups could access it under "know your customer" and usage-monitoring requirements.

6. Enforcement & Protections
   • Civil penalties apply for non-compliance with reporting, risk-assessment, or shutdown requirements.
   • Whistleblowers who expose violations are protected from employer retaliation.

7. Support and Opposition
   • Co-sponsors include the Center for AI Safety Action Fund, Economic Security Project Action, and Encode Justice, with backing from academic alignment groups and AI safety researchers.
   • Opponents include major industry trade associations—like the California Chamber of Commerce and Chamber of Progress—which argue it may entrench incumbents and raise compliance costs.

Next Steps
If SB 1047 passes out of its current committee, it will be heard by the Assembly Judiciary Committee before moving toward a full floor vote.

Bottom line: SB 1047 aims to strike a balance between managing worst-case AI risks (mass-casualty or systemic failures) and preserving California's innovative AI ecosystem, by focusing its rules only on the most compute-intensive, potentially high-risk models.

FIGURE 9.3 AI assistant's detailed response to user's query.

FIGURE 9.4 AI assistance sharing its source of information to ensure accuracy and trust.

Deployment

We package both frontend and backend as Docker services and wire them with *docker-compose*. The *.env* file controls:

- OpenAI API key
- Model choice (*o1-mini*)
- Data paths

Project Structure

```
├──. env                     # contains OPENAI_API_KEY, API_URL
├── docker-compose.yml       # orchestrates backend & frontend
├── requirements.txt         # Python deps for both services
├── data/                    # place all your PDFs here
│   └── *.pdf
├── backend/                 # FastAPI + indexing logic
│   ├── document_processor.py
│   ├── chroma_manager.py
│   └── main.py
└── frontend/                # Streamlit chat UI
└──  app.py
```

Afterword

The Future of Risk Management in the Era of Artificial Intelligence

Rapid expansion and integration of artificial intelligence (AI) systems across industries underscore the necessity for sophisticated, granular, and model-specific risk management strategies. Current risk management practices in AI predominantly rely on high-level regulations and guidelines, often lacking specificity and measurable thresholds. The future demands more precise metrics, targeted controls, and detailed validations to ensure that models remain ethical, faithful, accurate, safe, and fit for use. The crux of this can be found in some innovative research papers published at the time, see Table 10.1.

1. ***Metrics for Judging AI Models***

   Risk management will evolve to focus on explicit metrics for evaluating AI models, namely:

   - **Faithfulness:** Faithfulness evaluates how reliably a model's explanation matches its actual computation and outcomes. Metrics like fidelity scores, measured by comparing model-generated explanations to model behavior, will become crucial.

   - **Accuracy:** Detailed accuracy metrics, such as precision, recall, and F1-score, will be standardized to rigorously assess models against set thresholds.

DOI: 10.1201/9781003607298-10

TABLE 10.1 Summary Table

Risk Management Direction	References	Current Solutions and Guidelines	Regulatory Guidelines (Future Trends)
Faithfulness metrics	Molnar, C. (2020) "Interpretable Machine Learning"	SHAP, LIME	Standardized fidelity thresholds
Accuracy thresholds	Goodfellow et al. (2016) "Deep Learning"	Precision, Recall, F1-Score	Mandatory accuracy benchmarks
Validation techniques	Bishop, C. (2006) "Pattern Recognition and Machine Learning"	Cross-validation, stress testing	Standardized validation procedures
Parameter control	Rudin, C. (2019) "Stop Explaining Black Box Models"	Regularization methods, pruning	Regulatory parameter caps
AI safety controls	Russell, S. (2019) "Human Compatible"	Adversarial testing, anomaly detection	Mandatory robustness, kill-switches
Bias and ethical compliance	Mehrabi et al. (2021) "A survey on bias and fairness in machine learning"	Bias detection algorithms	Mandatory bias metrics and ethical compliance
Real-time monitoring	Amodei et al. (2016) "Concrete Problems in AI Safety"	Monitoring dashboards, continuous learning	Regulatory real-time monitoring requirements

- **Validation:** Robust validation methodologies including cross-validation, adversarial testing, and stress testing will be mandated, each with predefined performance thresholds to ensure reliability.

2. ***Parameter Control and Model Complexity***

   Another critical future direction is the explicit control of model complexity through regulation of parameters:

   - **Parameter limitations:** Overly complex models can lead to overfitting and decreased interpretability. Regulatory frameworks will likely enforce upper limits on parameter numbers relative to model usage contexts.
   - **Model interpretability:** Techniques such as layer-wise relevance propagation (LRP), SHAP values, and LIME will become standard to assess interpretability and to justify model complexity.

3. ***AI Safety Controls***

   Enhanced safety controls will be critical, especially for high-stakes applications.

   - **Robustness and resilience testing:** Future regulatory practices will mandate systematic robustness testing against adversarial attacks, anomalies, and input perturbations.
   - **Kill-switch mechanisms:** Explicit "kill-switch" mechanisms enabling swift model intervention or shutdown in unsafe scenarios will be developed and deployed.
   - **Anomaly detection:** Automated real-time monitoring systems to detect and address anomalous behaviors, ensuring continuous compliance and safety.

4. ***Additional Future Directions***

   - **Real-time monitoring and continuous learning:** Risk management will integrate continuous monitoring frameworks to dynamically assess model performance and adapt controls accordingly.
   - **Bias and ethical compliance metrics:** Automated bias detection and fairness metrics, such as statistical parity, equal opportunity, and predictive equality, will become mandatory.
   - **Collaborative AI risk networks:** Organizations will form collaborative networks sharing best practices, adversarial tests, and risk mitigation strategies to standardize and elevate AI risk management.

THANK YOU FOR JOINING US ON THIS JOURNEY

As we reach the final pages of this book, we want to extend our heartfelt thanks to you—our reader—for embarking on this important journey with us. In a world that is being reshaped by AI, your curiosity, commitment, and critical thinking are more vital than ever.

By reading through these chapters, you've not only deepened your understanding of AI and safety, but also taken a meaningful step toward becoming a more responsible architect of the future—whether you are a developer, policymaker, researcher, risk leader, or simply a conscious global citizen.

This book was never just about technology; it was about **trust**, **transparency**, and **the collective responsibility** we share in shaping intelligent systems that **respect** human values. *Your willingness to engage with these ideas gives us hope.*

We hope the insights, frameworks, and stories shared here will continue to serve as a compass—guiding your actions, sparking dialogue, and inspiring innovation rooted in ethics and impact.

Thank you for reading. Thank you for caring.

The journey doesn't end here—it evolves with every decision you make. Let's keep asking the right questions, and let's build better together.

Index

Note: Page references in *italics* denote figures, in **bold** tables and with "n" endnotes.

A

Abadi, M., 173n3
Abdalla, H. B., 46
Accountability, 12, 15, 38, 49, 126, 140, 142, 143, 147, 150, 154, 156–159, 161, 165, 171, 175, 177, 181
Accreditation in Public Relations (APR), 17
Accuracy, 146, 154, *187*, 188; *see also* Validation
Adam optimizer, 62, 64, 99n9
Adaptive governance, 167; *see also* Governance
Adversarial attacks, 167–168, 189
Adversarial training, 168–169, *169*; *see also* Training
Affordable Care Act (ACA), 17
AI Risk Management Framework (AI RMF), 3, 12, 13, 17, 163n9, 179, *180*
Algorithmic advancements, 26
Algorithmic bias, 6, 15, 16, 165–166; *see also* Bias
Algorithmic innovation, 24
Algorithms, 23, 55
Analysis
  regulatory text, 148
  risk, 35, 144
  sentiment and external risk, 144, 145
  unstructured data, 141
Anomaly detection, 36, 56, 141, 147, 154, 189; *see also* Detection
Anti-money laundering (AML), 147
Application-specific integrated circuits (ASICs), 41n3
Aristotle, 30
Artificial general intelligence (AGI), 34
Artificial intelligence (AI), 2, 20–42; *see also* Generative artificial intelligence (GenAI); Machine learning (ML); Risk management; Technologies
  assistant, 33, 183–187, *186*, *187*
  categories of, 29
  compliance practically, 149
  components of, *28*, **27–28**
  ethical, 37–39, 150–151, 169–172
  evolution, 30–34, *31*
  factors, *22*
  governance frameworks, 179
  humanity and businesses, 35–37
  human potential, 35, *36*
  innovation, 35–37
  major scientific phases, 30–34
  model auditing, 181, *181*
  natural to, 30
  overview, 20–29
  regulatory compliance, 147–148
  role of, 138–163
  socioeconomic impacts, 36
  strategic edge, 35–36
Artificial neural networks (ANNs), 32, 59–61, *66*, *69*, *71*, 98n4; *see also* Deep learning; Machine learning (ML)
Assets and reputation protection, 14
Attention mechanism, 26, 27, 41n4, 84

Autoencoders, 56, 57
Automation, 29, 35, 39, 139, 146, 148, 158, 175, 181; *see also* Technologies

B

Babbage, Charles, 30
Backend setup, 134, 185, 187
Backpropagation, 55, 62, 64, 98n6, 161–162n3
Bayesian models, 144
BERT models, 26, 34, 46, 84, 87, 94
Bias
  algorithmic, 6, 15, 16, 165–166
  detection, 151, 166, *166*
  and ethical compliance metrics, 189
  and fairness, 38, 156
  in hiring systems, 166
  mitigation, 145, 151
Big data, 24, 41n1, **45**
Bilingual Evaluation Understudy (BLEU), 120, 127, 131, 136n14, 137n18
Bill of Rights, 38
Black Box Machine Learning Models, 159
Board of Certified Safety Professionals (BCSP), 17
Bohr, Niels, 18n1
Buolamwini, J., 173n1
Business, 12, 14, 20, 24, 35, 144, 182n2
  continuity, 14, 162n6
  humanity and, 35–37
  teams, 145

C

Calculating machines, 30
California Consumer Privacy Act (CCPA), 14, 15, 38, 149, 161, 166, 172n4
Call detail records (CDRs), 45
Case studies
  of ethical ai and profitability, 169–172
  financial services, 181
  of NLP, 86–97
  RAG, 183–187
  real-world applications, 175
Catastrophic forgetting, 114
Causal language modeling, 105
Certifications, 3, 17, 19n6, 40
Certified Artificial Intelligence Practitioner (CAIP), 18
Certified Environmental Risk Assessor (CERA), 18
Certified Financial Planner (CFP), 18
Certified Information Privacy Professional (CIPP), 3
Certified Information Systems Security Professional (CISSP), 17
Certified in Risk and Information Systems Control (CRI/SC), 17
Certified Safety Professional (CSP), 17
Certified Supply Chain Professional (CSCP), 17
Certified Third-Party Risk Professional (CTPRP), 4
Chain-of-thought (CoT), 108, 110
Chain rule, 62, 98n6
Chatbot, 32, 35, 40, 131–132, 136n15, 183–187; *see also* Retrieval-augmented generation (RAG)
ChatGPT, 107, 112, 117, 118, 130; *see also* Generative pre-trained transformer (GPT); InstructGPT
Civil rights, 156
Classification report, 64, *65*, *68*, 72, 75, *76*
Claude, 107, 112, 118
Clean Air Act, 16
Clean Water Act, 16
Clinical forecasting, 83
Clustering, 56, 57
Collaborate cross-functionally, 141
Collaborative networks, 154, 190
Collective responsibility, 191
Colossal Clean Crawled Corpus (C4), 135n5
Commodity Futures Trading Commission (CFTC), 15
Common activation functions, *60*
Communication, 2, 170, 175–178
Competitive market status, 13
Compliance and regulatory obligations, 14
Compliance practically, 149
Comprehensive meta-review, 160
Computational advancements, 25
Computational considerations, 76
Computational power, 22, 24, 26, 165
Computation theory, 32

Computer vision, 29, 41n2
Compute Unified Device Architecture (CUDA), 25, 41n2
Conceptual fog, 43
Confusion matrix, 64–65, *66*, *69*, *71*, 76, *77*
Consent-aware data architecture, 149
Consent management, 148–149, 166
Consumer Financial Protection Bureau (CFPB), 15, 17
Continuous learning, 154, 189
Continuous risk monitoring, 146–147, 181; *see also* Monitoring
Controlling model output, 118–120
Convolutional neural networks (CNNs), 26, 29, 73–78, *73*, 99n10
  computational considerations, 76
  confusion matrix, *77*
  model evaluation, 75
  overview, 73–74
  with TensorFlow, 74–75
Cosine similarity, 122
COVID-19 pandemic, 4, 7, 16
CPUs, 25, 62, 76, 99n11
Crossdisciplinary, 167
Cross-entropy measures, 58
Cross-functional teams, 143, 149, 153, 178
Cumulative probability, 120
Customer trust, 172
Cybersecurity, 2, 3, 5, 12, 14, 15, 17, 145, 168
Cybersecurity and Infrastructure Security Agency (CISA), 15
Cybersecurity Information Sharing Act (CISA), 15

D

Dartmouth Conference of 1956, 22, 30, 32
Data, 124, 159
  analysis, 141
  consumer, 15
  driven AI, 33
  governance, 46, 49
  high-quality, 145
  hungry, 46
  infrastructure, 141
  interpret visual, 29
  monitoring, 167
  privacy, 15, 147, 148–149, 157
  quality *vs.* quantity, 105
  real-time, 141, 143
  robust, 15
  sequential, 78
  time-dependent, 79
  unstructured, 26, 27, 59, 141, 144, 148
Dataset, 46, 113–114
  multimodal, 46
  with sentiment labels, *89*
  text preprocessing, *91*
  training, 104, 156, 170
DBSCAN, 56, 57
Decision frameworks, 142
Decoder-only models, 105
Deep Blue *vs.* Kasparov, 33
Deep learning, 33, 51–99, 161n1
  ANNs, 59–61
  CNNs, 73–78
  components, 54
  features/representations/limits, 57–59
  historical milestones, 54–55
  machine learning, 51–52
  NLP, 86–97
  overview, 51–59
  reinforcement learning, 57
  rise of, 59
  RNNs, 78–86
  supervised learning, 51–55
  training neural networks, 62–70
  unsupervised learning, 56–57
DeepMind AlphaGo project, 26, 42n5
Deep neural networks (DNNs), 26
Dense vector retrieval, 124, 136–137n16
Deployment, 4, 12, 25, 36, 38, 39, 126, 134, 139, 151, 158, 170–172, 179, 181, 187
Detection, 189
  anomaly, 36, 56, 141, 147, 154, 189
  bias, 166, *166*
  cyber and IT risk, 145
  to decision, 141–143
  fraud, 15, 35, 151, 153, 168, 171
  privacy risk, *168*
Differentially private follow-the-regularized-leader (DP-FTRL), 170
Differential privacy (DP), 170

Digital public infrastructure (DPI), 35
Disparate impact ratios (DIR), 156
DistilBERT, 86, 93–94, 97
Dodd-Frank Wall Street Reform and Consumer Protection Act, 15
Domain-specific retrieval tasks, 116; *see also* Retrieval-augmented generation (RAG)

E

E-commerce, 46
Efficiency, 25, 26, 35, 153, 172, 175, 176, 181
Elastic cloud clusters, 25, 26
ELIZA, 22, 32
Embedding model, 126, 184
Emergence, 33, 107, 139
Emerging risks, 165–169
Empirical evidence, 104
Employment polarization, 36
Empowerment, 15, 142
Encoder-decoder models, 84, 103, 105
Energy and utilities, 153
Enterprise intelligence, 125
Enterprise risk management (ERM), 16, 17, 36, 145, 182n2
Enterprises, benefit for, *37*
Environmental Protection Agency (EPA), 16
Environment and library setup, 87
Ethical considerations, 37–39
Ethical design, 39
Ethical governance, 159, 165–169
Ethical guidelines, 171
Ethical integrity, 150
Ethical standards, 158
Ethics and regulation, 34
EU AI Act, 49, 127
Evaluation, 13, 47, 49, 86, 120, 122, 127, 152–154, 156–158
Evolution of intelligence, 30
Executive Order on America's Supply Chains, 16
Expert systems, 33
Explainability, 38, 125, 126, 141, 151, 157, 177

F

Facebook AI Similarity Search (FAISS), 127, 137n17
Fairness metrics, 171, 189
Faithfulness, 154, 188
Federal Trade Commission (FTC), 15, 16
Federated learning (FL), 167, 169–171, 173n7; *see also* Machine learning (ML)
Feedback loops, 145, 159, 165
Few-shot prompting, 108–110
Financial Risk Manager (FRM), 15, 17
Financial services, 153, 160, 181
Fine-tuned Language Net with T5 (FLAN-T5), 112–113, 117
Fishbone/ Ishikawa, 18n5
Floridi, Luciano, 139
Foundation model, 43, 86, 103–107
Fraud detection, 15, 35, 151, 153, 168, 171; *see also* Detection
Fusion cells, 3

G

Gaussian mixture models (GMM), 56
Gebru, T., 173n1
Gemini, 118
General Data Protection Regulation (GDPR), 14, 38, 157, 182n3, 184
General Problem Solver (GPS), 32
General-purpose architectures, 102
Generate original outputs, 134n1
Generative adversarial networks (GANs), 23, 161n1
Generative artificial intelligence (GenAI), 20, 21, 23, *23*, 27, 34, *53*, 100–137, 159
  augmented intelligence, 103–123
  defined, 100, 134n1
  ICL, 107–108
  LLMs, 103–123
  overview, 100–103
  RAG, 123–134
Generative pre-trained transformer (GPT), 26, 28, 34, 41, 46, 78, 84, 103, 104, 107, 108, 112, 135n2, 135n4; *see also* ChatGPT; InstructGPT

Genomics, 46
Global Association of Risk Professionals (GARP), 17
Goodfellow, Ian J., 161n1, 173n2
Governance, *49*
- adaptive, 167
- council, 171
- data, 46, 49
- drives, *7*, **8**
- ethical, 158, 165–169
- frameworks, 179–180
- policy, 46
- rules, 147

Government Accountability Office (GAO), 5, 14
Graphics processing unit (GPU), 25, 26, 41n2, 63, 99n11, 114

H

Harvard Online blog, 24
Health/healthcare, 22, 35, 150, 151, 165
- privacy, 167
- and safety, 16

Heisenberg, Werner, 18n1
High compute time, 114
High-quality data, 145; *see also* Data
Hinton, Geoffrey, 55, 139, 161–162n3
Hiring systems, 166
Homogenization, 107
Human/humanity, 5, 6, 20, 35
- annotators rank, 118
- and businesses, 35–37
- integrity/transparency/care., *39*
- loop systems, 151
- machines, 44
- potential, 35, *36*

I

Inclusive design and testing, 152
In-context learning (ICL), 107–108
Industry-specific applications, 153
Inferred risks, 167
Innovation, 35–37; *see also* Technologies
- algorithmic, 24
- humanity and businesses, 35–37

InstructGPT, 117; *see also* ChatGPT; Generative pre-trained transformer (GPT)
Instruction tuning, 112–113, **113**
Intelligence service, 30
Intelligent compliance, 148
Internet of Things (IoT), 167, 172–173n5
Interpretability techniques, 154, 162–163n8, 189; *see also* Techniques
Intuition, 7, 44, 62, 86
Investment, 16, 26, 34

J

Japanese fifth-generation computer project, 33
Job displacement, 39, 158

K

Kahneman, Daniel, 139, 162n4
Kernel methods, 55; *see also* Machine learning (ML)
Key risk indicators (KRIs), 147
Kill-switch mechanisms, 154, 189

L

Languages, 27, 83, 103, 118, 148, 165, 169, 177–178; *see also* Programming languages; Python
Large language models (LLMs), 78, 83, 100, *101*, 103–123, 105, 123, 185; *see also* Generative artificial intelligence (GenAI)
- and augmented intelligence architecture., *101*
- controlling model output, 118–120
- cosine similarity, 122
- CoT prompting, 110
- datasets, 113–114
- few-shot prompting, 109–110
- foundation models, 105–107
- full fine-tuning, 114, 117
- generator, 126
- ICL, 107–108
- instruction tuning, 112–113, **113**

LoRA, 115–116
major leaps in, 102
metrics/sampling strategies, 118
one-shot prompting, 109
PEFT, 115
pre-training, 102–103, **106**
prompt engineering, 108
prompt sensitivity, 111–112
quantitative evaluation metrics, 120
RAG *vs.*, **125**
real-world evaluation, 122–123
RLHF, 117–118
ROUGE, 120–121
scaling laws, 103–104
temperature, 119
zero-shot prompting, 108–109
Latent Dirichlet allocation (LDA), 56
Layer-wise relevance propagation (LRP), 189
Legal compliance, 159
Legal liabilities, 14, 142, 150
Leibniz, Gottfried, 30
Literacy, 3, 141, 145, 175
Local Interpretable Model-agnostic Explanations (LIME), 154, 189
Logic theorist, 32
Logistic regression, 55, 58, 59, 97n1
Longest common subsequence (LCS), 121
Long short-term memory (LSTM), 78, 81, *82*, 83, 86, 90–93
Low-Rank Adaptation (LoRA), 114, 115–116, 117
Low-rank adapters, 115

M

Machine learning (ML), 3, 6, 21, 23, *23*, 27, 28, 33, 43–50, 51–52; *see also* Artificial intelligence (AI); Federated learning (FL); Robotics; Technologies
big data, 45–47
defined, 47, 51
evolution of, 51–59
governance, 50
overview, 43
task–performance–experience, 47–48
taxonomy, 43
types of, *24*, *52*
Major scientific phases, 30–34
Manufacturing, 16, 147, 153
Mapping hypothesis, 44
Market collapse, 33
Masked language modeling, 105
Massive-scale pre-training, 102
Mastercard's AI Governance Framework, 171–172
Mathematical intimidation, 43
McCulloch, Warren, 32
Mean squared error (MSE), 58
Medical chatbot, 114
Memory, 44, 79, 81, 83, 92, 114, 115, 116, 123; *see also* Long short-term memory (LSTM)
Metrics/sampling strategies, 118
Mindset, 3, 143, 153
Misalignment, impact of, 177
Model auditing, 181, *181*
Model capabilities plateau, 105
Model complexity, 189
Model development, 49
Model evaluation, 75
Model explainability, 151
Model interpretability, 189
Momentum, 99n9
Monitoring, 4, 16, 49
continuous risk, 146–147, 167, 181
data, 167
real-time, 16, 141, 148, 154, 189
Monte Carlo simulation, 2, 6, 18n2
Multi-head attention, 84
Multi-level accountability, 156, 159
Multimodal datasets, 46

N

Narrow AI (weak AI), 29
National Artificial Intelligence Initiative Act, 15, 16
National Institute of Standards and Technology (NIST), 3, 12–14, 17, 39, 42n6, 49, 150, *152*, 157, 160, 163n9, 179, 182n4
Natural instructions (NI), 113

Natural language processing (NLP), 26, 29, 32, 33, 78, 86–97, 99n12, 100, 103, 122, 135n5, 141, 144, 147
Neural network, 25, 26, 29, 33, 59, 61, *61*, 62–70, 135n4; *see also* Machine learning (ML)
Noise: A Flaw in Human Judgment (Kahneman), 139
Noncompliance penalties, 147
Nonlinear activation, 60
Nonnegative matrix factorization (NMF), 56

O

Occupational Safety and Health Administration (OSHA), 16
One-shot prompting, 108, 109
Operational risk management, 16, 147; *see also* Risk management
Optimism and funding, 32
Organisation for Economic Co-operation and Development (OECD), 38, 151, 158, 179, *180*

P

Parameterefficient fine-tuning (PEFT), 115
Parameter limitations, 189
Perceptron, 32, 54, *61*; *see also* Neural network
Perplexity, 121, 122
Personal risk management, 17; *see also* Risk management
Pitts, Walter, 32
Policy
  audits, 149
  data-governance, 46
  governance, 46
  risk, *184*
Predictive modeling, 36, 141
Pre-trained foundation models, 105, **106**
Principal component analysis (PCA), 56, 57
Prioritize risks, 145
Privacy
  assurance, 171
  data, 15
  healthcare, 167
  risk detection, 166–167, *168*
  and security, 38, 157
Proactive responsibility, 151
Proactivity, 154
Probability distribution, 58, 119
Problem statement, 184
Profitability, 169–172
Program, pillars of, *48*
Programming for risk, 175
Programming languages, 39, 41n2, 165, 172n2; *see also* Languages; Python
Project Management Institute-Risk Management Program (PMI-RMP), 3
Project structure, 187
Prompt assembly, 126
Prompt-based task generalization, 102
Prompt engineering, 108, 111, 112, 117, 118, 129
Prompt sensitivity, 111–112
Prompt testing, 111; *see also* Testing
Proprietary knowledge, 125
Proximal policy optimization (PPO), 117, 118, 136n13
Public Company Accounting Oversight Board (PCAOB), 16
Public trust erodes, 150
Python, 164–173, *178*
  adversarial attacks, 167–168
  adversarial training, 169, *169*
  algorithmic bias, 165–166
  bias detection, 166, *166*
  emerging risks, 165–168
  ethical AI, 169–172
  ethical governance, 165–169
  FL, 169
  implementation, 166, 169, *169*
  mastercard, 171–172
  overview, 164–165
  privacy risks, 166–167
  profitability, 169–172

Q

Quantitative analytics, 4
Quantitative evaluation metrics, 120

Quantitative risk assessment, 144
Quantized LoRA (QLoRA), 115–116
Quantum technology, 18n1; *see also* Technologies

R

Raji, I. D., 177, 182n1
Real-time data, 141, 143; *see also* Data
Real-time monitoring, 16, 141, 148, 154, 189; *see also* Monitoring
Real-time sources, 145
Real-world device availability, 170
Real-world evaluation, 122–123
Real-world projects, 40
Recall-Oriented Understudy for Gisting Evaluation (ROUGE), 120–121, 137n19
Recurrent neural networks (RNNs), 26, 78–86, *79*, *80*, 86, 90–93, 99n13
Regular audits, 171, 181
Regulatory compliance, 127, 147–149
Regulatory intelligence platforms, 149
Regulatory mastery, 4
Regulatory text analysis, 148
Reinforcement learning (RL), 26, 52, 57
Reinforcement learning with human feedback (RLHF), 117–118
Reputation risk management, 16, 17, 144, 147, 151
Research papers, 41n4, 159–160
Resilience, 1, 2, 4, 7, 12, 14, 16, 144, 154, 189
Retrieval-augmented generation (RAG), 46, 102, 107, 117, 122, 123–134, 183–187; *see also* Chatbot; Generative artificial intelligence (GenAI)
  advantage, 125
  backend, 185
  conceptual pipeline, *124*
  critical for enterprises, 125–126
  deployment, 187
  document ingestion and chunking, 184
  embedding and indexing, 184–185
  FAISS, 127
  LLM *vs.*, **125**
  overview, 183
  problem statement, 184
  project structure, 187
  regulatory compliance documents, 127
  streamlit interface, 185
  technical building blocks, 126
Retrieval quality, 134
Retriever logic, 126
Reward model, 117, 118
Risk analysis, 35, 144; *see also* Analysis
Risk appetite, 4, 19n7
Risk-aware culture, 143
Risk management, 1–19, **8–11**, 40, 138–163, 174–182, *176*, *177*
  applications, 15–18
  bias and fairness, 156
  building common ground, 177–178
  communication divide, 176–177
  components of, *7*, 7–12
  continuous risk monitoring, 146–147
  cross-functional teams and workshops, 178
  decision detection, 141–143
  environmental and climate, 16, 18
  ethical standards, 150–153, 158
  financial, 15, 181
  fundamental purpose of, 6
  future of, 154–161, *155*
  health and safety, 16
  identification, 140–141
  implementing integrated, 179–181
  industry-specific applications, 153
  job displacement and societal impact, 158
  language, 177–178misalignment, 177
  nonnegotiable, 12–15
  operational, 16
  origins of, 5
  overview, 1–12, 138–140, 174–175, *176*
  personal, 17
  privacy and security, 157
  reputation, 16, 17, 144, 147, 151
  research papers, 158–160
  risk mitigation, 146
  role of, 140–154
  supply chain, 16
  transparency and accountability, 156–157

Risk mitigation, 13, 38, 141, 145, 146, 151, 153–154, 166, 190
Risk modeling, 81, 83
Risk policy, *183*; *see also* Policy
Risk spiral, 1
Risk thresholds and triggers, 142
Risk vigilance, 139
RMSprop techniques, 99n9; *see also* Techniques
RoBERTa, 59, 86, 93–94, 96, 97
Robotics, *20*, 29, 57; *see also* Machine learning (ML); Technologies
Robustness testing, 49, 133, 154, 158, 189; *see also* Testing
Rosenblatt, Frank, 32
ROUGE, 120–121, 127, 131

S

Sarbanes-Oxley Act (SOX, 2002), 16
Scalability, 154, 170
Scaling laws, 34, 103–105,
Scenario planning, 146
Scenario simulations, 141, 178
Schrödinger, Erwin, 18n1
Securities and Exchange Commission (SEC), 15
Self-instruct, 114
Self-supervised vision, 46
Sequential data, 78; *see also* Data
Shakey Robot, 32
SHapley Additive exPlanations (SHAP), 157, 189
Shlens, J., 173n2
Single perceptron model, *61*
Societal impact, 153, 158
Socioeconomic impacts, 36, *37*
Sociotechnical safety evaluation, 159
Span corruption/denoising, 105
Speed limit sign, 168
Stakeholder, 4, 12–14, 38, 141, 145, 150, 158
Strategic edge, 35–36
Streamlit interface, 185
Superintelligent AI, 29
Supervised learning, 51–55, 57
Supply chain, 2, 3, 5, 14, 16, 153
Support vector machines (SVMs), 33, 55, 58, 98n3
Sustainability disclosures, 147
Synthetic data engines, 46
Szegedy, C., 173n2

T

Technical building blocks, 126
Techniques
  CNNs, 29
  FL, 173n7
  interpretability, 154, 162–163n8, 189
  meta-learning, 114
  parameter- efficient tuning, 114
  RAG, 102, 123
  RMSprop, 99n9
Technologies, 12, 15, 17–18, 22, 24, 40, 46, 139, 161, 167, 179, 191; *see also* Artificial intelligence (AI); Automation; Innovation; Machine learning (ML); Robotics
Temperature, 118–119, 122–123
Tensorflow, 62–65, 74–75, 87
Tensor processing units (TPUs), 25, 26
Testing, 2, 88, 134, 149, 152, 154, 159, 189; *see also* Prompt testing
Text preprocessing, 87–89, 90, *91*
Text-To-Text Transfer Transformer (T5), 135n5
Theoretical work, 30–34
Threats
  cyber, 143
  emerging, 144
  vs. vulnerability, 6
Time-dependent data, 79; *see also* Data
Top-k/top-p sampling, 118–120
Train cross-functional teams, 149, 153
Training compute thresholds, 34, 160
Training *vs.* validation accuracy, *64*, 67, *68*, *70*
Train risk and business teams, 145
Transformer architecture, 26, 34, 41n4, 103, 135n2, 135n5
Transformer models, 34, 78, 84, *85*, 86, 97, 102

Transparency, 38, 125, 156–157, 191
Trust infrastructure, 4
T-SNE, 56
Turing, Alan, 32

U

UMAP, 56
Uniform client sampling, 170
Unstructured data, 26, 27, 59, 141, 144, 148; *see also* Data
Unsupervised learning, 52, 56–57
Utility preservation, 170

V

Validation, 28, *64*, 67, *68*, *70*, 88, 93, 154, 158, 188, 189
Vanishing/exploding gradient, 81
Vector store, 126, 184
Visualization, 46, 52, 143
Volume, Velocity, Variety, and Veracity (4 Vs), 41n1, 45, **45**

W

Weather prediction, 45
Weizenbaum, Joseph, 32
Workshops, 32, 178
World Bank, 182n5

Y

Yottabyte scales, 46

Z

Zero-shot engines, 102
Zero-shot generalization, 112
Zero-shot prompting, 107–109